Poverty and Charity
in Aix-en-Provence,
1640-1789

THE JOHNS HOPKINS UNIVERSITY STUDIES IN HISTORICAL AND POLITICAL SCIENCE

NINETY-FOURTH SERIES (1976)

Poverty and Charity in Aix-en-Provence, 1640-1789

Cissie C. Fairchilds

The Johns Hopkins University Press
Baltimore • London

This book has been brought to publication with the generous
assistance of the Andrew W. Mellon Foundation.

Manufactured in the United States of America

The Johns Hopkins University Press, Baltimore, Maryland 21218
The Johns Hopkins University Press Ltd., London

Library of Congress Catalog Card Number 75-36938
ISBN 0-8018-1677-7

Library of Congress Cataloging in Publication data
will be found on the last printed page of this book.

Contents

LIST OF TABLES

LIST OF FIGURES

Preface

The basic social problem of Old Regime France was the chronic, endemic poverty of the bulk of its population. The most important dividing line in French society was not that separating the privileged from the unprivileged, the noble from the mass of the Third Estate. This barrier was easily crossed by men of initiative and enterprise. Instead it was the line which separated the poor from the rest of society. This gap was almost impossible to bridge. What set the poor apart was the day-to-day, hand-to-mouth nature of their existence. Whether they were peasant smallholders and agricultural laborers of the countryside, or petty artisans and salaried workers in the towns, the poor were poor because their only resource was their labor, by which they could earn barely enough to keep alive from day to day. Unable to save, the poor had no resources to fall back on in times of trouble. Thus they were an easy prey to forces beyond their control: bad harvests, rising prices, periods of unemployment, even family problems like the illness of the major breadwinner or the birth of a new baby could leave them utterly destitute. Precarious as such an existence was, it was nonetheless the normal state of the vast majority of the population. In 1790 the Committee on Mendicity of the Constitutent Assembly defined the poverty level as an income of 435 *livres* or less to support a family of five.[1] By this criterion perhaps one-half of the French population of the Old Regime lived in poverty.

The poor were not, however, completely without recourse. Old Regime France boasted literally thousands of charitable institutions which dispensed a wide variety of aid for the old, the young, the ill, the orphaned, and the unemployed. These institutions were largely the product of the Counter-Reformation in the early years of the seventeenth century. This was a transitional period in the history of public assistance. The religiously inspired private almsgiving of the Middle Ages had been repudiated as ineffective, but the modern principle that the state was responsible for the material welfare of its citizens had not yet been established. This would come only with the French

Revolution. Although the emerging absolutist state increasingly viewed the poor as economic problems and as threats to public order, and therefore made pretensions toward regulating public assistance, the state was not yet powerful enough to do this effectively. With the absence of both Church and state from the field of aid to the poor, the resulting vacuum was filled by private local charities. These institutions were secular, although the donations they received were still religiously inspired. Usually municipal in scope, these charities were founded on the initiative of local notables, and supported by the local public at large. It was to such institutions, to the local *hôpital-général* or *bureau de charité*, that the poor could—and did—turn in time of trouble.

This book is a study of the charitable institutions of one French town, Aix-en-Provence. It begins with their foundation during the Counter-Reformation, and ends with their dissolution during the Revolution. It details the impulses behind their foundation, and describes how they were financed and administered. And it also explores the lives of the people they helped. The study is based primarily on the surviving records of the charities. These are the same sort of records charitable institutions of today accumulate: entrance registers, minutes of their board meetings, account books, and fund-raising pamphlets. Records of the local and central government and court records were also consulted.

Such a study is, I think, valuable in two ways. First of all, it will help us approach the reality of the immensely vast and important problem of poverty in Old Regime France. The poor are notoriously "inarticulate" and therefore hard for an historian to reach. They leave few memoirs, wills, or other standard historical documents. But charity records are one source which can bring us close to the poor. They can help answer such questions as: What percentage of the population depended on charity? What socioeconomic groups did these people come from? How did they feel about charity? What alternatives to charity were available to them? How effective was charity in relieving their poverty? Further, charity records can shed light on the daily lives of the poor: their family relations, homelife, recreations, and religion. Thus they can give a flesh and blood reality to a group which is all too often portrayed only through the abstractions of economists and sociologists.

Therefore one purpose of this study is to bring us closer to the reality of the problem of poverty in Old Regime France. But the study has another purpose also. To the historian, a problem like that of poverty in Old Regime France has two dimensions—that of reality and that of perception. The historian is interested in the reality of the problem itself, but equally important to him is the way the people of the time *perceived* that reality. It is on this secondary level of contemporary attitudes, or "mentalities," as the French would put it, that I also hope to make a contribution. For the charities of Old

Regime France were both the product and the reflection of a whole cluster of attitudes and assumptions about the nature of poverty, its causes and its cure, about the way the economy worked, about the Christian duty of charity, and about the role of the Church and the state in public assistance. Thus they are mirrors which reflect the major intellectual currents of Old Regime society. For example, because charitable giving was religiously inspired, changing popular attitudes toward religion are reflected in the changing level of charitable donations. Changes in charitable donations are a rough barometer of the impact, first, of the Counter-Reformation and, later, of the Enlightenment and deChristianization at the grassroots level. And because both the church and state had pretensions to ultimate control over the charities, we can see in their struggle reflections of the debates over the declining institutional role of the Church and the growing pretensions of the absolutist state. Thus the history of attitudes toward charity reflects many of the major themes of the history of the Old Regime.

This study is organized to reflect these two levels of interest—the reality of poverty, and the contemporary perception of that reality. Part I takes as its subject the charitable institutions themselves. The first chapter is essentially introductory, outlining the social and economic makeup of the city of Aix. Chapter II deals with the attitudes and assumptions behind the foundation of the charities. And Chapter III describes how the institutions were administered and financed, and the many and important roles they played in the community at large.

In Part II the focus shifts from the charities to their clients, the poor. Chapter IV describes the types of assistance available to the poor, and the types of people who received it. And Chapter V discusses the most important alternatives to charity for the needy—beggary and crime.

In Part III the focus again shifts. The two earlier parts describe an essentially static situation—they discuss the charities and their functioning during the institutions' heyday, from approximately 1680 to 1760. But after 1760 the traditional charities enter into a period of decline. Both the economic and social realities of poverty, and popular perceptions of those realities, change drastically after 1760. And these changes affect the charities adversely. Flooded by increasing numbers of the poor, paralyzed financially because of declining donations and general mismanagement, repudiated by public opinion, and subject to increasing control by the state, the charities were ineffective and indeed almost moribund after 1760. Chapters VI and VII detail these developments.

In a local study such as this, the problem of typicality inevitably arises. Are the problems of poverty in Aix the same as those in other areas of France? Does the pattern of heyday and decline of Aix's charities hold true elsewhere? Any historian of the Old Regime is all too well aware of the immense regional diversities in economic and social conditions which make it dangerous to proclaim the particular spot he studied as "typical." I am no exception. Aix was deliberately chosen because it differed from both provincial cities in northern France, like Bayeux, studied by Olwen Hufton, and large manufacturing cities, like Lyon, the subject of a work by Jean-Pierre Gutton.[2] There were many factors which made the conditions of poverty and charity in Provence unique. For example, town life was traditionally more important in the Mediterranean south than in the north, and religion more exuberantly baroque. Also, Provence was a *pays d'état*, which meant that the role of the royal government in public assistance was less than in a *pays d'élection*. Conversely, private charitable resources were probably more abundant in Provence than in the north of France. And, too, the Provençal practice of buying wheat from overseas, the so-called "grains de mer," meant that bad harvests and food riots were less of a problem in Provence than elsewhere. These and other features which made conditions in Provence unique will be pointed out in the text. Nevertheless, the general pattern described herein will, I think, be found applicable to a wider context.

For the sake of brevity, I shall skip the usual acknowledgments to professors, archivists, librarians, family, and friends. All of the people who helped with the preparation of this book know, I hope, how grateful I am for their assistance. But I would like to give special thanks to three people: first, to Professor Louise Tilly of Michigan State University, who read and criticized the manuscript at various stages and gave invaluable suggestions for its improvement; secondly, to my mentor, Professor Robert Forster of The Johns Hopkins University, who communicates his own immense enthusiasm for archival research, Old Regime social history, and France itself to his students, and whose patience with an independent and stubborn female graduate student is greatly appreciated; and, finally, to my mother, who typed the manuscript four times, almost without complaint. This book is dedicated to her.

PART ONE

Charity

CHAPTER I

Aix-en-Provence, "Ville Hospitalière"

In 1787 the famed English agriculturist and traveller Arthur Young passed through Aix-en-Provence. He did not stay long. While paying homage to the town as the home of both Monseigneur Gibelin, translator of the works of Priestley and the records of the Philosophical Society, and of the Baron de la Tour d'Aigues, pioneer of scientific agriculture, Young had little else to say about the city.[1] One feels instinctively that it was not the sort of place to attract a man so bent upon "improvement" as the good squire. Aix was, like most provincial cities of eighteenth-century France, a place where life moved slowly and change was long in coming. Indeed, Aix seems to have acquired in the late eighteenth century a reputation for lethargy and dullness even above and beyond that of most provincial French towns. The daughter of Mme. de Sevigné, the famed letterwriter, was wont to lament that "Aix is a true desert," and a local nobleman, the Comte de Villeneuve de Vence, complained poetically:

> Dans Aix, l'ennui, dès le lundi
> Vous mène jusqu'au samedi
> Sans vous laisser une heure fraîche.
> En vain, des langueurs du mardi,
> L'on espère, le mercredi,
> De pouvoir prendre sa revanche;
> Pas plus mercredi que jeudi.
> Bref, on y pleure le dimanche
> Sans avoir ri le vendredi.[2]

In 1787, M. Bouche, a progressive-minded *avocat* of the *Parlement* of Aix, felt impelled to defend his fellow townsmen against frequently made charges of lack of intelligence and initiative; his words could not conceal the element of truth in these accusations:

> The inhabitants of Aix all have genius, spirit, and taste; they are suited to feats of arms, to diplomacy, to abstract science, to the study of belles-

3

lettres, to commerce, to useful professions, to agreeable acts; but, in general little favored by the blessings of fortune, insouciant in character, stay-at-homes in habit, they know no other life than that of the Palais.[3]

Bouche was correct in stressing the importance of the "Palais"—the *Palais de Justice*—in the life of the town. Aix in the Old Regime was a town of Church, law, and charities, a "ville parlementaire" and a "ville hospitalière," as contemporaries called it. These traditional institutions dominated the town both economically and socially. Aix was one of those preindustrial provincial cities which E. J. Hobsbawm has described trenchantly as living by "battening on the surrounding peasantry and . . . by very little else except taking in its own washing."[4] In the city of 29,000 manufacturing was almost nonexistent; all of Provence had less cottage industry than was usual in France.[5] In 1787 Bouche noted, of the town, "as for manufactures, they are not very numerous . . . : the manufactures consist of Cadiz, serge, and other heavy cloths." Bouche bemoaned the fact that Aix lacked a cotton-spinning industry, which was in England in those years serving as the engine of the Industrial Revolution.[6] Similarly, Bouche deplored Aix's lack of a "grand commerce."[7] Aix had been long since eclipsed in the role of commercial center by the great seaport of Marseille, some twenty miles away. Marseille in the late eighteenth century numbered some 90,000; its commercial ties stretched not only throughout the Mediterranean and the Levant but across the Atlantic as well.[8] In the face of such competition Aix dwindled to the status of a regional market, a point where the products of Provence, especially the region's famous olive oil, were exchanged for the manufactured goods and salt fish of Marseille.[9] Such commercial activities remained on a very small scale, and supported only a fraction of the town's population. In 1695 only 58 of Aix's 29,000 citizens were described as substantial merchants, "marchands," and only three of these were *négociants* engaged in large-scale wholesale trade.[10]

Aix survived economically because it was an administrative center for Church and state, a place like Bayeux and Angers, where the revenues drawn by these institutions from the surrounding countryside were circulated to support a population of tradesmen and artisans.[11] Aix was, first of all, an administrative center of the Church. Its cathedral, St. Sauveur, a supremely ugly building dating in part from the sixth century, was the seat of the Archbishopric of Provence. In regard to its revenues, this was apparently one of the less attractive of the French archepiscopal sees; at any rate, when Daniel de Cosnac, chaplain to Monsieur, brother of the king, was chosen archbishop in 1687, he complained, "I could better console myself if the king had named me Archbishop of Albi. *That* is a benefice of very considerable revenue."[12] The Archbishopric of Provence brought with it, however, considerable temporal power. The archbishop was ex officio *procureur-né* of the

Parlement of Provence, and president of the *Assemblée des communautés,* a body with representatives from all the villages of the province. Thus he rivalled the intendant for influence in provincial affairs. Since the days in the mid-seventeenth century of Michel Mazarin, brother of the great cardinal, the archbishops of Provence were more widely known for political acumen than spiritual goodness. They played a political role not only locally but nationally, at court. In 1695 the compilers of the *Capitation* noted the archbishop as "in Paris"; this was the usual state of affairs.[13] But even when the archbishop was not in residence in his palace, the presence of an archepiscopal see was an economic boon for the town. The cathedral housed in 1695 a staff of 64, excluding domestics; among these were 14 canons and 19 beneficed priests, all nobles, whose spending helped support the town's luxury trades.

The cathedral was, of course, far from the only church in Aix. Around 1770 the Curé de Rilly wrote of Aix, with only slight exaggeration, "one can't walk a hundred feet without running into a church, and we counted at least 300 convents."[14] In all, the various churches, chapels, and charities of the city supported some 100 priests. Besides this complement of secular clergy, Aix boasted 29 religious houses, 15 of them male and 14 female, with a total population of 912. These religious houses ranged in size from the 6 men of the Feuillants, housed in the fashionable quarter of Mazarin-St. Jean, to the 59 women of the Sts. Maries de la Visitation, in outlying Bellegarde.[15] Some of these religious orders provided important educational services for the town—for example, the Oratorians—and also the Jesuits, who ran the Collège Royal du Bourbon, which educated the sons of Aix's nobles and administrators. Others were merely a refuge for the nobility of the surrounding countryside. In all some nine percent of the town's population were ecclesiastics. But while this proportion was substantial, it did not begin to approach the number of those who were administrators of the state.

Aix was a focal point for the various overlapping webs which characterized bureaucratic organization under the Old Regime. The town was "the capital of Provence"; literally a capital city in the Middle Ages, when Provence had been independent, and capital of the pays d'état after Provence was incorporated into France at the end of the fifteenth century. As such it housed the governor, lieutenant-general, and intendant of the province, as well as two sovereign courts, the Parlement of Provence, and the *Cour des comptes, aides, et finances,* plus innumerable officials of the various fiscal agencies, the *controlleurs des domaines,* the *visiteurs des gabelles,* the agents of the *bureau de tabac,* the *eaux et forêts,* the *grenier de sel,* and the mint. Further, Aix was the *chef-lieu* of its *viguerie,* and therefore boasted a *sénéchaussée* court, and a branch of the mounted police, the *maréchaussée.* In all some 1,172 holders of administrative positions lived in the city in 1695.[16] If their families and servants are added, it appears that over 20 percent of the town's population relied directly or indirectly on administrative positions for their existence, not counting the many artisans and shopkeepers who earned a living by catering to their needs (see Table 1.1).

Table 1.1. Socioprofessional Makeup of Aix, 1695

Occupation	Number of households		Percent of total	
Church				
Regular	828		7.4	
Secular	217		1.9	
Total		1,045		9.3
Nobility		452		4.0
Administration				
grande robe*	239		2.1	
petite robe	515		4.6	
Other	418		3.7	
Total		1,172		10.5
Liberal professions, bourgeoisie, merchants		582		5.2
Arts and metiérs		2,495		22.3
Servants		3,063		27.3
Agricultural laborers		1,998		17.8
Beggars		394		3.5
Total		11,201		99.9+

*Of these, 140 were nobles.
+Percentages rounded.
Source: Coste, *La Ville d'Aix,* 2:712.

The dominance of the administrators in the life of the town was easily visible in sections like the Villeneuve quarter, an area of modest houses near the tall, brooding Palais de Justice, which contained both sovereign courts, the sénéchaussée court, the *Bureau des finances,* and the prisons. Almost every building in the Villeneuve quarter housed an avocat, procureur, or tax official anxious to live near his place of work. One street alone, the Grande Rue du Boulevard, counted 21 avocats in 1695.[17]

The dominance of the administrators was even more obvious in the most fashionable areas of the city, the cours Royale (today the cours Mirabeau) and in the quarters of St. Jean and Mazarin. Newly developed in the 1640's, blessed with the wide, straight streets, the squares, fountains and vistas which epitomize the most progressive notions of seventeenth-century urban planning, these areas were dominated by the great hôtels of Aix's robe nobility, the 200 *présidents* and *conseillers* of the two sovereign courts. These attractive areas were sights which drew visitors then as today. In 1739, Charles de Brosses, président of the Parlement of Dijon, in his description of the town, noted:

[The quarter] of the *gens de condition*, which covers a great part of the town, is magnificently built; most of the houses are tall, built in the Italian manner and beautifully ornamented . . . the streets are wide, straight and filled with beautiful fountains; small squares planted with trees to give shade are everywhere; in sum, this town is very attractive, and is the most attractive in France, apart from Paris.[18]

The tourist of today is likely to share de Brosses' enthusiasm. The cours, lined with tall shady sycamore trees, and ornamented with no less than three bubbling fountains, which give an illusion of coolness even at the height of the Provençal summer, is much the same now as it was then, although a Monoprix supermarket stands at present on the site of the convent of Notre Dame de Miséricorde. The hôtels built by the *parlementaires* still dominate the south side of the cours, their severely elegant facades broken only by occasional witty touches of ornamentation: the male caryatids, found only in the region of Aix, which support the doorframes and grimace under the weight they bear. And in the quartier Mazarin similar hôtels line the place des Quatre Dauphins, so named for its fountain, carved with four gambolling dolphins. These areas are the sights which the tourist thinks of as most typical of Aix, with perhaps the exception of the brooding, distant Mt. Sainte-Victoire, immortalized by Aix's native painter, Cézanne.

Within these elegant hôtels the robe nobles led lives of a luxury which few members of the traditional military nobility could match. By the end of the seventeenth century the *grande robe* had been completely assimilated into the traditional nobility, and had come to dominate the whole Second Estate through wealth and influence. The major division among the nobles of Provence was not between robe and sword, but rather between the nobles who possessed fiefs, and thus held the privileges, including fiscal exemptions, accruing to them, and those who did not. The nobles of the robe were in most cases wealthy enough to buy fiefs. Of approximately 600 noble heads of households in Aix in 1695, 50 possessed fiefs, and of these 37 were robe nobles.[19] As landlords the robe nobles controlled perhaps 20 percent of the land of Provence.[20] In 1730, for example, M. de Bayer, Marquis d'Argens, and procureur-général of the Parlement, was lord of the 1,140 communicants of Eguilles, while Président of the Parlement Ragusse was seigneur of Mimes, and M. de Meirnet, conseiller in the same court, held the village of St. Marc in fief.[21] Arthur Young's acquaintance, Baron de la Tour d'Aigues, enjoyed an estate worth some 2,000,000 livres and had an annual income of 86,000 livres. But his fortune is exceptional, for his family, the Brunys, had been négociants in Marseille.[22] Probably more usual was a yearly income of 3,000-5,000 livres. At any rate, the robe nobles had enough money to dominate "high society" in a provincial capital. The robe nobles had the most imposing households in Aix. In 1695, Scipion d'Agut, Président of the Cour des comptes, employed 12 servants: one cook, one nurse, one chambermaid, three other maids, three lackeys, one sedan-chair carrier, and two clerks.[23] One président of the Parlement employed a total of 17. While such large staffs of servants were unusual, présidents of the Parlement employed an average of nine servants each, while the average for présidents of the Cour des comptes was over five, and counsellors of the Parlement averaged almost four. This is in contrast to an average of 1.45 for the rest of the nobility of Aix, and 0.24 for the town as a whole.[24]

The 450 other nobles who lived in Aix were for the most part not nearly so wealthy, although their levels of income varied widely. Most of them were not fief-holders. There were among Aix's nobles four *chevaliers*, 136 *écuyers*, 88 "nobles," and 124 army officers. Those who could boast the most ancient lineage were the 37 Knights of Malta, connected with the church of St. Jean de Malte, which gave its name to the quartier St. Jean. Few of these lesser nobles could afford the great hôtels in the fashionable quarters and the retinues of servants of their robe counterparts. They lived in less fashionable areas throughout the city, often in apartments of only a few rooms.[25] Their furnishings were more apt to be comfortable rather than luxurious. For example, when Dlle. Magdelaine Jeanne Bonnard, daughter of a noble and sister of a canon and of the French consul-general at Smyrna, died in 1775, she left an estate of household furniture, including a walnut wardrobe and silver candlesticks, worth only some 200 livres.[26] While some of these nobles were quite wealthy for the provinces—the estate of Jean Baptiste Maximin Le Gros, who died in 1782, totalled 72,474 livres, and included *rentes* on the commune worth 20,030 livres, and 37,988 livres of rentes to private individuals—others were actually impecunious. In 1695, four "nobles" were classified in the *Capitation* as poor, including two orphan daughters of a noble who "lived by the work of their hands."[27]

All but the poorest of the nobles shared the enjoyment of Aix's social season, which usually began in December when they moved into town from their country estates.[28] Despite Aix's reputation for dullness, the town offered many amusements: a badminton court, a theater, whose lovely comedienne was frequently accused of leading the cadets of noble houses astray, and many gambling dens. The town also offered opportunities for less frivolous socializing, through its penitent groups, and, later, through the Masonic lodges which replaced them in popularity in the last years of the Old Regime. These organizations allowed the Aixois to get together to satisfy what one historian has called an urge to "sociability typical of the people of the Midi," while at the same time performing good works and spreading enlighten-ment.[29] In addition the city nobles enjoyed a round of social calls, salons, and balls, paced by the judicial calendar and centering on the social circle of the intendant. On the whole, the life of Aix's nobles and administrators must have been quite pleasant.

It is an exaggeration, but only a slight one, to say that the rest of the town existed to serve the needs of these nobles and administrators. At the end of the seventeenth century Aix was, for the most part, a town of the rich and their servants, with few elements which could be termed "middle class." Households which could be thus classified numbered only nine percent of the 11,201 households in Aix in 1695, as table 1.2 shows. The merchants were

Table 1.2: Aix's Middle Classes, 1695

Lawyers	451
Other liberal professions	
Doctors	30
Surgeons	63
Apothecaries	28
Professors and schoolmasters	26
Bourgeois	199
Merchants	58
Bankers	3
Small shopkeepers	175
Total, including lawyers	1,033
Percent of total population	9.1%

Source: Coste, *La Ville d'Aix*, 2:712, 769-838.

almost infinitesimal in number—only 58 in 1695. So too were those who practiced in the liberal professions, if we leave aside the 277 avocats, 139 procureurs, and 35 *notaires* who are best classified among the administrators. Apart from the lawyers, the liberal professions consisted only of a handful of doctors, surgeons, and professors drawn to Aix by its university. Not much more numerous were the true "bourgeois," as the term was used in the ancien régime, those who did not work but lived off their incomes as *rentiers*. In 1695 these numbered 199 households. These people were most likely former avocats or merchants. Their scale of living was pleasant but modest; one, but only one, owned a fief. Most shunned the more fashionable and expensive quarters, and lived in modest apartments in the older parts of the city. They employed one servant, or perhaps none at all. In sum, the middle classes of Aix were neither numerous, rich, nor powerful.[30]

Aix was thus a city of the rich, and of the *menu peuple* who served them. Indeed, the largest single socioprofessional group in the city was that of servants, who numbered some 27 percent of the heads of households in 1695.[31] This total includes public servants, such as soldiers, sailors, and *gardes de police*. The omission of such types leave 22 percent, or some 2,500 households, of those properly classified as domestic servants. Among these there were wide variations in wealth and status; the washerwoman who hired herself out for a few sous a day had little in common with a great noble's proud domestic, who might at his death leave a valuable estate of clothes, house-hold furnishings, and jewelry.[32] Table 1.3 illustrates the differentiations among the servant class. Especially noticeable are the large number of *servantes*. These could be of two types. They might be the maids-of-all-work employed in the minor noble or bourgeois households which kept just one

Table 1.3. Servants in Aix, 1695

Not lodged with master	
Washerwoman	18
Fine laundress	1
Manoeuvre	1
Porteurs de chaise	225
Litter-carriers	19
Carters	2
	266
Lodged with master	
Servantes	1,046
Garçons de boutique	293
Valets	275
Chambermaids	225
Lackeys	142
Clerks	73
Tutors	58
Femmes de service	56
Apprentices	27
Porteurs	9
Doorkeepers	14
Maitres d'hôtel	4
Nurses	4
Scullery boys	3
Kitchen aid	1
Baker	1
Grooms	2
Sommelier	1
Sécretaires	2
Carter	1
	2,237
Total	2,503

Source: Carrière, *La Population d'Aix*, pp. 85-86.

servant, for only the largest and wealthiest households could afford special-ized domestics like valets or lackeys. Or they might be female workers in various domestic industries, especially the textile industry; such women often lived in the households of the master craftsmen and were known as "ser-vantes." They were among the poorest paid of all of Aix's wage-earners. Another minor point to notice: the large number of porteurs de chaise. In Aix only a handful of the very rich kept a carriage; the rest made do with a sedan chair.

Second only to the servants in number were the artisans and small shopkeepers, who made up approximately 22 percent of the households in the town in 1695. The trades and crafts they practiced were bewildering in their variety. The Capitation roll lists 140 different categories. Carpenters, shoemakers, weavers, bakers, glovemakers, pasta-sellers, pullers of teeth, fountain cleaners, mule drivers, musicians, sievemakers (there were four in Aix in 1695), dyers, spinners, wool-carders, workers in glass, pewter, leather, wood, iron, pottery—the list is endless. Most widely practiced were the trades of *tailleur d'habits* (a total of 190 in 1695), shoemaker (170), plasterer (118), and joiner (108).[33]

Usually the artisan had his atelier in his home, and worked alone, or with one or two helpers. Only in the textile industries was there evidence of units of production larger than the family workshop. In the woolen and linen industries the putting-out system prevailed. Masters bought the raw materials and distributed them to the artisans, often women, who performed each step of the production operation, carding, weaving, dyeing, etc. Such industries were not on a large scale. Aix had only a handful of masters, and some 30 to 50 craftsmen attached to them. The production cycle was carefully regulated by the gilds. In 1751, for example, the gild of the wool carders demanded an *arrêt* of Parlement to prevent dyers from performing tasks normally done by carders only.[34]

How widespread or effective the gild system was among the other arti-sans of Aix, it is impossible to say. Certainly artisans were encouraged to organize gilds by the government, for its own fiscal purposes; this was the practice not only of the royal government, but also of the municipality, which hoped to collect a tax for the participation of the gilds in the *fête-Dieu* procession. But we have records of organized gild activities in only 17 crafts. Doubtless the system was more widespread than this indicates; in 1695 some 16 percent of the artisans, scattered in 55 different trades, identified them-selves as masters, while nine percent were labeled apprentices.[35] But we do not know precisely how many of Aix's trades had gilds, or if these gilds were becoming more exclusive during the eighteenth century.

Aix's artisans lived modestly. They could rarely afford servants. Arti-sans who worked in the same trade often lived together in the same neighbor-hood, usually in the meanest areas of the town, the medieval Corps de Ville, and its surrounding quarters. All 67 of Aix's tanners, for example, practiced their malodorous craft on the street lying between the quarters of Cordeliers and Villeverte, which bore their name. Similarly, Aix's locksmiths congregated on the rue des Chaudronniers, which in 1695 housed at No. 1 a glassmaker, at No. 18 a cabaret, at No. 19 a locksmith, at No. 23 two metalworkers and another locksmith, at Nos. 24 and 26 three more locksmiths. Butchers and fishsellers, of course, lived in the Corps de Ville near the marketplace, while those artisans and shopkeepers who dealt in the luxury trades often settled in the quarters of St. Jean and Mazarin, for the convenience of their fashionable clientele.[36]

In the least densely populated quarter of the city, the Faubourg, beyond the walls, and in the poor quarters of Bellegarde and Cordeliers, near the city gates, lived that portion of Aix's population classified as rural: 18 percent of all the households in 1695.[37] The modern tourist, whose view of Mt. Sainte-Victoire is obscured by concrete apartment complexes, may find it difficult to believe, but during the seventeenth and eighteenth centuries Aix had within its city limits many patches of green: squares, gardens, commons, and even open fields. These were cared for by Aix's rural population, the gardeners, and above all the day laborers, the so-called *travailleurs*. Most travailleurs owned a bit of property, either in the town or in its surrounding fields (*terroir*). Peasants owned about half of the land in Aix's terroir, while nobles held 25-30 percent, 20 percent was in the possession of the bourgeoisie, and the remaining 6 percent was owned by the clergy.[38] But apart from a few well-to-do peasants, (called in Provence *ménagers* or *bastidans*, because they often lived apart from the peasant villages, on their own land), who owned substantial plots of from 5 to 15 hectares, most peasant plots were very small.[39] A travailleur would own only enough land for a few rows of wheat or vegetables or a vine or two. Such a plot would not produce sufficient food to sustain the travailleur and his family. Therefore the travailleur would go to the marketplace on hiring day to seek employment in the countryside during planting or harvesting, and if he found work, he would leave the city gates before dawn to labor all day in the fields. Agriculture in Provence was more specialized, and therefore more labor-intensive, than elsewhere in France. The standard staple crop, wheat, was grown, but so were a number of other crops—vines and olive and chestnut trees. Provence did not produce enough grain to feed its population, and therefore imported wheat both from other areas of France and from abroad, even in years of good harvest. When harvests were meagre, municipal authorities in the towns of Provence were careful to insure an adequate supply of these *grains de mer*.[40] The wheat imports were paid for by exports of wine and Provence's famous olive oil, used for both cooking and light. The vines and olive trees needed a lot of attention, and many travailleurs were employed in their care. During the winter, when such agricultural employment was hard to find, the travailleur might turn his hand to a petty craft; Aix in 1695 housed travailleurs who were also masons, woodcutters, mule-drivers, and furriers.[41]

The Aix of such menu peuple—the travailleurs, the artisans, the servants, who formed almost 80 percent of the population—was a very different city from the Aix of the rich and privileged. Its landmarks were not the cathedral, the Palais, the cours, but rather the marketplace and the local cabaret, where the artisan or travailleur might stop to have a pot of watered wine after his days' labor. The lives of these menu peuple were not paced to the judicial calendar or the fashionable season, but rather by the market days (Tuesdays and Saturdays), the fairs (Aix had three, of five days each, one starting on December 4, the feast day of Ste. Barbe, one on February 9, the day of Ste. Apollonie, and the third in the spring, before the fête-Dieu)[42] and the great religious feasts, Christmas, Easter, All Saint's Day, the fête-Dieu, which brought them holidays and processions. The spaciousness and serenity of the quarters St. Jean and Mazarin had no counterparts in areas like the Corps de Ville, Bellegarde, Cordeliers, and Villeverte, where the menu peuple lived. These quarters had been the center of the town in the Middle Ages, and in the seventeenth and eighteenth centuries they kept their medieval appearance. These were areas of narrow, twisting streets lined with the old-fashioned deux-fenêtre houses, small and cramped, crowded with many families, each living in a few small rooms. Houses in Aix contained an average of over nine persons each in 1695. There were some which contained as many as 40. The quarters with the highest averages were the poor quarters of Villeneuve and Villeverte.[43]

The people who made their homes in such houses lived poised precariously on the brink of destitution. Wages of travailleurs and other day laborers were so low that if a man and his wife both worked steadily throughout the year they could barely support themselves, let alone their children.[44] And all too frequently work was hard to find, or the breadwinner fell ill, or prices rose, or a new baby came, or something else happened to upset the delicate family budget. It is true that skilled artisans usually could earn a higher wage, when they found work. But they too had their problems. Their trades suffered from overcrowding. Could a town like Aix, after all, support 190 tailors and 170 shoemakers? Aix in the Old Regime was, as Michel Vovelle has said, "an urban milieu in crisis."[45] Its lack of economic diversity, its position of feeding off the nobles and administrators, who in turn fed off the surrounding countryside, made it highly vulnerable to the perils of underemployment. When disaster struck, how could the poor artisan or travailleur survive?

Charity is the answer. During the Old Regime approximately 20 percent of the people of Aix received some sort of organized public assistance (see

Chapter IV). By 1789 Aix had 28 charities (see Chapter II). If a man were ill, he could get aid from the hôtel-Dieu, the Miséricorde, the Incurables. If he were insane, the Insensés would care for him, and if he were blind, he could turn to the Hôpital St. Joachim. The Charité would give him bread if he were starving, care for him in his old age, or take in his children if he fell ill or could not support them. The Corpus Domini de St. Sauveur and the Miséricorde would pay for a dowry for his daughter or an apprenticeship for his son. If he were in financial trouble he could pawn his few belongings at the Mont-de-Piété, and if he were beset by legal difficulties, the Conseil Charitable would provide free legal aid. If this failed to help him, the Oeuvre des Prisons would bring him clothing and food during his incarceration. When he died the Penitents Gris would bury him.

These charities were important to Aix for many more reasons than the aid they gave to its most unfortunate citizens. The charities were as much a part of the town's tradition as its archepiscopate and its Parlement. Aix was a "ville hospitalière" as well as a "ville parlementaire." As the town's most famous historian, Pierre-Joseph de Haitze, wrote in 1715, "Nothing is more noticeable than the fact that the soil of the town has always been favorable to works of charity." Aix had "at all times" been "animated by a spirit of charity."[46] The first hospital in Aix was probably founded in the sixth or seventh century, and from the eleventh century on, the city was never without some form of charitable organization.[47]

In the seventeenth and eighteenth centuries the charities of Aix were deeply interwoven in the fabric of municipal life. Their buildings were local landmarks in which the Aixois felt great civic pride. The hospital-general, La Charité, for example, was considered by many to be "one of the most beautiful ornaments of the town."[48] Designed, at least according to local tradition, by Vauban, it was esteemed by even the nineteenth-century citizens of Aix as "the most beautiful *maison centrale de correction et de travail*" in all of France.

This truly royal monument, surrounded by high walls and decorated with a magnificent facade, situated along the most beautiful promenade outside the town of Aix, and facing due north, offers four separate great courts, shaded by high leafy trees, and watered . . . by bubbling fountains, decorated with dolphins.[49]

It is little wonder that during the construction of the Charité some people objected that it was "too magnificent a building for the lodging of the poor"; an objection met by apologists for the Charité with the retort that, although Heaven was even more beautiful, the poor were allowed lodging there.[50]

As familiar to the townspeople as the buildings of the charities were their inmates. What inhabitant of Aix could fail to recognize as they marched in the procession the orphan boys cared for in the Petit Betheléem, dressed in red "in honor of the incarnation of the eternal word" and thus popularly known as the "Enfants Rouges? " Who would not know by sight the Penitents Gris, dressed in their robes, masks and pointed hats (shaped rather like a dunce cap), made of coarse gray cloth, when they, as a charitable duty, accompanied to their final resting place those too poor to pay for a proper funeral? [51] The funeral procession of a wealthier citizen, an écuyer or an avocat en la cour, would probably include the easily recognizable black-robed figures of the proud rectors of one of the city's major charities— the Charité, perhaps, or the Miséricorde—since a small donation to the charity could buy their participation. For example, a mere 18 livres given to the Miséricorde in 1688 would guarantee the presence at a funeral of 13 former rectors of the organization, and of eight of the rectors currently in office, bearing candles decorated with the crest of the hospital— a fine show in an era when the length of a funeral cortege was a mark of social status. [52]

Ceremonial appearances of the charities were not limited to funerals, for one of the maxims of the charities was "that processions will be held often; the whole town takes pleasure in them." [53] In seventeenth-century Aix all important events—the major religious feasts, such as Easter and the fête-Dieu, and secular celebrations like the royal births and marriages—were marked by processions in which all the gilds and corporations of the town took part. These processions gave the love of pageantry characteristic of Provençal life full rein. Every charity was proud to participate in these colorful occasions. The rectors and inmates of the charities dressed in special costume, and all marched behind a banner bearing the crest of the institution. That of the Oeuvre des Prisons, for example, was bordered in blue satin printed with fleur de lys, and had on one side a picture of the Virgin as Notre Dame de Piété, hovering over a prison, and on the other John the Baptist catechizing his fellow inmates in the prisons of Herod. [54] The order in which the charities marched was a major indication of prestige, and disputes over rank frequently arose, causing even fistfights between rectors of rival institutions, and necessitating mediation by the archbishop or the Parlement. [55]

These ceremonial appearances of the charities are only a minor, if colorful, aspect of their role in municipal life. Far more important was the involvement of the institutions in the economy of Aix. Like Aix's churches and convents, the charities were major consumers, although in contrast to the convents and monasteries, they purchased not luxuries manufactured by Aix's artisans, but basic necessities such as wheat and other foodstuffs, wool, and coarse cloth. [56] The charitable institutions also played an important economic role as employers. All of them needed a minimum of supervisory personnel, including the inevitable porter to guard the door. The institutions which cared for the sick also employed a medical staff of physicians, surgeons, and nurses. The very largest of the charities, such as the hôtel-Dieu and the Charité, encompassed numerous workshops, which manufactured not only almost everything necessary for their own use, but also surpluses for sale. They thus offered employment to master bakers, shoemakers, tailors, and weavers. Further, because they had the right to grant the *maîtrise,* or mastership, after a certain period of service, these charity workshops provided an opportunity to rise for those who found the gild system of apprenticeship closed to them.[57]

Apart from their roles as important consumers and employers, the charities figured vitally in the economy of Aix as landowners. Because the legacies of the pious to the charities frequently included parcels of land, over the years the charities came to control many urban properties and much valuable agricultural acreage in the town's hinterland. Thus the charities took the role of landlord for many a poor peasant who might, in time of disaster, be forced to seek their aid.

One further economic function was performed by the charities of the town. Aix, primarily an administrative rather than a commercial center, had in that preindustrial era few opportunities for investment aside from land. One of the few alternatives available to the small investor was a rente, or lifetime annuity, purchased from one of the charities. These rentes seemed attractive investments, for the financial needs of the institutions drove up the interest rates—levels of eight and even 12 percent were not uncommon— while the income from the charities' lands, and from their own rentes invested in such safe institutions as the Clergy of France and the Estates of Provence, seemed to guarantee payment. Domestic servants looking for an investment for their meagre life savings, artisans saving for their daughters' dowries, and elderly demoiselles seeking a way to live respectably off their incomes, all found them irresistible investments.

The charities of Aix were uniquely *municipal* institutions, objects of civic pride to the town as a whole. They were important economically to all levels of society, not merely to the poor, and were in turn supported by all levels of society, not only the rich. They played an important role in the town's religious life; one could be buried in their cemeteries or have masses said in their chapels for the souls of the dead. The charities even performed some duties of municipal government, for *archers* nominally under the control of the Charité had the official duty of arresting beggars in the streets and clearing them from the churches. Thus the charities were very important institutions in the Aix of the Old Regime.

This is a study of the charities of Aix and of the poor they helped. Aix in the Old Regime was, to paraphrase Disraeli, two cities, divided into the very rich and the very poor. Yet these two cities were bound together by myriad ties of mutual dependence, and of these, the charities were one of the most important. They bound together the rich and poor in a "perpetual commerce of charity,"[58] and thus softened social antagonisms. But after 1760 Aix's municipal system of charity broke down. There were, as we shall see, many factors behind the collapse, factors as disparate as the financial mismanagement of the charities, changing attitudes toward charity work and even religion, and the centralizing initiatives of the royal government in the field of public assistance. But whatever its cause, the collapse of its charities left Aix a splintered society of mutually antagonistic social groups on the eve of that great social upheaval which was the French Revolution.

CHAPTER II

The Charitable Impulse

Aix's system of charitable assistance for the poor was essentially a product of the cluster of attitudes and assumptions about poverty and charity which prevailed during the French Counter-Reformation, in roughly the first half of the seventeenth century. These years were a period of transition, when attitudes toward poverty and charity were changing rapidly. Three factors combined to produce this change. The first element was ideological: the Counter-Reformation itself, which created a renewed interest in Christian-inspired charitable endeavors, and in a moral reformation of the poor. The second was economic. The worsening economic conditions of the late sixteenth and early seventeenth centuries greatly aggravated the problem of poverty, and therefore forced it on public attention. And the third factor was political and administrative. The emerging absolutist state developed pretensions to control in the field of charity, long the exclusive purview of the Church. But changes in attitudes are rarely swift or clearcut. Old assumptions continued to coexist side by side with the new. Together they formed the immensely complex constellation of attitudes which form the subject of this chapter. But before tracing them, we must see how and when Aix's charities came into being.

Most of Aix's charities date from the first half of the seventeenth century. Because of this the year 1640 makes a convenient starting point for this study. Before 1600 Aix had only four charities. All provided care only for the sick. Oldest of Aix's hospitals was the leprosery, St. Lazare (naturally located outside the walls of the town), which dated from the middle of the thirteenth century. By 1600 St. Lazare was in decline, the scourge of leprosy having abated from its peak in the Middle Ages. Next in date was another relic of medieval Aix, the hospital St. Eutrope, founded in 1469.[1] St. Eutrope was a very small hospital—its patients numbered only six—which cared for so-called "hydropiques,"[2] victims of dropsy. Larger and more important than either St. Lazare or St. Eutrope was St. Jacques, the hôtel-Dieu, or hospital, which provided treatment for all types of the ill. Founded in 1519 by the banker Jacques de la Roque, St. Jacques could accommodate

18

over 200 patients in its roomy building. One of the three major charities large and important enough to be designated by the title of "hospital-general," the hôtel-Dieu enjoyed the largest endowment and the proudest tradition of all Aix's charities.[3] Last of Aix's charities established before 1600 was another large enough to be called a hospital-general. This was the Miśericorde. From its beginning in 1590 the Miśericorde provided food and medicine to the ill who for some reason could not go to the hôtel-Dieu and had to remain at home. The Miśericorde also gave alms to the so-called *pauvres honteux,* those unfortunates whose social position made begging shameful, and it provided dowries and apprenticeships for those whose parents were too poor to pay for them.[4]

Thus all of Aix's charities founded before the year 1600 catered primarily to the ill. Other types of poor, the able-bodied unemployed, the orphans, and the aged, had to rely on private alms which they begged in the streets or at the doors of the rich. But this situation changed in roughly the first half of the seventeenth century, when many new charities were established to care for a broad spectrum of the problems of poverty. The founding in 1590 of the Miśericorde, which provided a variety of charitable services, was a significant portent for the future.

The century of Aix's greatest charitable endeavor opened in 1600 with the rebuilding of the hospital St. Eutrope by Michel Jualne, a merchant of Aix. The year 1629 saw the foundation of Filles du Bon Pasteur, a charity which housed repentant prostitutes. This was followed in 1637 by the foundation of a Mont-de-Piété, or pawnshop, where both rich and poor could pawn their household goods without paying interest. The next year saw the beginning of two more charities, one, called the Oeuvre de la Propagande de la Foi, avowedly intended to woo indigent Protestant children to the Catholic faith, and the other, the Maison Hospitalière des Filles Religieuses de la Miséricorde, to provide dowries for girls too poor to enter convents.[5] About this time another pious work, the Oeuvre de la Redemption des Captifs, also had its beginning. The purpose of this charity was to buy the freedom of Christians held captive by the infidel Turks.[6] The year 1640 saw the foundation of three charities, the Refuge, the Providence, and La Charité. The Refuge housed women arrested for prostitution, while the Providence gave shelter to women turned out by their families, usually for lewd behavior.[7] More important than these two *oeuvres* was La Charité, the third and last of Aix's major hospitals-general. The Charité was intended by its founders to be the crown of Aix's system of charities. It housed orphans, the aged, and the able-bodied unemployed, and it also distributed bread every Sunday to the poor of the city.[8] Thus the first 40 years of the seventeenth century had seen the foundation of eight new charities, seven of these having their beginnings in the three years between 1637 and 1640. This period was truly one when the spirit of charity—and the desire to found charitable organizations—seemed to pervade Aix.

In the 1680's Aix experienced a similar outburst of charitable endeavor, which added seven new foundations to the city's roster of charitable institutions. These included asylums for orphan boys and girls (Petit Bethléem and the Pureté), and the insane (the Insensés), as well as charities to aid prisoners (Oeuvre des Prisons) and to provide legal counsel for poor people involved in law suits (the Conseil Charitable). These years also saw the foundation of a penitent group, the Penitents Gris, who provided for the funerals of the poor, and of bureaux de charité in each parish, which distributed bread and clothing at the local parish level.[9]

After the 1680's the impulse to found charities weakened. No major charities would be founded in Aix in the eighteenth century. Admittedly the period from 1700 to 1789 saw the beginning of six new charities, but four of these were the work of one pious archbishop, Brancas, and represent his attempt to regain for the Church the initiative in the field of charity.[10] The two others were minor foundations, a hospital for so-called "incurables," founded in 1724, and an institution for the blind, founded in 1782 in imitation of the famed hospital Quinze-Vingts in Paris.[11] But by and large the system of municipal charity in Aix was a product of the seventeenth century, and more precisely of the two great outbursts of charitable endeavor in the late 1630's and 1680's.

It is important to note that only four of these charities, Archbishop Brancas's foundations, were religious institutions, and that none was founded or run by the royal government. Most of Aix's charities were totally private and secular institutions, founded and administered by local laymen. This was a reflection of current attitudes about the proper roles of the Church and state in public assistance. By the early seventeenth century the Church's control of charity, traditional since the Middle Ages, had been successfully challenged, and the emerging absolutist state hoped to fill the resulting gap. But neither the resources nor the philosophy of the newly powerful state allowed for a nationwide, centrally administered, state-supported system of public assistance. So in practice the state left the field to private initiative. We can trace the grassroots impact of this debate over the proper institutional roles of Church and state in their struggle for control of the charities of Aix.

Legal basis of the pretensions of both Church and state for the control of charitable administration was the fact that in the law charities were considered "minors," to be overseen by a tutelary power. The Church's claim to exercise such power was based on tradition, and harked back to the church's undisputed control of charity in the Middle Ages. In medieval Aix, as everywhere in France, charity was a function of the Church. In the thirteenth century all eight of Aix's charities were founded and controlled and held in benefice by ecclesiastics. The archbishop of Aix exercised, as did each bishop in his diocese, a tutelary power over all hospitals in his jurisdiction except those run by the independent hospital orders. This did not mean that he personally conducted the day to day administration of the organizations; rather he could appoint rectors, receive their ceremonial promise to administer the hospital faithfully, and inspect the yearly rendering of the hospital's accounts.[12]

This ecclesiastical domination of charity did not last. The wars and economic disasters of the latter half of the fourteenth century destroyed all but three of these ecclesiastical charities. When peace and prosperity returned in the mid-fifteenth century, the hospitals were re-established, but for the most part under lay rather than ecclesiastical control. In the fifteenth century Aix boasted six hospitals. Two were governed by religious orders, and one was the benefice of the cathedral chapter, while three were totally lay organizations. The reasons for this shift to lay control are hard to pinpoint, but doubtless primary among them were the incompetence of ecclesiastical administration and the abuses of the benefice system. The churches and priories which held the charities in benefice often appropriated hospital revenues for their own use.[13] The publicity given such abuses by Protestant polemicists during the Reformation—and indeed the whole Reformation attack on the powers of the Church—most probably contributed as well to this shift toward secularization.

Important also was a growing consciousness on the part of the urban bourgeoisie of the problem of poverty. Spurred by the writings of humanists like Juan Luis Vives, who emphasized that charity was the duty of all, laymen and religious alike, as well as by the sight of the misery all around them, the merchants of almost every major town in western Europe began in the late fifteenth and early sixteenth centuries to establish new charities, which they, and not the Church, would control. The best example of such new foundations, indeed the prototype for most of them in France, was the Aumône Général of Lyon, dating from 1531. This institution was founded and administered solely by Lyon's rich merchants.[14]

Aix, too, showed evidence of this new trend toward the secularization of charity. In 1532 a bourgeois *marchand*, Jacques de la Roque, founded Aix's hôtel-Dieu. De la Roque's will specified:

> that . . . I have had and have the idea, the intention, the will that this hospital will be, is and must be, in all times and as long as the world will last, private, profane, lay and not at all ecclesiastic, for this I formulate and I specify repeatedly my will and my intention. . . and I impose this absolute condition in the construction, foundation, titling, annexation and aggrandizement of the aforesaid hospital, of the products and revenues of my property for the poor of Jesus Christ who can come in great crowds into this hospital,

that there will not intervene and cannot interfere expressly, tacitly, wittingly or in any other manner, any authority, consent and permission of our very holy seigneur the Pope, of his very reverend seigneur the archbishop of Aix, or of any other ecclesiastic, of whatever rank. . . .

This strongly worded prohibition was followed by other clauses designed to guarantee its effectiveness. De la Roque's will expressly forbade that any of the hospital's property be made into a benefice. No ecclesiastic was to be elected rector, or to oversee in any way the work of the lay administrators. This trend toward secularization of charitable institutions continued until the beginning of the seventeenth century. The Miséricorde, founded in 1590, included no clerics among its rectors.[15] In the face of such widespread opposition the archbishop dared not attempt to exercise his traditional supervisory powers over the hospitals, which lay in abeyance in these years.

By the mid-sixteenth century, the royal government had moved to fill this apparent vacuum. Increasingly concerned with poverty as a cause of public disorder, the French state in these years began its two-century-long struggle to wipe out mendicity. The effectiveness of its measures toward this end depended to a large extent on the existence of well-administered hospitals in every town. To insure adequate administration, the royal government began to exercise the tutelary powers over the charities formerly held by the bishops. An edict of December 19, 1543, citing clerical mismanagement of the works of public assistance, specified that the accounts of charities be rendered to *"bailiffs, sénéchaux, prévosts, chastelains"* in the royal service rather than to the bishops. This provision was repeated in the ordinances of January 15, 1545, February 26, 1546, July 25, 1560, April 1561, and in articles 65, 66, and 67 of the famous Ordinance of Blois of May 1579 on hospital administration.[16]

In Aix this royal supervision over the charities was readily accepted. The Grand Bureau of the hôtel-Dieu was created in 1559 to receive the accounts of the hospital, and to authorize borrowing and the reception of legacies. The personnel of the Grand Bureau was composed totally of *gens du roi*, including one president, six conseillers, and one procureur-général of the Parlement, as well as members from the Cour des comptes and the avocat and the procureur des pauvres. The archbishop was not present at the Grand Bureau.[17]

Beset by the far more vast problems of the Reformation, the Church at first seemed prepared to sanction this usurpation of its powers in the field of charity. The council held at Cologne in 1533 was ready to accept the rendition of hospital accounts to local magistrates. But the regenerate Church which arose from the Council of Trent did not surrender its prerogatives so easily; the decrees of Trent specified that bishops alone had the power to supervise the financial affairs of the charities.[18] In succeeding Estates-General and Assemblies of the Clergy, the clergy constantly repeated its demand that bishops preside over the grands-bureaux which received hospital accounts.[19] Agitation over this issue was especially fierce in the 1690's, but Louis XIV resisted clerical pressure and, in edicts in 1695 and 1698, reiterated the rights of royal magistrates to oversee the charities.[20]

It is noteworthy that the royal government never went further in its pretensions than this attempt to assert its supervisory control—a sort of watching brief—over the charities. The king's government did not itself found or administer any institutions of public assistance. The absolutist state of the seventeenth century lacked the resources, both financial and bureaucratic, for a state-supported system of public assistance. It also lacked the inclination. The early modern state exercised its functions through existing private bodies rather than its own bureaucracy whenever possible; the possible contradiction of interests between these bodies and the state, obvious to the modern mind, did not occur to the king's men of the sixteenth and seventeenth centuries. Thus in reality royal policy in the field of public assistance was to leave the problem to private initiative. The epitome of this policy is the royal edict of 1662, which ordered that hospitals-general be established in all cities, but did nothing further toward their foundation.[21]

Thus Aix's charities were the result, not of royal policy, but of private initiative. They were founded by the local notables of the early seventeenth century. What inspired these men to establish charities?

Doubtless one factor was a new awareness of and concern for the problem of poverty. The simple brute facts of popular misery increasingly forced themselves on the attention of the rich and well-born at the end of the sixteenth and the beginning of the seventeenth century. Aix was ravaged by the plague in 1580 and 1630; these outbreaks caused untold misery among the menu peuple, and left crowds of the destitute in their wake.[22] Bad harvests in the 1620's and 1630's made countless more turn to beggary to survive. So many beggars infested Aix in 1623 that the guards on the city gates were doubled to keep them out; the guards were increased again in 1625.[23] In 1630 the revolt of the Cascaveoux brought home to many the extremes to which misery might drive the desperate populace. Starving agricultural laborers from the nearby countryside flocked to Aix, and there joined with the artisans of the town in riot and pillage. For three days they ran wild, burning and sacking the houses of the rich.[24]

Thus the increasing misery of the poor forced itself on public attention. But this was only one factor which underlay the growing concern with the problems of poverty. Another and even more vital element was the influence of the French Counter-Reformation. The religious revival of the early seventeenth century stimulated a return to the traditional Christian duty of charity. The post-Tridentine Church took a renewed interest in charitable endeavor. Giants of the Counter-Reformation, such as St. Vincent de Paul and St. Jean Eudes, focused attention on the problems of poverty through their preaching and writing. Both founded charities themselves and encouraged the charitable giving of the pious.[25] The Counter-Reformation also stimulated charitable acts because they were one obvious and easy route to the heightened personal spiritual satisfaction which was its goal, as presented in the works of figures such as St. François de Sales and Pierre Berulle.

The major channel through which the notions about charity of the figures of the Counter-Reformation reached Aix was the Company of the Holy Sacrament.[26] This secret *cabale des dévots,* with its branches throughout the country and its tentacles deep into the magistrature and the royal government, was highly concerned with the organization of charity and improvement of the moral state of the poor. It was the local branch of the Company of the Holy Sacrament, founded in Aix in 1638, which took the lead in the organization of the majority of the charities in seventeenth-century Aix. Its role was most noticeable, perhaps, in the foundation of the hospital-general in 1640. It is the attitudes and the assumptions of the French Counter-Reformation, as channelled through the Company of the Holy Sacrament, which underlay the system of public assistance which functioned in Aix until 1789.

To point to these underlying causative factors—increasing popular misery, and a spiritual climate which fostered an awareness of and sympathy for the problems of the poor—does not, however, go far toward explaining the form which this outpouring of charity actually took. For the charity of this period had certain distinct characteristics which set it off from that of the past. For example, charity before the seventeenth century had been a matter of almsgiving by private donors directly to the poor; the rich man gave bread or coins to the beggar who came to his door. But in the seventeenth century the gifts of the wealthy came to be channelled through charitable institutions. This institutionalization of charity explains the profusion of charitable organizations founded in the seventeenth century.

A second major change from earlier forms of charity was that not only charity but the poor themselves were to be institutionalized. In the Middle Ages only the sick actually entered charitable institutions to live. But in the seventeenth century, orphans, the aged, beggars, and prostitutes were all to be confined within the walls of institutions. And this brought in its wake the third major change, for the institutionalization of the poor made possible the surveillance of their moral condition. According to traditional concepts of charity the poor man was morally no different from anyone else; indeed it was the rich and not the poor who were in moral danger. But seventeenth-century thinkers popularized the notion that poverty was apt to lead to idleness and thence to debauchery and vice. The charities set about preventing this. The one institution which perhaps epitomizes all of these new trends is the hospital-general, an invention of the early seventeenth century, popularized by the Company of the Holy Sacrament. The hospital-general was intended to wipe out beggary. The indiscriminate private almsgiving which encouraged beggary would be eliminated when all beggars were confined in hospitals-general, where they would be taught the rudiments of religion and set to work. But if the hospital-general was the most characteristic product of these new ideas, all the charities of the seventeenth century reflected them to some extent.

To understand why charity in the seventeenth century took this particular form, we must explore the attitudes and assumptions behind it. These are best revealed in the pamphlets issued by the charities themselves, in justification of their foundation, and for the purpose of fund-raising. These pamphlets were written usually by ecclesiastics connected with the charities, or by especially devoted—and literarily inclined—rectors. Because these pamphlets were designed for the purpose of fund-raising, it is probable that the arguments they present were calculated to appeal to the assumptions of their audience—the pamphlets would have been ineffective otherwise. We can therefore assume that the ideas they elaborate were actually held by the people of Aix.

Yet were these truly "popular attitudes"? Before we say that they were, we must consider carefully who the audience for these pamphlets actually was. Internal evidence indicates that the pamphlets were designed to appeal primarily to the rich potential donor—the écuyer or parlementaire who might bequeath to the charity a fine piece of land or a substantial rente on the Estates of Provence. It is true that the pamphlets emphasized that no one was too poor to be exempt from the duty of Christian charity, and it is a fact that the charities of Aix were supported financially by all classes, the poor as well as the rich (see Chapter III). Yet it is doubtful that the pamphlets reached many of the artisans or small shopkeepers of Aix, who were for the most part illiterate. In Aix in the seventeenth century probably only slightly more than ten percent of the population could even sign their names.[27] Further, the pamphlets were written in French, while the menu peuple of seventeenth-century Aix clung tenaciously to Provençal. It is possible that these factors need not have been as restrictive as they appear. Perhaps the arguments presented in the pamphlets were repeated verbally—in Provençal— by the rectors of the charities during their weekly *quêtes* for funds in the churches and marketplace. There is no proof of this, however. It is best to assume that the audience whose attitudes these pamphlets reflect was a relatively small proportion of the population of Aix.

Yet the ideas found in these pamphlets are as near to truly "popular" attitudes as the historian is likely to get—much nearer, at least, than the analyses of royal legislation and the writings of individual intellectuals which are usually employed as sources for "attitudes" about the care of the poor. These pamphlets do not present a sophisticated and coherent theory of the causes of poverty and the best means for its relief. Instead they reflect the cluster of often incompatible assumptions about such various matters as the just organization of society, the religious duty of charity, the shamefulness of poverty, the necessity of work, and the sin of idleness, which lay behind the formation and continued existence of Aix's charities in the Old Regime.

What is striking about these pamphlets is first of all how old-fashioned they are. If charity took a new form in the seventeenth century, the arguments in its favor were still the traditional Christian ones, propounded by the Church since the days of its foundation. These pamphlets still quoted the Church Fathers of the fourth and fifth centuries, men such as Caesar of Arles, Clement of Alexandria, Gregory of Nyssa, St. Basil, St. John Chrysostom, and St. Augustine, whose writings formed the basis of the traditional teachings of the Christian Church about poverty and charity.[28] Charity was still presented as a Christian duty. The pamphlets of the charities argued that charity was the crown of Christian virtues because it, of all the virtues, was that which most directly imitated God Himself. *"Deus charitas est"*:[29]

Mercy among men, oldest daughter of charity, and the second mother of all good works, is a most excellent virtue which we imitate, as nearly as we can in our fickleness, the high and supreme Mercy which is in God.[30]

God's mercy was manifest in Jesus Christ, who had "given all his Blood on Calvary, to create in the Redemption of all men the greatest of charities."[31] Man could only hope to imitate this infinite charity by being merciful toward those less fortunate than himself. The more wretched the object of charity, the more generous and unselfish the gesture of the donor, and thus the greater the spiritual satisfaction involved. To give an example of this conviction, the Oeuvre des Prisons argued that its alms were, of all charitable acts, the "most spiritual," for the objects of its works were clearly the most wretched sinners.[32]

Christ Himself had set His followers an example of love and sympathy for the poor. He had lived on earth as a poor man, "not only poor, but indigent, and in a state of misery, of need, and worthy of our compassion." He commanded His followers to love the poor, for in so doing they would show their love for Him: "he who had aided the least of them, has aided me."[33]

Those who gave in true imitation of Christ gave without thought of personal gain, except for a feeling of spiritual satisfaction. But apparently, despite the religious revival of the Counter-Reformation, this totally unselfish charity was rare. The Christian concept of charity had always contained an element of personal self-interest; the charities doubtless found this a most effective argument in favor of generosity toward the poor, for it was blatantly stressed in their literature. Charitable acts were presented as a guaranteed road to salvation:

Christ promised Paradise to those who help the poor, he condemns to eternal flames those who abandon them; he declares blessed those who are merciful; he threatens with Hell the implacable misers and those who are harsh towards the poor: because men are judged on the basis of their charity, and if the poor plead our cause at the Tribunal of divine Justice, we have nothing to fear.[34]

Almsgiving was not simply a suggestion for the good Christian; it was rather an obligation. Charity was not merely one of the virtues which contributed toward the soul's salvation; it was the sine qua non. As St. John Chrysostom warned, " 'Perform a thousand good works, nonetheless if you have harshness toward the Poor, you are unworthy of God's mercy toward you,' " and St. Leo added, " 'Though you have faith, chastity, temperance and still more virtues, though you have most excellent merit, all that will profit nothing, if you are not merciful toward the poor.' "[35] A lack of charitable zeal would condemn a soul, but its presence would insure salvation. As one pamphlet put it, quoting St. Prosper, " 'Charity distinguishes the Elect from the Condemned.' "[36] "A tender soul sensible towards them (the poor) is a predestined soul .... what blindness to lose an immortal crown for having refused to the poor that which we must abandon when we die.' "[37]

This promise of the "immortal crown," of "Paradis Ouvert" (as one pamphlet was entitled), to those generous to the poor was obviously one of the charities' most effective fund-raising appeals, and was constantly repeated. Often it was couched in economic metaphor, doubtless in the hope of striking a responsive chord in the hearts of the rich. A donor was invited to form a "société d'action with God and the Angels," the most profitable of speculations an investor could hope to make. " 'Lands, buildings, banks return four or five percent; but one earns much more with charity, God being obliged to pay one hundred to one.' "[38]

Charity then was a way for a rich man to buy salvation. The rich were well advised to worry about the state of their souls, for the Church had always been uneasy about the morally corrupting effect of wealth. This is revealed in the Church's teachings on usury. The wrongs of making loans at interest were far from a dead issue in the early seventeenth century. In 1637 the Confraire de Notre Dame d'Esperance founded a Mont-de-Piété, or pawnshop, in Aix. The purpose of its foundation was stated to be "as much for the conversion of usurers, as for the aid of poor families."[39] Apparently it retained popular support in this endeavor until the end of the century.

The Church's concern with wealth was part and parcel of its view of the proper organization of society. Apparently in seventeenth-century Aix the traditional medieval image of society as the mystical body of Christ still prevailed. This was made explicit in one charity pamphlet:

No one can be ignorant of the fact that God has put all men in a society which makes a body (*corps*) of which each is a member, from which it follows that all property (*biens*) was destined by Providence for their needs . . . . that each has that which is necessary for him; because since property is not held in common among men, and equal sharing among us is neither just nor possible, it always just and necessary that each has some part of the property which was made for all, and that no one lack at least that which is necessary for shelter, food, and clothing, since all are members of the Body of society, and must take part in the obligations that this membership demands. . . . [40]

This passage provides a concise summary of the still current medieval theories of the origin and distribution of property and the obligations which its ownership entailed. The medieval canonists had argued that God created the fruits of the earth for the use of His creatures: this implied that they were to be shared equally among men, and that all men had a right to that which was necessary for their existence. But the canonists could not quite bring themselves to condemn the existence of private property rights; such a sweeping condemnation would, after all, destroy the very fabric of their contemporary society. (As their seventeenth-century adapters stated, "Equal sharing among us is neither just nor possible.")[41] They did stress, however, that individuals had a right only to that which was strictly necessary to their existence. The remainder, "superfluities," were to be shared by others in time of need. No one should lack the basic minimum which made it possible to sustain life.[42] As a seventeenth-century theorist stated:

It follows from these principles, that those who find themselves in need of things absolutely necessary for life and who are unable to earn these by their work have a title and a *natural right* to that which is necessary to their needs of the goods which God has given to others, and since it is not permitted to take these goods, if they are not given, it is an indispensable law that those who are able to succor the poor, give them that part (which is necessary for their existence) . . . . and acquit this duty.[43]

Charity is thus absolutely necessary to the proper functioning of society; it is the means by which the inequalities inherent in the system of private property are corrected. The God of justice and mercy "would not have permitted in the world the distinction of Poor and Rich, if not to unite the Faithful through a perpetual commerce of charity."[44] Charity was thus a sort of social glue, which bound by mutual ties of obligation the rich and the poor.

Each party to the charitable act gained: the poor received the wherewithal to stay alive, while the rich won salvation. These arguments were the traditional Christian arguments for charity, arguments given a new appeal by the religious revival of the Counter-Reformation. They help explain why charity was so prevalent in this era. What they do not explain is why charity in the seventeenth century took the particular, *institutionalized* form that it did.

THE NECESSITY OF ENFERMEMENT

In the last years of the seventeenth century the rectors of one of the new charitable institutions, the hospital-general La Charité, published a pamphlet defending the principle of institutionalization:[45] of caring for the poor in an institution, rather than through private almsgiving by individuals. Institutionalization, the pamphlet stated, was more conducive to public order, for it did not encourage the large crowds of beggars who swarmed in doorways and infested the churches. Secondly, institutionalized charity was cheaper: a gift of one lump sum would replace the thousands of tiny donations to beggars, donations which, for all their small size, added up to being very costly. Finally, and most importantly, the institutionalized charity allowed discrimination in the matter of who received alms. A rich man could not investigate carefully all those who came to his door, to see if they truly deserved his aid. But a charitable institution could made such investigations, and could channel aid only to fit recipients.[46]

The idea that such discrimination was necessary provided the main impetus behind the institutionalization of charity and the attempt to abolish private almsgiving. This idea was fairly new in the seventeenth century. In traditional Christian charity little effort was made to discriminate between the "worthy" and the "unworthy" poor. All who demanded alms were to receive them. There were, of course, even among the Church Fathers, notions about what sort of people were the most fit and proper objects of charity. According to the canonists, one's first concern should be for one's family— charity did indeed begin at home. From there it spread in ever-widening circles to include one's nearest neighbors, one's fellow townsmen, and, ultimately, all Christians.[47] Special attention was to be given to the very old and the very young, to widows and orphans, to the ill—to all those who were unable to care for themselves and thus had special need of protection. In the Middle Ages the terms "paupers" and "les pauvres" had connotations of feebleness, of incapacity to care for oneself, and were used as antonyms of "potens," a man free in himself who needed no protection.[48] Help was also to be given to those of good birth who had fallen on evil times, for they experienced a sense of shame at their poverty which did not affect those born into a humble station.[49]

In seventeenth-century Aix these priorities of almsgiving were still accepted. It was commonly acknowledged that one's primary duty was still to one's family.[50] The sick, the orphans, and the aged were, of course, still the objects of special attention. So too were those of good family who had fallen on evil times. The Miséricorde, besides distributing food and medicine to the ill in their homes, also made distributions of money to those whom they termed the *pauvres honteux*—"persons of good family" who "suffer impatiently humiliating want and pitiful poverty," who fear that their sad position will become common knowledge and who would choose to "die of hunger, being ashamed to ask for alms."[51] Since it was humiliating for those accustomed to a respected station in life to be reduced to relying on the charity of others for their existence, the Miséricorde was careful to distribute its aid to those classified as pauvres honteux only in strictest secrecy.[52] Such secrecy was necessary only in the distribution of alms to those pauvres honteux, however; for one of the menu peuple to be reduced to living off charity was not nearly so humiliating:

... among the honteux one often sees men born in down, formerly covered with gold, with silk, lying today on straw, dressed in old rags ... how full of anguish such people must be! ... But those of *le peuple* are inured ... to working, to suffering, no embarrassment remains to them, they do not blush for shame to proclaim their misery, they describe it without pain, and even with pleasure when they receive some aid.[53]

Thus for some poverty was their natural state; hard work and suffering were all they could expect of life. For them the acceptance of alms was not "shameful."

Even among the menu peuple, however, further distinctions had to be drawn. These are revealed in the rules of the charities. First of all, people who were not residents of Aix were ineligible for aid from the municipal charities;[54] the principle that each community should be responsible for its own poor was an axiom of public assistance in the seventeenth century. Also excluded from charity were "valets and servants still in the houses of their masters." The traditional form of the household obviously still prevailed; a master had complete responsibility for the care of members of his household struck by illness or old age. A further exclusion was made in the case of those suffering from venereal disease. The Miséricorde would not aid them, although the hôtel-Dieu admitted them.[55] The sin of these people was so blatant to preclude them from the consideration of many Christians.

More important than these rather technical distinctions was the basic division between those who deserved help and those who did not. The aged, the very young, and the ill, of course, deserved help. But what was to be done about those who formed the heart of the problem of poverty in early modern

France: the able-bodied poor who because of unemployment or crop failure faced disaster unless helped by charity? It was in respect to this type of poor—the so-called *pauvres valides*—that attitudes changed most radically in the seventeenth century.

The problem lay in the difficulty in distinguishing between those who were reduced to beggary through unavoidable natural circumstance and those who begged from laziness, who found dependence on alms easier and more pleasant than working. Even in the Middle Ages, supposedly the era of indiscriminate charity, this distinction had been drawn, and the wilfully idle were considered unworthy of charity, which would only encourage their irresponsibility.[56] The change which occured in the seventeenth century was that this distinction between those reduced to beggary through circumstance and those who begged by choice was made less often. Increasingly, *all* of the able-bodied poor were considered wilfully idle. A life of labor was Adam's curse and God's commandment: man must earn his bread by the sweat of his brow.[57] Those who did not work disobeyed the law of God.

That the seventeenth-century Aixois drew this conclusion did not mean that he was totally unaware of the way in which his economy operated. It was accepted that sometimes men truly could not find work, especially in winter, "when there is no employment," "when frost and bad weather prevents them from working."[58] For agricultural laborers winter was of course necessarily a time of idleness; even those who possessed another skill—those who might work occasionally as carters, or perhaps carpenters—might find it difficult to carry out these trades because of bad weather. But admission that seasonal unemployment might exist was as far as these pamphlets were prepared to go. If a man was reduced to beggary even in winter, it was quite likely to be his own fault. He might have wasted what he had earned when work was abundant; "peasants during good weather should make some reserve for bad weather, and not pass Sunday in a Cabaret."[59] He might not have been able to find employment because he was a negligent or unfaithful worker.[60] Finally, he might have been offered work but refused it:

A person of merit and of virtue whom one could name, needing fifteen peasants during the rigors of last winter, and going where there were a great number: "My friends," he said, "I need fifteen of you to bind up branches in the country, and I will give you twelve sous per day." There was not one of them who would go to work; they all responded in a mocking tone: "We can earn more than thirty by doing nothing, with the fine métier that we exercise [i.e., begging]."[61]

The poor still have a "natural right" to alms if there is no other means to keep them alive.[62] But to give charity in any other circumstance—to give them alms when opportunities for work exist—merely encourages wilful idleness. This was the most telling argument against the traditional practice of indiscriminate almsgiving. But an institutionalization of charity could prevent this. For with the municipal charities of the seventeenth century not only charity but also the poor themselves were to be institutionalized. That is, the idle beggars would be swept from the streets and confined in institutions, specifically in the new hospital-general, La Charité. This process of institutionalization was known as "enfermement" or "renfermement," and it was the most distinctive feature of the charitable impulse of the seventeenth century.

The advantage of enfermement was that it would put the idle to work. The poor confined in the care of the hospital-general would be made to work, weaving cloth, knitting stockings, making shoes, baking bread in the various ateliers attached to the hospital. They would be made "accustomed from the earliest age to a life of labor." Those reduced to begging for their living would be transformed into "good artisans for the public, and good valets and servant-girls for private persons."[63] This hoped-for transformation of course drew its inspiration partly from the doctrines of the mercantilists; setting the idle to work would, it was hoped, increase productivity and thus insure prosperity. But more influential, I believe, than the theories of the mercantilist writers was the slow diffusion of what would in Protestant countries be termed the work ethic. Man was born to a life of labor, and if he worked hard he would prosper. If the people themselves were slow to accept the necessity of work, enfermement was an obvious way to inculcate the work discipline. (see Chapter IV).

As used by these writers, the term "work" or *"travail"* had overtones of pain and fatigue, of "the painful effort of one who carries a heavy weight on earth."[64] To the founders of the charities work was not merely an occupation; it also had moral overtones. It was a "penitence for sin."[65] This illuminates another, and most important, aspect of enfermement. If the movement to shut the poor in workhouses was partially economic in motivation, it was also spurred by a very real concern for saving the souls of the poor. This concern with the spiritual well-being of one's fellow man was a natural part of the religious revival of the early years of the century: St. Vincent de Paul, for example, sent missions to the poor. The foundation of the Charité provided an institutionalized method of helping the poor toward salvation. Such help was considered very necessary. The poor were deemed completely ignorant of even the simplest tenets of religion:

One sees everywhere infinite crowds of the poor in public places, at the doors of churches and in other meeting places, who for the most part know nothing of what the Holy Church and the Holy Fathers say we must know about the Mysteries of the Faith, the pain of damnation, the Unity and Trinity of God, the Incarnation, the knowledge and the usage of the Sacraments. . . . These wretches who live among Christians as ignorant of Christianity as the Turks, and often more vicious than these Infidels . . . [will be damned.] [66]

Not only did living in poverty deprive the poor of the religious instruction necessary for their salvation, but it also encouraged their tendency to sin. Idleness bred vice. The poor lived in a

criminal idleness, which is for them the source of all vices: lying, perjuring, blasphemy . . . continual grumbling, quarrels and frequent injuries, drunkness, and impiety. . . . They neglect all the Sacraments: they almost never know the sanctity of marriage, and live together in a shameful fashion. They neglect the instruction of their children. [67]

Even crime could result from living in poverty and idleness: these factors had a tendency to "multiply larcenies, thefts, and murders." [68] A medieval canonist had stressed that "Poverty is not a kind of crime." [69] But to the supporters of enfermement poverty was, if not itself a crime, definitely a forcing ground for criminals. The poor were all sinners, and most were potential criminals. Much of this railing against the criminal tendencies of the poor was inspired by social fear. One of the pamphlets supporting enfermement paints a horrific picture of the consequences which would occur if mendicants were allowed to infest the city:

This crowd of insolents attacks day and night in the country—crops, animals, property; when they gather together they engaged in debauchery . . . they commit a thousand mischievous acts and such horrible crimes that they draw the scourges of Heaven, to the great detriment of the public . . . when they are assembled here in great number if the least occasion presents itself they excite or aid in public seditions, thefts, pillages of houses. [70]

Enfermement provided a way to protect the public from these scourges by locking away the possible criminals. Just as work was useful for the poor both in itself and as a penitence for sin, so too was enfermement useful both to protect society and to correct the poor, who were now increasingly thought of as sinners and criminals who deserved punishment. Emmanuel Chill has stressed the penal aspects of the hospitals-general: the strict regulation of the lives of the inmates, the harsh punishments for those who disobeyed the rules. [71] Members of the Company of the Holy Sacrament viewed with a distaste amounting almost to repulsion the irregularity of the lives of the poor. Their debaucheries seem to put them outside the bonds of civilized society. [72] Michel Foucault has in fact argued that the major impulse behind enfermement was an attempt to isolate the poor from civilized society, to prevent their idleness and debauchery from "infecting" the healthy elements of the social body. [73] With this attitude, the poor have almost ceased to be considered as human beings. As Philippe Ariès put it, "The repugnance of the rich [for the poor] preceded the shame of poverty," and this repugnance made it easier for the plan of confining the poor in the hospitals-general to gain support.[74]

How could this repugnance be squared with the sympathy shown toward the poor in the early years of the century, with the conviction that the poor were fellow members of Christ, "nos semblables, nos frères," that those who had fallen lowest, like prisoners, were those most in need of Christian charity? This old sympathy and the new harshness were not as irreconcilable as might be supposed. Many people, especially members of the Company of the Holy Sacrament, held both attitudes at once. This was possible because they were careful to distinguish between those whom they termed the "true" and the "false" poor:

It is necessary to distinguish between two sorts of poor: the poor of Jesus Christ, and the poor of the Devil. The poor of Jesus Christ are patient, humble, modest and content with the state in which Divine Providence has placed them. . . . The poor of the Devil are enemies of good order, do-nothings, liars, drunkards, and lechers who have no other language but that of the Devil their father.[75]

It was only the "vrai pauvres," and "pauvres du Jésus Christ," who deserved Christian charity. "One must admit to aid only the 'véritables pauvres,' and those who live as good Christians, it being unreasonable to distribute the legacies of the pious to the impious, to the enemies of God, who are those who foolishly persevere in vice, and who live in crime."[76] Only the true poor are legitimately entitled to alms; alms given to the false poor rob the true poor of the necessities of life. The false poor should instead be locked up in the hospitals-general, where their souls will be saved through work and religion. Obviously great care was necessary to distinguish between the two types of poor. All charities stipulated that the recipients of their aid be carefully investigated. Their dwellings were visited and their neighbors questioned to make sure that "they are truly poor" and that "they live as good Christians."[77] "If the rectors learn that the poor whom they aid live in scandal or in impurity or in drunkenness or in revenge or that they do not frequent the Sacraments. . . . their alms will be taken away."[78] Only the true poor deserve Christian charity.

This distinction between true and false poor was an ideal solution for the problems posed by an era when attitudes toward poverty were changing. It made possible a reconciliation between the old attitudes and the new. Supporters of enfermement could emphasize the traditional Christian arguments in favor of charity, and show all the traditional Christian sympathy toward the poor, with, of course, the stipulation that only the true poor were worthy of such consideration. This ability to annex the Christian rhetoric was very useful, for as we shall see, the traditional arguments were still widely accepted and very persuasive.

Examples of how the propagandists for enfermement manipulated the old rhetoric abound. To those who might object that Christ had said that the poor we always have with us, the pamphlet *Mendicité abolie* pointed out that Christ had not meant this to refer to mendicants. Similarly, in answer to the objection that no beggar should be refused alms, since doing so would be refusing Christ, who had lived on earth as a poor man, the pamphlet stated that Christ had never lived in the "idleness of a bad life" which characterized the false poor.[79]

The proponents of enfermement realized how difficult it would be to eradicate the traditional attitudes overnight. Besides trying to adapt the traditional rhetoric to support the new ideas, they also attempted to answer in advance any objections which might be raised by those who clung to the old conceptions of how charity should be conducted. To those who could not see what was wrong with giving alms in the old, open-handed fashion, the propagandists of the Charité pointed out that it was against the laws of the kingdom (and therefore against the commandment of God, who had stated that earthly laws should be obeyed) to encourage beggary by giving alms. Those who argued that the old system was better because the sight of the wretchedness of the poor was apt to stimulate generous giving were told that surely the sight of the socially prominent rectors of the charities humbly soliciting funds would be much more edifying. Finally, those who felt it "strange" that the poor should be locked up when they had done nothing more than demand the alms to which they traditionally had a right were told curtly that it was stranger still that people would tolerate a crowd of dangerous, criminal beggars in their midst.[80]

These attacks failed to destroy belief in the traditional attitudes. The propagandists of the Charité were unable to convince people of the necessity of enfermement. The Charité did not gain true popular support for over forty years after its foundation in 1640. This is true despite the fact that after 1656 the policy of the confinement of beggars had all the weight of the royal government behind it. For the Company of the Holy Sacrament had managed to convert royal officials to its views that confinement of the poor in hospitals-general was the only proper organization of poor relief; the foundation in 1656 of the Hôpital-Général La Charité in Paris marked the beginning of a governmental assault against beggary carried out under the Company's inspiration.[81] The next step came in 1662, when a royal edict ordered that "in all cities and *faubourgs* of our kingdom, where there is not yet a hospital-general established, the establishment of such a hospital be undertaken immediately."[82] But despite this support of the royal government, the Charité in Aix won little popular approval. Private charity persisted, and

beggars still infested the streets of Aix. It was only with the second, or
so-called "grand" enfermement of 1687 that this situation changed. For this
attempt at enfermement was accompanied by an immense propaganda effort
which sought to involve the whole town in the success of the movement.

On October 12, 1686, the royal government issued an ordinance
designed to resuscitate the policy of arresting beggars found on the streets
and enclosing them in the hospitals-general.[83] In Aix this ordinance would
doubtless have suffered the fate of its predecessors, had not the Jesuit
preacher Père Chaurand arrived in January 1687, prepared to mount a campaign from the pulpit in favor of the attempt at enfermement. Chaurand, a
brilliant orator, had earlier made his reputation by popular crusades against
Protestantism, but in the 1670's he switched his interest to the field of
charity. From then until his death in 1697, he wandered all over France
preaching in favor of the extinction of mendicity and the enclosure of the
poor in hospitals-general. There is evidence, for example, of missions to
Normandy and Brittany in the early 1680's. In all, Chaurand is credited with
founding or assisting in the foundation of no less than 126 hospitals-general
and bureaux de charité throughout France.[84]

Chaurand's appearance in Aix was recorded by an eyewitness, the
indefatigable Pierre-Joseph de Haitze. According to Haitze's account,
Chaurand began his campaign with a series of revivalistic sermons in the
Cathedral "on the necessity of enfermement of poor as much for their temporal as their spiritual well-being, and also for the good and holy police of the
town." The text of his sermons has not survived, but reportedly he dwelt at
length on the "extraordinary libertinage in which these scoundrels lived."[85]
At any rate, Chaurand's oratory was very effective, for a quête for funds
undertaken among the audience a week after the sermons began yielded more
than 8,000 livres to help the Charité meet the expenses of enfermement. Not
content with this success, Chaurand inspired his fellow Jesuits to mount
similar campaigns in the parish churches.[86]

The highlight of Chaurand's campaign was a true masterstroke of public
relations: the organization of a giant procession in which all those who had
contributed to the Charité were invited to take part. Haitze has left a description of the procession, with its long series of carts filled with furnishings for
the Charité, so many indeed that there were constant traffic jams and accidents along the route. In the procession also marched all the artisans who had
gratuitously contributed their labor to make the hospital ready for its new
inmates. This rallying of the apparently hitherto reluctant artisans to the
cause of enfermement Haitze saw as evidence of a "supernatural operation of
a true spirit of charity to which nothing is impossible."[87] The grand enfermement was overwhelmingly successful; between seven and eight hundred
beggars were confined to the hospital-general during this period. Yet not even

Chaurand's propaganda efforts could completely eradicate the old attitudes toward charity. Private almsgiving to beggars persisted even into the eighteenth century. In 1702 the directors of the Charité had to appeal to the archbishop of Aix to pronounce against this private charity which so prejudiced the work of the hospital-general.[88]

This persistence of traditional modes of behavior points up emphatically the fact that the municipal charities of Aix founded in the seventeenth century were products of an era of transition in attitudes toward poverty and charity. The charities were halfway houses between traditional Christian *charité* toward the poor and the secular, state-supported system of public assistance which would come into effect with the French Revolution. The impetus behind the charitable impulse of the seventeenth century was still religious, but many of the features of traditional Christian charity, especially indiscriminate private almsgiving, were gone. The institutionalization of the care of the poor was a new development, and it represented the first step toward the eventual emergence of a state bureaucracy of institutions for public assistance. But these institutions were different from their successors. First of all, they were still administered and supported by private individuals. And, secondly, their primary concern was for a moral policing of the poor. In the seventeenth century poverty was still viewed primarily in a religious context. Charitable donors were concerned with saving the souls of the poor as well as their bodies. It would be only after 1760 that this tendency to view poverty in a religious context gave way to a conviction that it was a purely economic phenomenon. When this happened Aix's municipal charities would lose their raison d'être, and this would be the first step in their destruction and their replacement by a national system of public assistance.

CHAPTER III

Administration and Finances

With regard to their administration, the charitable institutions of Old Regime France presented a paradoxical picture: while they were the keystone of the royal government's policy of public assistance, they were at the same time privately controlled bodies, almost completely independent of outside interference. Their mode of financing, through the gifts of local private donors, guaranteed this autonomy. And the private and local nature of these institutions made possible their many close ties to the local community. For they played numerous important roles in municipal life; they were employers, consumers, landowners, banks, and even social clubs. This chapter will explore the administration and financing of the charities, and point up the many and varied roles they played in their local community.

THE RECTORS

Daily administration of the charities was the responsibility of their governing boards of rectors. The number of rectors on the board of a charity in Aix varied between eight and 34. Their term of office varied also: the eight rectors of the Pureté were chosen for life, while in the other charities the rectors served terms of one, two, or three years. Except for those of the bureaux de charité, who were elected by their parishes, incoming rectors were chosen by those already in office. These elections were usually held on All Saints' Day. In theory, nominations were made a week before the elections. Voting was by secret ballot. Actually this election procedure was often merely pro forma: an outgoing rector often handpicked his successor, and his right of choice was respected by his colleagues. The charities were thus governed by a self-perpetuating oligarchy.

"Nothing is more important for the hospital of the Miséricorde than the proper choice of its rectors, because good administration depends uniquely on that."[1] All the charities agreed with this sentiment, and all made careful provisions regarding the type of person eligible to become a rector. For example, in its rules of 1688 the Miséricorde specified that its rectors must be

chosen from among the *gens de bien* of the city, who love the poor, who have zeal, leisure, reputation, probity, gentleness, firmness, some free time from business, and substantial property. *Gentilshommes,* Avocats, Bourgeois, Marchands and Notaries are the only persons who can fill the offices of rector.[2]

Usually, however, the long enumeration of personal qualities was omitted; only the social status necessary for rectorship was specified. For example, the Charité stipulated that two of its rectors be ecclesiastics, and the rest "Gentilshommes, Officers, Avocats, Marchands or Bourgeois."[3] Similarly "Gentilshommes, Avocats, Procureurs, Notaries, Bourgeois and Marchands" were eligible to become rectors of the Oeuvre des Prisons.[4]

It is obvious that certain social groups were considered especially suitable as rectors, the gentilhomme, the avocat, the most substantial of the merchants and bourgeoisie. The humble notary found a place in this exalted company because of the charities' need for accurate records: the secretary of a charity was invariably a notary. Aside from this, no attempt was made to insure any financial or administrative expertise. Those considered fit to administer were the members of the social groups from which the ruling classes of French society had always been drawn—the gentilshommes, and the robe nobility which manned the royal administration. They had by definition the qualities of honor, probity, and disinterested concern for public welfare thought necessary in rectors. They also had the necessary wealth, although riches alone would not make a man eligible to be a rector: the Incurables allowed those who had donated a bed to the hospital to become "honorary rectors," but only if "they were of a state, condition and quality to be elected rectors."[5] In sum, charity was the duty of all Christians, regardless of social class, but not all social classes were capable of administering a charity. This attitude is illustrated by the explanation offered by the Oeuvre des Prisons for a brief period fo crisis it experienced in the 1660's. The charity had prospered as long as

one was careful to employ in that Oeuvre only men of great distinction, or at least above the vulgar. But when one admitted indifferently all sorts of people, not only did the Oeuvre no longer subsist on its former footage: far from making the progress it had promised, it fell into such a state that it could scarcely sustain itself. This setback happened only through the lack of leaders zealous to have the statutes of the Company observed. I think how responsible before God are those who treat this sort of office with this carelessness, and esteem it the least of their affairs.[6]

This conviction that the vulgar were unsuitable to the administration of charities had not always been held. The new secular charities of the sixteenth century had been founded by men whose social rank was no higher than that of merchant. Even women—automatically excluded from the administration of the charities in all roles but that of donor in the seventeenth century—had participated in the foundation and direction of charities a century earlier. As a historian of the Miséricorde noted in 1709:

Providence aroused, for the foundation of the Miséricorde, not the great of the world, not even people of some distinction, but small merchants, notaries, and women of that station in order to show that, even in such vast enterprises, human grandeur is not necessary to make them succeed; and all honor is due these people.[7]

This statement is borne out by a list of the rectors of the institution. From 1600 to 1622 only men described as "bourgeois" or "marchands" were elected rectors. But in 1622 the social composition of the rectorate changed: the first écuyers and avocats appeared. The écuyers, avocats, and various governmental officials increased in number during the 1620's, 1630's and 1640's. Not, however, until the 1650's did they make up the majority of the rectors. They retained this majority position throughout the rest of the seventeenth century.[8]

It is difficult to account for this change. One possible explanation is that it is a change in appearance only. Because of the inflation of offices which occurred in the first half of the seventeenth century (reaching its height in the 1640's), it is possible that the same families continued to provide rectors as before—that these families merely purchased an office as they prospered. It seems unlikely, however, that this was true for more than a few families. A more convincing explanation of the change lies in the possibility of a changing concept of the prerequisites of social status. The activities of the Company of the Holy Sacrament in the 1630's and 1640's had made charity a fashionable enterprise for the nobility, especially for the rising nobles of the robe. Thus an interest in charity was de rigueur for the robe noble of the 1640's. It is likely that such types simply crowded out the marchands and bourgeois on the boards of the charities. If this were true, the widespread notion that only gentilshommes and avocats were fit to administer charities might be viewed as justification of a fait accompli: charity was an activity favored by certain social groups, and therefore these social groups seemed especially suited to charitable endeavors. The rectorship of a charity, especially of one of the major hospitals-general, undeniably had a certain social cachet: the rewards it brought—the respect of one's fellow-townsmen, the place of prominence in the fête-Dieu procession, the accompaniment of one's fellow rectors to one's final resting place—were undoubtedly attractive.

In turn, the charity doubtless derived prestige (useful in raising funds), from the presence on its bureau of a *président à mortier* of Parlement or a Chevalier of the Order of St. Louis. Most probably this reciprocal relationship of prestige explains why the charities became socially exclusive in the seventeenth and eighteenth centuries.

Whatever the reasons, the governing boards of the charities were by 1700 clearly filled with the parlementaires and petty nobles who so dominated the social and economic life of Aix. An analysis of the social status of the eighteenth-century rectors of the Charité illustrates this trend. Of the 24 original rectors of the Charité (chosen in 1641), five were either bourgeois, marchands, or notaries.[9] From 1720 to 1760 these types seem to have almost completely disappeared: the charity was administered by the avocats and judges of the Parlement, and by the "nobles" and écuyers. A second change in the social composition of the rectorship took place after the financial crisis of 1760, when the charities appear to have become simultaneously less, and more, exclusive in makeup. On the one hand the bourgeois and marchand reappeared on the board of the Charité, perhaps the result of the institutions's effort to recruit financial support and financial expertise in the wake of its money problems. And on the other hand, the number of rectors who were nobles of the sword increased, and for the first time titled nobles sat on the Charité's board. These developments might have resulted from an effort by the Charité to repair its tarnished public image by attracting prestigious names to its bureau.[10]

Why were the avocats and écuyers of Aix willing to become rectors? The considerations of status mentioned above were doubtless very influential factors. Bound up with these was the influence of a family tradition of charitable endeavor. Seats on the charities often passed from father to son, son-in-law, or nephew through succeeding generations. An example of this is the service of the Rostolan family, great nobles of the robe, at the Charité. A Rostolan was rector of the Charité in 1720-21. In 1739 his eldest son was elected rector. In 1743 this Rostolan was replaced by his younger brother. In 1744 Ducaire, described as the father-in-law of the eldest Rostolan son, was chosen. Then in 1751 the younger brother returned to serve again.[11] While some families were, like the Rostolans, closely identified with one particular institution, others contributed rectors to many different charities. For example, the du Chaine, Barreme, the Lieutaud, the de Laurens and the Seguiran families, all of the robe nobility, supplied more than one rector to both the Pureté and the Charité in the seventeenth and eighteenth centuries.[12]

Certainly these considerations of status and family tradition were more compelling motivations for the rectors than any possibility of monetary gain. Admittedly the rectors of the charities apparently tried from time to time to use the labor of the inmates of the charities on their own projects for their own profit.[13] It is also possible that the rectors awarded the contracts for grain and other supplies of the charities to friends and relatives for a consideration; at least the rectors of the Charité were accused of this in 1763.[14] But probably only a very few of the rectors used their position for financial gain. Indeed, as we shall see, men were far more likely to lose money when they became rectors.

If a few men became rectors because of financial gain, and many more because of considerations of status and family tradition, probably many others were impelled by a genuine feeling of duty towards those less fortunate than themselves, whether this was motivated primarily by religious teachings, as in the seventeenth century, or by the secular humanitarianism of the philosophes of the eighteenth century. Certainly many of the rectors devoted much of their lives to charitable service. Some were re-elected repeatedly, despite provisions against this in the rules.[15] For example, at the Charité the abbé Meyronnet, who had been a rector off and on during the 1730's, was appointed a "rector Surnumeraire" with the special duty of running the institution's *fabrique de Cadiz,* a charge he filled devotedly for almost twenty years, until the fabrique's dissolution.[16]

The great sense of duty which impelled men such as Meyronnet to devote their lives to charitable service becomes more obvious when one examines the disadvantages of the charge of rectorship. First of all, being a rector might constitute a heavy financial burden. It was expected that rectors would favor their charities in their wills, and that they would come to their rescue in cases of emergency.[17] Further, it was possible that the rectors might be held personally responsible for the debts incurred by the charities. During the financial crisis experienced by the Charité in 1760, the creditors of the institution threatened to sue the rectors personally in an attempt to recover their money. The rectors defended themselves by stating that the regulations provided that, when the rectors signed legal documents, "their signature obliges only the Charité, and not those that sign."[18] Apparently the question was never decided in a court of law. This threat remained, however, as a deterrent to those who might become rectors.

Aside from these financial burdens, the duties of rectorship had other unattractive aspects. One was the sheer amount of time involved. All rectors were expected to be present at the twice-weekly meetings of the bureaux, at which the administrative decisions concerning the functioning of the charities were taken. When the charities were hired to take part in funeral processions, the rectors were expected to participate. Finally, most rectors had other and even more time-consuming supervisory duties as well.

The rectors were responsible for all aspects of the administration of the charity. The main organ through which they exercised this responsibility was the bureau, often termed the "bureau ordinaire" to distinguish it from the supervisory grand bureau. All the rectors were members of the bureau, which usually met twice a week, typically on Sunday and Thursday. After the recitation of prayers, the bureau tackled its administrative tasks. The bureau had to pass on the eligibility of the poor who applied for aid. It had to approve the hiring of hospital personnel, the purchasing of supplies, the borrowing of money. The bureau made decisions concerning the administration of the property owned by the hospital, and oversaw the innumerable lawsuits concerning its legacies. In short, the bureau handled all administrative matters. Decision in the bureau was by majority vote.

There are indications that discussions in the bureaux were often heated and even acrimonious. At least the Miséricorde found it necessary in 1671 to make the following provision about the conduct of the bureaux:

In the aforesaid Assembly it is not at all permitted that the Rectors injure each other, rather they must treat each other with honor and respect . . . and they will not carry arms in the aforesaid Assembly.

And in the case that there is in the aforesaid Assembly a riot among some of the Rectors all the others must make peace, and not let them leave the Chamber without embracing and forgetting everything.[19]

These differences of opinion over policy would have shed useful light on attitudes toward charity and poverty. Unfortunately they are not recorded in the minutes of the bureaux. Concerned with harmonizing their differences, the rectors preferred that they present the picture of a united front in decision-making. At one point in the records a note that there had been "bien des contestations" over an issue was crossed out, and replaced by the milder "diverses opinions."[20] Once a policy was decided, all the rectors apparently united around it.

THE SEMAINIER

While the bureau was effective for making policy decisions, it was far too cumbersome to oversee with the necessary strictness the day-to-day administration of the charities. This responsibility rested instead on the *semainier*. This office was held by each rector in turn, for, as its name suggests, a week at a time. During this week the semainier lived at the institution, or at least was constantly available for consultation. He presided over the assemblies during the week, and he made tours of inspection, insuring that all functioned smoothly. He settled petty administrative disputes. He had custody of the keys to the storeroom and treasury, and signed the receipts for the purchase of supplies. The semainier derived his authority from the fact that he was an emanation of the bureau. While he had absolute authority over the paid employees of the charity, he in turn was accountable to the bureau for his actions.

SECRETARY AND TREASURER

Apart from the attendance at the bureau, and rotating duty as semainier, each rector had certain specialized duties as well, connected with various areas of the administration. For example, the rector chosen as treasurer had the task of keeping the accounts. The Charité stated at one time that as for its treasurers, "the good ones are rare."[21] This seems unduly severe; the surviving account books reveal the treasurers as meticulous, if occasionally weak in basic arithmetic. The treasurer had to render his accounts every year to representatives of the Parlement, the Cour des Comptes and the municipality —a precaution designed to insure honest administration. This was not really necessary. The vast majority of the treasurers seem to have been honest men. There is only one recorded example of peculation. In 1755 M. de la Touloubre, a former university professor and a substitute for the *gens du roy*, fled across the border to Avignon, taking with him 28,000 livres he had stolen from the Mont-de-Piété during his 26-year term as treasurer.[22] M. de la Touloubre's dishonesty was unusual, however.

Each charity also had one rector, usually a notary, who served as secretary, and kept the records of the deliberations of the bureaux, of the admission of the poor, and of the legal documents connected with the gifts and legacies, and with the administration of the charity's property. This was one of the most vital of the administrative tasks, for in the charities precedent rather than innovation was the keynote of administration: the rectors had constant recourse to their records for precedents in the handling of thorny administrative questions, and for supportive evidence for the legal battles in which the charity was engaged. It is therefore not surprising that the Miséricorde carefully set forth the qualities necessary for a secretary:

A secretary must have some free time from business, have a fine memory, be laborious, vigilant, active and assiduous. . . . It is very necessary that the Secretary write well; because the Registers remain forever in the Archives, and it is sometimes necessary after a long period of years to have recourse to them . . . one finds them very difficult to read when they are badly written and one often loses much for the lack of being able to decipher badly written Registers.[23]

This is an opinion with which the present-day historian can most heartily concur.

The other rectors also had specialized duties, depending in their nature on the type of aid offered by the institution. Most charities had some rectors who specialized in financial affairs, some who handled the awarding of supply contracts, and some who supervised the leasing of the properties belonging to the charities. The avocats often supervised the conduct of court cases in which the charities were involved. This was an especially important activity at the Conseil charitable, which provided free legal service for those too poor to pay. Many of the Charité's rectors acted as overseers for the various workshops, or fabriques, in which the inmates were employed. At the Miséricorde, which distributed food and medicines to the poor and ill throughout the city, much of the rectors' time was spent visiting their assigned areas, supervising the work of doctors and surgeons connected with the institution, and urging the ill to make a last confession. Similar admonitory visiting was a part of the duties of the rectors of the Oeuvre des Prisons, who daily listened to the prisoners' complaints, and urged the unhappy inmates to repent and reform. In all the charities the rectors were responsible to their fellows in the bureaux for the conduct of these specialized tasks.

How efficient were the rectors as administrators? Such a thing is almost impossible to gauge from the surviving records; administrators do not as a rule record their shortcomings for the benefit of future historians. A few indications suggestive of the rectors' attitudes toward their duties, however, have survived. First of all, the assemblies suffered from the chronic absenteeism of the rectors. Most of the bureaux of the Charité were attended by only three or four rectors. Repeatedly, outgoing rectors of the Charité were described as "absent for a long time."[24] Another indication that many of the rectors did not take their duties seriously is the fact that the Charité found it necessary to write into its rules the provision that:

One will never read the Gazette during the time of the Bureau, nor the News, nor anything else which would stop or interfere with the succor of the poor, which will always be spoken of in a serious manner, as one speaks of important affairs.[25]

It is probable that the majority of the rectors, having agreed to serve on the charities for reasons of social connections and prestige, regarded the institutions as little more than social clubs, and left the actual work of administration to the few who took their office seriously. On the whole these seem to have done an adequate job.

EMPLOYEES OF THE CHARITIES

Apart from the rectors who voluntarily acted as the executive officers of the charities, each institution had a paid staff which carried out the tasks necessary for its daily existence. Although these staffs varied according to the function of the individual institutions, they typically included: (a) at least one curé or priest to care for the souls of the poor; (b) a medical staff, usually consisting of doctor, surgeon, and apothecary; (c) a financial staff: a supply agent, a rent collector for the hospital properties, a lawyer who guarded the charity's interests in court; (d) master craftsmen—such as bakers, shoe-makers, weavers—who made the charity self-sufficient by allowing it to manufacture the food and clothing it needed on its own premises; and (e) a host of subordinate employees in various menial positions: doorkeepers and guards, gardeners and carters, cooks, washerwomen, serving girls, nurses to care for the sick, and *inspecteurs* and *mères* to handle discipline among the inmates.

THE PRIESTS

Most prestigious of all the paid employees of the charities was the *aumônier,* or priest. His position was always listed first in the rules and in the hospital accounts; he sat at the head of the staff table in the refectory. The respect accorded to the priest doubtless stemmed from the primacy of religion in the life of the charities; the rectors constantly proclaimed that the main concern of the charities was the saving of the souls of the poor, rather than feeding and clothing their bodies.[26]

The duties of the priests reflected this concern. Almost all charities made the partaking of communion a condition for entrance, or for receipt of bread, medicines, and other aid. Besides administering communion, the priest was expected to give last rites to the sick, and to catechise the children. Most of the charities had their own chapel, in which the priest was expected to hold daily services, and to officiate at the masses endowed by individual donors. Since these masses might amount to as many as two hundred for each donor, the duties of the priest were time-consuming.[27]

The smallest charities tended to rely on the voluntary assistance of curés from the various parishes of the town, but most charities employed their own priest, retained on a full-time basis and paid from the charities' funds. The hôtel-Dieu had four, all reformed Augustinians, while the Charité usually had at least two.[28] The priests were quite well paid. Those at the Charité usually received 132 livres a year; at other institutions salaries ran as high as 300 livres.[29] At first sight this does not seem very tempting; after all the *portion congrue*, universally considered a bare minimum necessary for subsistence, was 300 livres until 1768, when it was raised to 500 livres.[30] But the charities provided food and lodging in addition to the salaries. This made them attractive opportunities for those members of the lower clergy who, because of their low birth and spotty education, could normally expect only the poorest parishes as their lot. The archbishop was frequently consulted in the selection of candidates, and he of course had to pass on the orthodoxy of each applicant.

If none of the charities' priests have left a mark as outstanding preachers, all seem to have performed their duties conscientiously. This was doubtless all that was necessary. Religion in the charities was a matter of rote, of saving souls by instilling in them, through endless repetition, the basic minimum of religious teaching necessary for salvation. Obviously priests with education and ambition would prefer the challenges of a cure in an individual parish, where there was more scope for initiative, and a chance of being noticed by one's ecclesiastical superiors. But for those whose alternatives were the poorest country parishes, a position in a charity brought a modicum of security and prestige.

MEDICAL PERSONNEL

Those charities which cared for the sick naturally employed a medical staff, usually consisting of a doctor, a surgeon and an apothecary. The large hôtel-Dieu employed four doctors and five surgeons, while the Miséricorde, which provided medical care for the poor confined to their homes, had four doctors and four surgeons on its roster. The Charité had no medical personnel; it sent those inmates in need of medical attention to the hôtel-Dieu.[31]

Highest in prestige of the medical personnel were the doctors or *médecins*. They were usually recruited from the Faculty of Medicine at Aix— the Miséricorde required that those "of the University" be given preference— and were usually bourgeois, or even "nobles hommes." Their salaries were quite low: the Miséricorde paid its doctors twenty *écus* a year in 1671; in the eighteenth century the usual wage for a doctor at the hôtel-Dieu was only eighty livres. Food and lodging were not included. These small salaries were possible because a doctor devoted only part of his time to the care of the poor; he also treated his rich private patients, or taught at the University. Apparently positions at the charities were much sought after. Candidates were selected by the rectors; the Miséricorde felt elaborate precautions necessary to prevent bribery of the rectors by eager candidates. The Miséricorde also specified that, "If it is recognized that two are of the same capacity, the one who is gentlest and most charitable must be chosen."[32]

At the hôtel-Dieu and the other hospitals, the duties of the doctors consisted of examining the patients upon admittance and making the rounds of the hospital twice a day.[33] The doctors associated with the Miséricorde were required to visit the ill daily in their homes, to prescribe remedies, and see that the apothecary provided them, and to urge the ill to make their confession.[34] The doctors were also warned to be alert to unmask those who merely feigned illness in order to qualify for the food distributed by the charity to convalescents.[35] To accept a fee of any sort from a patient suggested by the Miséricorde was strictly forbidden.[36]

Inferior in prestige—and often in salary—to the doctors were the surgeons. Usually a charity had the same number of surgeons as it had doctors; the surgeons, however, often received slightly lower salaries. For example, at the Incurables in 1766 the doctor received 30 livres a year, while the surgeon's salary was only 24 livres. Similarly, the Insensés paid their doctor 36 livres and their surgeon only 30 livres.[37] The surgeons were usually considered mere subordinates of and aides to the doctors. In large part, this lesser prestige accorded to surgeons was due to the fact that surgery was still considered a craft; surgeons were trained by apprenticeship rather than in the universities. Indeed, the hôtel-Dieu in Aix provided an apprenticeship program for students in surgery, and had the right to grant the maîtrise. After six years of service the candidate underwent an examination by a board of four doctors and four surgeons. The examination consisted of three parts: first, an hour-and-a-half oral examination on theory and practice; second, a practical demonstration of operating techniques on a cadaver, and third, another demonstration on the dressing of wounds. According to the hospital records, only a few candidates presented themselves, and most of them were very unskilled.[38]

The duties of the surgeons attached to the charities were similar to those of the doctors. At the hôtel-Dieu, the surgeons were required to make their rounds twice a day. The surgeons attached to the Miséricorde were expected to visit daily all those in need of their care, and to perform all necessary operations themselves. The latter point was much contested. In 1671 the Miséricorde noted, "There are often complaints that the surgeons have most of the bleedings and other operations performed by their apprentices, and that they cripple many of the poor."[39]

Lowest in the hierarchy of the charities' medical staff was the apothecary. He too was a mere craftsman, and indeed little more than a glorified shopkeeper, who had charge of the supply of drugs in the hospitals' "boutiques." The apothecary was expected to fill accurately the prescriptions of the doctors and surgeons, and to make in their company a yearly inspection of their supplies to see that they were still potent. The apothecaries were strictly forbidden to dispense drugs to any of the staff members or rectors without a doctor's orders.[40]

The quality of the medical care provided by the charities was doubtless quite low. Given the charities' preoccupation with economizing—it was their credo that a "spirit of economy" was appropriate to the administration of charities—it can be safely assumed that the organizations were willing to finance only what they considered the bare minimum of medical care. After all, as the charities constantly emphasized, their main concern was with the spiritual and not the bodily welfare of the poor. Also, it is obvious that all the medical personnel neglected the poor in favor of their richer private patients. One can picture them making their hurried, careless rounds before rushing away to more lucrative fields.

As for the types of treatment given, they varied little from the standard seventeenth- and eighteenth-century practice, with its emphasis on purging and bleeding, and its neglect of such essentials as adequate sanitation and ventilation. This assured a high mortality rate (see Chapter IV). Although it might be assumed that charity hospitals would furnish fruitful opportunities for experimentation with new methods, none of the doctors attached to the hospitals of Aix seem to have been interested in such things, at least before the 1760's. Admittedly the doctors occasionally accepted patients in whose diseases they were especially interested—for example, those suffering from the "putrid fevers" which received so much medical attention in the eighteenth century.[41] But the hospitals themselves discouraged any sort of experimentation because it disrupted their routine. In the hôtel-Dieu, dissections were allowed only from October 15 to April 15, and only with the permission of the semainier. Medical students were not permitted in the dormitories to observe the patients, although the University and the students themselves repeatedly attempted to get this ban lifted. In 1745 they were momentarily successful, as the Parlement ordered the hospitals to admit them. The ban was quickly restored, however, when the rectors reported that the students "committed many indecencies with the female patients and even argued insolently with the rectors."[42] Thus while the doctors of Paris and Montpellier flirted with new methods, those of Aix remained mired in old routines.

FINANCIAL PERSONNEL

Under this rubric are grouped the various paid employees who aided the rectors in the financial administration of the charities. These included, first of all, the agent who had charge of collecting the rents and other debts due the hospitals. This could be an unpleasant and even dangerous task; for example, on June 19, 1749, the agent of the Charité was attacked and beaten when he tried to collect a pension.[43] Far safer were the tasks of the financial personnel inside the hospital. Usually each charity had an *économe*, who had charge of the storerooms and distributed the daily supplies—always closely supervised by the semainier. In larger institutions like the Charité, the économe's duties were often shared among several officers. Thus in the late seventeenth century the Charité employed: (1) a *dépensier*, who kept a record of the inmates working in the fabriques, and also of the grain ground in the hospital's mill; (2) an *inspecteur des bleds*, who kept an account of all wheat used by the baker, and distributed the bread to the économe; (3) the économe, who in turn distributed the bread to the inmates, and the rice and vegetables to the cook. The économe's duties also included gathering all the human waste material of the hospital and selling it for fertilizer.[44]

These economic officers were well paid, relative to the other employees of the charities. As an example, the agent of the Charité received a salary which ranged from 159 to 400 livres a year.[45] Doubtless it was hoped that an adequate salary would discourage peculation. These jobs required at least a modicum of education. This fact, combined with the higher salaries, probably insured that these positions were filled by people who were relatively well off: those who came from the milieu of prosperous craftsmen or shopkeepers. Unfortunately there are few sources which tell us about the recruitment for these positions. Indeed, the only evidence available is that on March 7, 1784, Charles Henry Jaubert, described as a "bourgeois de cette ville," was chosen économe of the Insensés at a salary of 200 livres per year.[46]

CRAFTSMEN

Frequently charities had their own bakers, millers, tailors, shoemakers, weavers, and other craftsmen who worked in shops directly attached to the institutions. This arrangement was advantageous to the charities in two ways. First of all, the products produced in their own workshops cost the charities less than they would if purchased on the open market. Secondly, the charities required that their craftsmen train selected inmates—usually young orphan boys—in their craft. This also saved money for the charities, since they did not have to pay apprentice fees to other masters.

Relations between the charity and its craftsmen were governed by a contract drawn up at the beginning of the craftsman's tenure. This contract specified the salary (which might range from 50 to over 300 livres) and the term of service. Most frequently the master was required to live in the charity. Conditions pertaining to his room and board were given, and, since he was in such close contact with the inmates, it was specified that he be of "good morals" and live so as to set a "good example." If the man was married, he was not allowed to bring his wife into the charity. According to the terms of his contract, the craftsman had to accept as apprentices the orphan boys selected by the rectors. The contract also specified which tools were furnished to the master by the charity, and the prices which he could charge for his products. When the needs of the charity were met, the crafts-man was free to take extra orders from the townspeople.[47]

Often the charities employed in their fabriques men who had not yet received their maîtrise. The charities had the power to grant this after six years of satisfactory service. The charities thus offered a chance to gain the status of master to those who found the ordinary paths of advancement in the gild system closed to them because they were not the sons or nephews of masters. Frequently those who presented themselves for service in the charities were former inmates of the institutions, orphan boys who had learned their craft through apprenticeship arranged by the charities but who could never otherwise rise higher than *compagnon*.[48]

Naturally the gilds of the town disliked this infringement of their monopoly, and, whenever possible, sabotaged the advancement of those who had earned their maîtrise through the charities. Thus in July, 1746, Aix's gild of shoemakers refused to receive as a member a shoemaker who had been granted his maîtrise by the Charité. Similarly, the weavers of Aix protested against the right of the weaver associated with the hospital to train pupils.[49] The town's gilds made several efforts to suppress the Charité's right to grant the maîtrise, but since this was protected by royal letters patent the attempts were unsuccessful. Thus the maîtrise program of the charities would continue to provide what was perhaps the only path of upward mobility available to the very poor.

SUBORDINATE PERSONNEL

For the poor who lacked the skill to become master craftsmen, one other opportunity for bettering their lot was open: that of employment in a subordinate position in one of the charities. All these institutions employed innumerable gardeners, carters, cooks, washerwomen, porters, and guards. These positions were usually filled by the very poor. Some were former servants, like the three men who became *aides infirmiers* at the Insensés: a "domestique de profession," a "cy devant serviteur," and a man described as "cy devant au service de M. de Monier et ensuite à l'hôpital la Charité."[50] Others had formerly followed various of the lesser trades: they were porteurs de chaise, peddlers, tinkers.[51] The geographical origins of these people follow the pattern of those of the poor confined to the charities as vagrants: the barren areas of the Comtat Venassin, and Genoa, source of so many of the migrants who wandered across southeastern France, provided employees as well as inmates for the charities. Thus the line between the unemployed vagrant and the employee of the charity was very blurred. Indeed, often the charities hired their former inmates. For example, in May, 1781, a "cy devant detenue" of the Insensés, Lucrese Mouttet, widow of Davin, was hired as a servant at 48 livres a year. The archers of the Charité, whose duty it was to arrest the poor vagrants loitering on street corners and in churches, were almost invariably chosen from among the inmates of the institution.[52]

The attractions of these positions certainly did not lie in the job itself. The tasks were usually menial and boring. Life was almost as harsh for the subordinate employees of the charities as it was for the inmates: the only advantage the employees enjoyed was a slightly better diet.[53] Nor did the attraction of employment in the charities lie in high salaries. The wages were minute—the mère des femmes, at the Charité, for example, received 54 livres per year — and for the most part remained unchanged throughout the eighteenth century, although the last twenty years before 1789 were marked by rapidly rising prices, and although other salaries rose during that period.[54] The major attraction of the charities as employers lay in the fact that they provided both food and lodging—an obvious boon in an era of rising prices—and security in old age. The charities invariably gave their old employees lodging until their deaths, often providing a small pension as well. The records of the Charité for January 29, 1764, note that

The mère has come to ask the Bureau to allow her to pass the rest of her days in the institution and to be nourished there with the other mères on an annual pension of 100 livres. The Bureau has accepted her proposition because of the services that she has rendered during the course of thirty years and those that she could still render by her residence in the institution.[55]

This promise of security in old age was doubtless very appealing to the charity orphans, or to the itinerant traders who had no family to care for them when they grew too old to work. Of all the occupations open to the poor, only that of domestic servant offered a similar promise of security, and even that was problematic. A master could change his mind, or his heirs could ignore his request to care for his old servants. The charities as continuing institutions were not subject to such individual whims.

Most important of the subordinate personnel of the charities were the supervisory personnel: the mères and inspecteurs who were responsible for the conduct of the inmates. They had the duty of making sure the daily routine ran smoothly: they kept order in the dormitories and during meals, they saw to it that the poor performed their allotted tasks during working hours, and they inflicted punishment when necessary.[56] The supervisory positions of the charities combined the duties of teacher and jailer. It was emphasized constantly that their major duty was to set a good example. The Charité specified, "Both mères must watch carefully that all the community, whether women or girls, live modestly and in a Christian manner; bringing them to this by their own example."[57] Even the craftsmen in the fabriques were exhorted to act always as fitting examples for the inmates. This faith in the utility of good examples was typical of seventeenth-century social thought. It was considered the duty of those endowed by God with superior rank and wealth and their accompanying attributes of honor, trustworthiness, and piety to set examples of correct behavior which would inspire their inferiors to emulation. So too the employees of the charities, endowed with superior authority, were to live as examples.

Often, however, mere force of example was not enough to make the inmates behave, and the administrators had to resort to punishment. Punishment in the charities was not haphazardly inflicted. It was specified that, "Punishments must be prudent, and never bizarre or ridiculous, time-wasting and unprofitable."[58] Punishment too would teach by example; public reprimands would discourage others from misbehaving. Since punishment was so important a device, it could not be used recklessly. Employees of the charities, even the supervisory personnel, could not order punishments at their own whim. There are many examples of officers who were reprimanded for punishing inmates without the permission of the rectors.[59]

If the rectors often had to restrain and even reprimand their employees, they were careful to do so in a manner which would not undermine the authority of the officers. It was necessary to maintain "the subordination and respect of inferiors in regard to superiors."[60] Therefore it was the rule that:

One will never reprimand . . . the Officers in front of the Poor; but always in secret. . . . One will never receive in public any written complaint of the Poor of the Town against the Archers, nor of the poor of the maison against the officers; but only in secret, so that the poor cannot take advantage of it and become insolent.[61]

Thus while the employees of the charities had sufficient power to guarantee the respect and fear of the inmates, the rectors retained the ultimate authority.

In this chapter we have considered the charities as administrative entities. We have described who their administrators were, how they were recruited, and the bureaucratic apparatus with which they functioned. But the rectors and employees did not regard the organizations they served in this light. To them a charity was a "famille;" this is the term always used to describe the Charité in its minutes. The use of this term is understandable. The family was after all the paradigm of authority most familiar to Old Regime France. God's authority over the beings He created was paternal; the king's authority was paternal; and so too on a lesser plane, the authority of the rectors over the poor of the charities was paternal. A father had the duty to feed and clothe, guard and protect his children, and the duty to punish them for their own good. So too must the rectors of the charities provide for their inmates—and punish them if they misbehaved.

If the rectors had the role of fathers in the charities' "famille," the poor were most definitely treated as children. We have seen in Chapter II that in the seventeenth century the poor were considered as somehow not whole men, not capable of caring for themselves and therefore in need of special protection. They lacked the qualities which made possible self-control; they had "neither piety, nor education, nor honor."[62] The poor had to be taught like children, by punishment and example. They had to be raised to honor work and religion. The minutes of the charities were constantly preoccupied with problems of the behavior of the poor.

The concept of the charity as a "famille" was central to the existence of the municipal charity. The municipal charity was an institution which bound together rich and poor, rectors and inmates, with mutual ties. It made the poor a part of society, a part of the family of man.

FINANCES

No aspect of the administration of the charities absorbed more of the time and energy of those who ran them than that of finances. The records of the deliberations of the charities show that most of the discussion at meetings of the charity bureaux centered on money problems. Charity finance was not just a simple matter of raising money through donations from the public. The charities were complex financial institutions, which played the roles of employers, consumers, landowners, and bankers in their local communities. It is to these functions of the charities that we now turn.

BUYING SALVATION: THE DONATIONS
OF THE PIOUS

Primary among the financial resources of the charities were of course public donations. Most charities began their existence with a large donation from their founder. For example, when the merchant Jacques de la Roque founded Aix's hôtel-Dieu in 1519, he made the hospital his universal heir, except for minor legacies to his wife and other relatives.[63] Similarly, when André de la Garde, procureur-général in the Parlement of Provence, decided in 1722 to start an institution which would care for the so-called "incurables" ignored by other hospitals, he made its future financially secure with a gift of 18,000 livres.[64] Such gifts, reinvested in lands or rentes, provided steadily increasing incomes for the charities each year.

Throughout a charity's existence, the pious donations it received each year were a major financial asset, although their relative importance usually declined as a charity developed more diversified economic resources. Thus in 1702 the Charité stated that pious legacies had formed its principal source of income for the preceding eleven years.[65] But by 1751 such gifts formed only five percent of the Charité's total resources (see below). For the smaller charities, which lacked the wide range of assets of the larger institutions, pious gifts continued to be of importance. Such donations provided 30-35 percent of the total yearly revenue of establishments like the Oeuvre des Prisons and the Insensés; for the very smallest, like the Mont-de-Piété, the proportion rose as high as 75 percent.[66]

Why did people give to the charities? The answer is simple. People made charitable donations in an attempt to buy salvation. Fear of the punishments of Purgatory was the keynote of religious belief in seventeenth-century Aix. This theme dominated religious iconography: the walls of the churches and chapels of Provence abounded in depictions of Judgement Day, Purgatory, and the torments of the damned. The saints who had intercessory powers, especially the Virgin Mary as intercessor with her son, pleading for His mercy toward sinners, were favored objects of devotion. The dying left legacies for hundreds, and even thousands, of masses to be said for the repose of their souls.[67]

To the concerned sinner, the charities held out the hope that a charitable bequest might bring salvation. The fund-raising pamphlets of the charities promised this explicitly (see Chapter II). Charity, they stated, opened the gates of Paradise. When a person gave to a charity he in effect bought a guarantee that the hundreds of the poor whom he had helped would plead his cause before God on Judgement Day. The poor were traditional intercessors. Their prayers were thought to be especially agreeable to God. And they were also considered especially effacious in removing a soul from Purgatory. The frequent presence of 13 poor men, symbolizing the 13 apostles, in funeral corteges of baroque Provence testifies to the role of the poor as heavenly intercessors.[68] Thus when one made a donation to a charity one not only performed an act which was virtuous in itself, but one also bought the prayers of the poor, powerful pleaders before God's throne of Judgement. That this was the purpose of many charitable donors is obvious from the formulas in which charitable bequests were couched in wills. Such bequests most often included a stipulation that the institution aided say a certain number of prayers for the soul of the deceased benefactor. For example, Magdeleine Bonnard, the daughter of a noble, who divided her estate between the Pureté, the Filles Orphelines, and the poor of the parish of St. Esprit, asked that each of her beneficiaries celebrate 100 masses for the repose of her immortal soul.[69]

If hope of salvation was the most important stimulus to charitable giving, it was not the only one. Philanthropic motives — a genuine concern for the poor and helpless—and, less altruistically, worldly pride, played a role as well. A donation to a charitable institution was one way to ensure that one lived in the memory of one's fellows as a good and generous man. The administrators of the charities recognized this as a natural human desire, and, if in pamphlet literature such as *Mendicité abolie*, they deplored charity undertaken for the sake of vanity as unChristian, in practice they encouraged it by every means at their command. Most charities had arrangements whereby a donor might make a special foundation, always to be identified with his name. At the Incurables patrons who made large donations were considered as having "founded" separate beds in the institution. A gift of

3,000 livres or more entitled its donor to be founder of a bed, and also an "honorary rector" of the charity. For 5,000 livres, or its equivalent, a rente bringing in an income of at least 200 livres a year, a philanthropist could gain the right to choose the occupant of his bed, a right which could be bequeathed to his heirs in perpetuity.[70] Those who gave over 1,000 livres to the Charité were entitled to have their portrait painted and hung in the main hall—at their own expense, of course. Thus the charities were very adept at bartering prestigious honors for hard cash.

Pious gifts might take two forms: first, legacies, and second, donations made during the charity's quête, or fund-raising drive. Charitable legacies came from people in all stations of life. Michel Vovelle, who has made an exhaustive study of the surviving wills from eighteenth-century Provence, found that in Aix in the first half of the century no less than 70 percent of the wills included some sort of charitable legacy.[71] And these legacies came from all social classes. While gifts from the rich parlementaires and the nobles predominated, the charities also received legacies from many humbler sorts, like Jean Louis Dorée, a tailor, who in 1744 left the Pureté 500 livres.[72] Donors left the charities not only money, but also houses, lands, rentes, furniture, religious paintings, clothing and even public offices.[73] Such legacies were often more trouble than they were worth, for the rectors had to inventory and auction off the real possessions, and to inspect the houses, fields and mills, and decide whether it would be more profitable to keep or sell them.

Such legacies frequently brought in their train one further problem, more expensive and time-consuming than all the rest: lawsuits. In a land where litigation was a national sport, and in a town where every other person one met seemed to be a lawyer, few families were willing to accept without a fight a relative's bequeathing to the poor that which might be better enjoyed by his own kin. Almost every large—and many small—charitable legacies were contested. Such suits often dragged through the Parlement for years, ever increasing in expense and complexity. A typical case was the legacy of Catherine Chambon, the difficult history of which spanned almost the whole of the eighteenth century, and was still unsettled when the Revolution swept away all the property of the charities.[74] The trouble arose when Sieur Randolphe Chambon, Seigneur de Velaux, made a will in 1723 making his two daughters, Marie Anne and Catherine, equal heirs to his estate, although the eldest, Marie Anne, received the *terre* of Velaux. When Sieur Chambon died in 1725 his wishes were carried out and his estate divided. The two sisters lived together into old age. Marie Anne died in 1761, leaving as her heir a distant relative, the Dame d'Albertas. Catherine died the following year, having bequeathed her portion of the Chambon estate to the Charité. After her death the Dame d'Albertas promptly sued the Charité for 20,000 livres. Her claim was based on the fact that, sixty-three years before, in 1699,

Catherine had been married with a dowry of 40,000 livres. Never consummated, the marriage was annulled in 1701, and the dowry returned to Catherine. Mme.d'Albertas maintained that the dowry was a part of Sieur Chambon's estate, and therefore should have been split between his two heirs. The Charité argued that Chambon had given the dowry outright to Catherine, and that it was her property, which she could will to the Charité if she wished. The case continued unsettled for at least another twenty years.

In cases such as this, the odds were in favor of the charity. The rectors of the charities embodied some of the finest legal talent in Aix. And further, by the customary law of Provence the interests of the "poor" were to be favored in any legal contest.[75] The loss of this legal advantage of the poor was one of the most important ways in which the charities suffered financially from the Revolution. This process is illustrated by the history of the legacy of Jean Baptiste Maximum Le Gros. In 1782, LeGros, the son of a "noble," left his whole estate of 72,000 livres to the Charité, stipulating only that his brother, a priest, be given a life interest. But by the law of 17 *nivoise an* 2, which reformed inheritance laws in favor of immediate relations, the brother was able to claim the entire estate.[76]

If the legacies created friction between the charities and the public at large, the other form of pious donation, the quête, brought about many quarrels among the charities themselves. A quête was a fund-raising drive, very much like those undertaken by charitable institutions today. The rectors, dressed in the costumes and insignia of their charity, and carrying the traditional leather *tronc*, or poor-box, stood in the churches during services or went from house to house, demanding alms. The rules of the Miséricorde described the proper demeanor for its rectors:

They walk slowly; they demand in a loud, firm and intelligible voice, "Pour les pauvres malades"; they carry a small basin to receive the gifts; they are modest and civil; they display a charitable gentleness and honest manners which are inseparable from administrators of this hospital.

They always carry in their purse change to accommodate people with only coins of large denomination . . .

However painful the quête is for the Rectors, particularly for those who have several churches in their share, they must conquer sleep to arrive at the first Mass; they must remain standing, resisting fatigue and lassitude; they must be patient and constant in order to assist at the last Mass . . . They must . . . . visit all the corners and the chapels of the Churches; and be attentive and vigilant to discover benefactors, and to neglect no one.[77]

The rules of the bureaux de charité added firmly that, "The quête undertaken for the poor being a sainted and religious work, they [the rectors] must never drink in the houses where they make a quête, nor must the householders give them anything to drink, for fear that an action of sanctity become something profane and scandalous."[78]

So frequent were the collections for charities in Aix that they were almost impossible to avoid. A citizen of the town going to church on Sunday would be met outside the door by a rector of the Charité; once inside, he would be approached during the service by a collector from the Miséricorde, the institution which had the exclusive right, granted by Parlement, to make their quête during the period of the service "from the beginning of Mass until the elevation of the Holy Sacrament."[79] Since "it seems there are already too many people passing basins during that time, and the public is not only incommoded in its prayers, but also crowded and shoved," fund-raising efforts of the rectors of the Oeuvre des Pauvres Prisonniers were restricted by Parlement to the time during "the chant of Vespers or the Saluts or Benedictions."[80] And church was not the only place where quêtes were made. The citizen would be approached in his home by rectors of the hôtel-Dieu and the Charité in January. From the Sunday after the Feast of Our Lady in February until February 25, the feast of St. Mathias, it was the turn of the Refuge. The Mont-de-Piété made its annual quête from the first Sunday in March until March 19, the feast of St. Joseph, while the Insensés made its drive the first week in April. Then came the turn of the Oeuvre de la Propagande de la Foi, the Incurables, the Bon Pasteur.[81] In the 1780's, when because of the dullness of Aix's social season few of the prominent land-owning families left their country estates for town until the end of January, the beginning of the annual round of quêtes was postponed by mutual agreement until February, so that all charities might have a fair chance at the available pickings.[82] In their pursuit of funds the charities were not above using methods which would today be called the "hard sell." The Charité, for example, sent out the youngest and most pathetically appealing of its children to solicit funds.[83] The charities even resorted to outright subterfuge. The institution for the redemption of Christians taken captive by the infidel Turks, not one of the most popular of the charities, greatly increased the yield of its quête one year when its rectors disguised themselves and infiltrated the churches, pretending that they were collecting for the Miséricorde! [84] The charities constantly quarreled over fund-raising prerogatives, and even over such matters as precedence in processions, since precedence meant prestige, and prestige brought money into the charity's coffers.[85] These fund-raising efforts might have elements which appear comical to us, but to the charities of the Old Regime the whole business was deadly serious. Pious donations were one of their major sources of income. But the institutions had other resources as well.

OTHER RESOURCES OF THE CHARITIES

In the investment of the proceeds of their legacies and quêtes, the charities acted under the same assumptions as did private individual investors of Old Regime France. Like most private investors the charities were what George V.

Taylor has called "proprietary capitalists."[86] They preferred investments which brought a steady, if moderate, income, to the more profitable but risky and "undignified" business ventures. The favored fields for private investment in the France of the ancien régime, were, first of all, land, and secondly, rentes, or annuities. The rente was an arrangement by which, in return for a capital sum, which he alienated permanently to the borrower, an investor received a yearly income, either in perpetuity (the *rente constituée* or *perpetuelle*) or for a lifetime (the *rente viagère*).[87] Private investors probably preferred land above all else, but for a charity, land, which needed at least a modicum of supervision, might be troublesome. The rente, which provided an assured income with no fuss at all, was much more appealing and was indeed the ideal investment for a charity.

The major role of the rente in charity finance is illustrated in Table 3.1, which is derived from the inventories of charitable resources demanded by the revolutionary government in 1790, as a prelude to nationalization. As this table shows, in all cases except the Mont-de-Piété, whose main income came from the sale of objects left for pawning, the charities derived well over half, and occasionally all their income from rentes.

Who issued these rentes which were such popular investments for the charities? Almost all the public and semipublic bodies in Old Regime France, from the royal government down to the most minor court or gild, sold rentes. The charities, favoring diversified holdings, usually owned a wide variety. The Charité, for example, in 1790 held 173,515 livres capital in rentes on such issuing institutions as the Hôtel de Ville of Paris, the provincial estates, the

Table 3.1. Income of the Charities, 1790

Charity	Yearly income, rentes			Total yearly income			% of income from rentes
Oeuvre des Prisons	2022/	9/	11	3522/	9/	11	57
Pureté	4348/	8/	0	7504/	13/	0	58
Orphelines	5295/	0/	0	7865/	0/	0	67
Mont-de-Piété	727/	0/	7	20275/	0/	0	3
Incurables	17701/	13/	6	22973/	16/	5	77
Refuge	0			4433/	0/	7	0
Ste. Marcelle	865/	0/	0	865/	0/	0	100
Enfants Abandonnées	2388/	0/	0	2388/	0/	0	100
Conseil Charitable	762/	10/	6	887/	7/	10	86
Insensés	1253/	5/	4	1653/	5/	4	76
Aveugles	7420/	19/	0	10283/	3/	10	73

Source: A.M., LL 349, Déclarations et Inventaires des Hôpitaux et oeuvres diverses, 1790-92.

commune of Aix, the Parlement of Provence, the *Secrétaires du Roy*, the *Trésoriers-Généraux de France*, the local Cour des Comptes, the local Jesuit college, the Clergé de France (a true blue-chip), five different local gilds, and a convent.[88] Most popular for the charities were rentes on the provincial and communal governments and on the Clergé de France—these were the equivalents of General Motors and AT&T stocks in the portfolios of today's universities and foundations.

In addition to those issued by public bodies, the charities also "bought" rentes "on" private individuals, that is, lent to private individuals capital sums at interest. In 1790 the Charité had rentes on 72 different people.[89] Unfortunately the existing records gave no indication of the social status of the individuals who borrowed money from the charities. But it is probable that most of them were merchants who needed capital for business ventures, or bourgeois or nobles wishing to invest in land. Because of the still primitive state of the joint-stock company, and the lack of banks and other credit facilities, loans from institutions like the charities were almost the only recourse, aside from private partnerships, for the financing of commercial ventures. Thus the charities played the role of banks in provincial France. But most charities preferred to invest in public or semipublic institutions rather than private parties. Such investments seemed to hold the promise of payment for an indefinite future; few investors of Old Regime France would not believe that an institution like the Estates of Provence would not exist for all time.

In addition to their rentes, the charities also derived income from the real property they owned. Charities owned a substantial amount of urban property, and bits and pieces of farmland scattered around the countryside. While their holdings did not approach those of the Church, they were nevertheless large enough to arouse envy on the eve of the Revolution.

Most of the charities owned the building they occupied. In addition, the Charité had substantial property near its headquarters, called the "garden," which it leased for 800 livres a year, and a flour mill, also rented out for 150 livres. The Charité also owned a few houses in the country.[90] The Oeuvre des Orphelines owned an inn, and three buildings in Aix, leased as apartments and shops. These real estate holdings brought this charity rents of 2,570 livres a year.[91] The Mont-de-Piété owned what were described as "five houses in the country."[92] These properties came to the charities through inheritance rather than purchase. For their own new investments, charities preferred the rente.

Charities also found a financial resource in the labor of their inmates. Each charity catering to the able-bodied hired out the labor of its inmates to private entrepreneurs. Behind such a policy was the desire to make the charity self-supporting, for the charities lost no chance to economize. But those who ran the charities also hoped that if the poor were taught a skill they would be inculcated with a love of work which would keep them safe from the moral dangers of idleness (see Chapter II). Most of these entrepreneurial activities involved textiles. The Charité, for example, housed in succession, as fashion dictated, lacemaking, silk manufacturing, a workshop which made "Cadiz" cloth (a printed wool), wool carding and stocking-making. The contract between the charity and the entrepreneur was that typical of the putting-out system: the entrepreneur supplied the tools and material, and the charity the labor. The product was split, with the entrepreneur getting the lion's share. The Charité sold its share of the goods from a stall on the cours Royale, the main "avenue" in Aix.[93]

In theory, at least, the charities enjoyed yet another source of income, the government subsidy. The king, as "father of the poor," was traditionally generous towards charitable institutions. Royal bounty usually took the form of attributing the income of a tax—frequently one newly created—to a charity. Thus it was really not the king but his subjects who paid. To give an example of such a royal gift, in 1660 the Charité was given the right to the product of the tax on dice, playing cards, and tobacco in Provence. In 1675 this was converted to an annual pension of 4,000 livres from the *ferme-général du tabac*, and in 1720 the pension was transferred to the *Cinq Grosses Fermes*. Other bounty which came not from the king but from his subjects was the gift in 1687 of all the property of the Protestant churches of Provence.[94] The royal government was no more prompt in its payment to the charities than to any of its other creditors; from the 1740's on, the pension from the Cinq Grosses Fermes was constantly in arrears.[95]

Apart from the princely gifts, the charities also received from the royal government payment for the care of those who entered the charities under various royal ordinances. For example, the hospital-general was entitled to four sous per day (later raised to five sous for the healthy and seven sous for invalids) for every beggar who entered the institution under the royal ordinance of July 18, 1724.[96] Similarly, the Refuge received a subvention of three sous (raised to four and one-half in the 1770's) for every prostitute imprisoned there.[97] But these subventions covered scarcely half the cost of caring for each inmate (see below). Further, these allotments were, like all other obligations of the royal government, frequently in arrears. The Charité was still trying to collect, in the 1780's, sums due under the ordinance of 1724.[98] This certainly did not help the charities when they experienced their financial crises, as most would after the 1760's. But to see why the charities experienced financial difficulties, we must examine their expenses.

EXPENSES

The cardinal rule which governed the internal expenditures of the charities was simple: all was to be done with "a good and holy economy" appropriate to a charitable institution.[99] Furthermore, those who ran the charities of Aix firmly believed that the poor, being naturally prone to idleness, would flood the charities unless conditions of life within the institutions were much more grim than those which they could expect on the outside. Therefore the inmates of the charities were provided with only the minimum of food, clothing, and shelter necessary for existence.

The poor of the Charité received three meals a day: at 9:30 A.M. a breakfast, consisting of a bowl of soup made with peas, lentils, rice and a bit of olive oil, at noon a déjeuner of brown bread (*pain bis*) and a glass of red wine mixed with water, served in the workshops so that no working time would be lost, and at 6:00 P.M. the final meal of the day, the *souper*, consisting of more soup, bread, and wine. The total daily bread ration for each inmate was one nine-ounce loaf. Only the ill ever tasted meat.[100] Every effort was made to keep expenses low. The food was prepared and the bread baked in the Charité's own kitchens. Supplies were purchased as cheaply as possible, in bulk and at wholesale prices. The rectors searched all the nearby markets for the cheapest wheat; wine was purchased right after the harvest each year, when it was the least expensive. The rules of the Charité specified that only good quality merchandise be bought, "to prevent the illnesses and corruptions which rotten supplies give the poor," but it is doubtful if this rule was always observed. Another rule specified that the oldest supplies must always be used up first.[101] If any items of food were too expensive, the poor simply did without them; in 1747, for example, the Charité's rectors deemed wine too costly, and reduced the inmates' ration rather than purchase any.[102]

Economy was similarly the rule in the provision of clothing and shelter for the inmates. For example, the inmates of the Charité received only one suit of clothes, made in the Charité's own workshops from the cheap, coarse cloth woven on the premises. The clothing of the men was blue, while the women were dressed in "a deep plum color."[103] In 1742 the *bombes* or bustles on the women's dresses were done away with, not for reasons of fashion, but because this would cut the cost of the material by over one-half.[104] In theory every inmate was given a pair of leather shoes, again made in the Charité's own workshops. But in practice when financial difficulties arose this expensive item was often eliminated, leaving the inmates barefooted.[105] To save on soap, the clothing of the inmates was washed only once a month. As might be expected, this created many difficulties with vermin. In November 1749, the rectors were forced to expel one Mathieu Veran because vermin tormented him so much that he could not work.[106] The administration was equally niggardly when it came to supplying fuel to heat the dormitories in winter. Complaints about the cold were constant. In December 1749, it was decided to keep the fabriques open on Sundays, since only by working could the inmates keep warm.[107] And in January 1754, the rectors complained of the disorder in the kitchens, caused by all the women and girls who crowded there near the heat of the ovens.[108]

Given such parsimonious management, one would expect that the cost per inmate was very low. This was indeed the case. In 1767, the Charité required for its 151 poor the following supplies:

240 *charges* of wheat at 30# / charge	7,200 livres
200 charges of grapes at 7-1/2# / charge	1,500
75 *quintaux* oil at 24# measure unspecified	600
Wood and vegetables for soup	1,250
Soap	130
Salt	25
Olives, vines	1,350
Cloth, shoes	2,000
Medicine	25
Other	3,250
Total	17,330[109]

This gave a total yearly cost for each inmate of 114 livres, 14 sous per year, or between six and seven sous per day. This figure is probably the norm for most charities.[110] It is noticeably less than the minimum amount needed for a poor man to survive outside the charities, which was about 15 sous per day in the 1780's (see Chapter IV).

With those low costs, plus the large revenue, it would seem that the charities could easily balance their budgets and even show a profit. But this was not so. The actual costs of caring for the poor were only a small portion of the total expenses of a charity. As we have seen, in 1767 the Charité's inmates cost the institution 17,330 livres. Total expenses for the year, however, reached the sum of 44,295 livres, 5 sous, 1 denier. On what was the other 28,000 livres spent? One expense which was not calculated in the cost per inmate was the salaries of the charity's staff. These, however, amounted to little more than 1,000 livres.[111] In fact the extra costs did not arise from the internal administration of the charities. Rather they resulted from the charities' activities as bankers—from the sums they borrowed, in the form of rentes, from the people of Aix. Paying the interest on these rentes, and not the costs of caring for the poor, was the Achilles' heel of charitable finance.

THE CHARITY RENTE

Any deficits in the budgets of the charities were made up by money borrowed from private investors through the medium of the rente. Rentes were the only type of loan legal in Old Regime France, where the strictures of the medieval Church against usury still discouraged the lending of money at interest. The rente was not affected by such prohibitions for, in theory at least, it was not a loan, since the principal was never repaid. The charities owed both major types of rentes. In 1762 some 20 percent of the capital borrowed by the Charité was in the form of "rentes viagères," or lifetime annuities. In this type of rente the lender turned over a certain capital sum to the borrower; in return the borrower paid him a percentage of the sum—it was quite high, usually 9 or even 12 percent, depending on the age of the lender—for as long as lived. When he died the borrower got clear title to the principal. But as a rule charities preferred the other form of rente, the "rente constituée" or "perpetuelle." As its name implies, this rente was perpetuated, that is, it continued after the original buyer died; he could bequeath it to his heirs. This sort of rente paid a lower interest, usually 4 or 5 percent. In 1762, 42 percent of the rentes of the Charité were rentes constituées.[112]

The remainder of the money borrowed took the form of a special rente, peculiar to the charities. This was the "rente avec donative." This rente was perpetual, but it had a special feature which set it apart from the usual rente constituée. The original buyer stipulated that part of the capital be donated to the charity on his death. Typical is the example of Marguerite Feissole, a former servant of the Conseiller de Nibes, who asked that when she died 166 livres of the 400-livre rente she bought in 1750 from the Charité would be donated to the hospital.[113] Some 20 percent of all rentes sold by the Charité in the years 1745 to 1750 were "rentes avec donatives."[114]

The charity rente was usually quite small in size. Analysis of the lists of rentes sold by the Charité in the years 1745 to 1762, 795 in all, reveal that, while some rentes ranged as high as 6,800 livres, the average rente was approximately 800 livres, and the median 600 livres.[115] Rentes of 200 livres or under were very common (they formed 20 percent of the total) and some were as low as 50 livres.[116] How very small these capital sums are becomes obvious when we consider that a livre was worth approximately one dollar, U.S., and that a 200-livre rente at five percent brought in a yearly income of only ten livres, while the income from a 50-livre rente was only two and one-half livres. The income from even the median rente of 600 livres was only 30 livres.

Charity rentes, with their rates of interest 4 and 5 percent, did not yield large incomes. Their attraction for the investor lay rather in the way they combined modest material with great spiritual advantages. Investment in a charity might buy salvation in the next life, as well as yield an adequate income in this one. Further, the charity rente was an investment of utmost, unquestionable respectability, doubtless endorsed by the clergy and leading members of the community. No accusation of sordid profit-making could be made against its buyer. Finally the charity rente had the advantage of being one of the few forms of investment accessible to the so-called "petites gens": it was the type of investment they would have heard about locally, and a charity would willingly accept the small sums they had available for investment.

Who then could be influenced by these attractions to invest in a charity? Examination of a list of charity rente-holders will give us some clues. Three such lists have been preserved: records of all those who bought rentes from the Charité in the years 1745-50, 1750-56, and 1756-62. An analysis of these rente-holders according to their social class appears in Table 3.2.

This table yields few surprises. Noticeable is the absence of the very wealthy, who had large amounts of capital to invest. Commercial loans, business partnerships, shares in ships engaged in overseas commerce, or even loans to "financiers" all promised higher returns than the charity rente.

Table 3.2. Holders of Rentes on the Charité, 1745-62

Social class	Number of rente-holders	% of total capital owned
Titled nobles, seigneurs, army officers	26	3.3
Écuyers	20	2.5
Parlementaires	10	1.3
Lawyers, office-holders	80	10.2
Other liberal professions	8	1.0
Bourgeois	42	5.3
Master craftsmen, marchands	79	10.0
Journeymen, small shopkeepers	18	2.3
Servants	56	7.1
Ménagers	7	.9
Travailleurs	1	.1
Minors	3	.4
Clergy	65	8.2
Charitable organizations	19	2.4
Inmates of the charities	4	.5
People identified only by honorific title	211	26.8
Women without honorific titles	130	16.5
Unidentified males	9	1.1
Total	788	99.9
Total Females	436	55.3

Source: A.D. (Aix), XXI H, II B 15, "Rentes," 1745-50; II B 16, "Rentes," 1750-56; II B 17, "Rentes," 1756-62.

Nobles obviously preferred to invest any surplus capital in land. Noble families might use a charity rente to provide a fixed-money income for a dowager, a spinster daughter, or a younger son. Younger sons who joined the army often invested what was left of their portion from the family settlement in a charity rente, as did, for example, Messire Ignace de Galliard de Bayons, chevalier of the Order of St. Louis and formerly of the grenadiers of the Flanders Regiment, who owned a 4,000-livre rente on the Charité which gave him an income of 160 livres a year.[117] But most nobles with surplus capital made the bulk of their investment elsewhere.

This was also true of the parlementaires, avocats and other judicial office-holders. Admittedly they form a fairly large number of the purchasers of rentes. Yet their numbers are nowhere near what might be expected of the social group which so dominated the city of Aix, both numerically and economically. The wealthy avocat was far more likely to buy an ennobling office, and an already noble parlementaire to buy a seigneurie which would give substance and dignity to his "state," than to invest in a rente on a charity. This social group, like the nobles, might buy a charity rente to provide for a dowager, a spinster daughter or a younger son. Indeed, in the period 1745-50, 27 of the 43 rentes purchased by this social group were held by women.[118] Probably, too, an avocat or parlementaire might make a token investment in a charity as a gesture of civic duty, for such people had always played prominent roles in the foundation and direction of Aix's charities. But, like the nobles, they placed the bulk of their investments in more prestigious land, especially titled land.

If the charity rente was largely ignored by the very wealthy, it had a definite appeal for certain other types of investors. One of these was the clergy, who were doubtless attracted to the charitable rente by the prospect of performing a Christian act of charity while at the same time receiving a modest income. Most of the clerical rente-holders belonged to the comfortable middle clergy—priors, canons, beneficed priests, doctors of theology who taught at the University. The simple country curé was of course too poor to buy a rente. Many of the clerical rente-holders were not individuals but institutions; local convents and monasteries often invested some of their capital in the charities.

Charitable rentes were probably most attractive to the bourgeois who lived modestly on his income, and to the merchant and master craftsman who hoped some day to become a bourgeois himself. As the table shows, such people formed the bulk of the Charité's rente-owners. Their prominence becomes even more apparent when we consider that most of the people identified in the lists only by the honorific titles of "Sieur," "Demoiselle," and "Dame" fall into these categories.[119] The attraction of the charity rente for such people doubtless lay in its respectability; few other types of investments apart from land or offices (which they probably could not afford) were more removed from sordid profit-making.

It is only to be expected that the true rentier class should provide a large number of the Charité's investors. More surprising is the almost equally large number of rente-holders among the menu peuple, the journeymen, the small shopkeepers and servants, the ménagers, and even travailleurs and inmates of the charities.[120] This is surprising because it is not usually realized that such people might have any surplus income to invest. Most historians seem to assume that if such people had any money, they kept it in a sock under the mattress. Admittedly their investments were usually quite small. The median of the rentes purchased by servants was 300 livres, compared with a median of 1,000 livres for the nobles, and 600 livres for all social groups combined.[121] Such a sum probably represented the whole life savings of someone like Marguerite Philip, servant of the curé of Gardanne, who owned a 300-livre rente which yielded her an income of six livres a year.[122] A charity rente was the obvious investment for such a servant saving for her old age, or for a garçon cordonnier hoping to provide a dowry for his daughter, or for Anne Conif, widow of François Jourdan, a weaver, looking for a way to invest the proceeds of the sale of her husband's effects.[123] Investment in land or a commercial venture would be out of the question for such people, whose horizons did not extend beyond their small shop. Charity rentes were by contrast safe and widely known; the charities were eager to accept their small sums of capital.

One further fact about the charity rente-holders deserves mention: over half of them were women. Female rente-holders are not exclusive to any one class: they are found in all social groups, from widows of écuyers to servants. This suggests that women in Old Regime France had a far greater degree of financial independence, and controlled far larger amounts of money, than is usually thought. Historians most often stress the paternalistic aspects of Old Regime society, and portray women as having no legal right to own property and thus completely subordinate financially to their husbands. But innumerable widows and spinster daughters controlled considerable amounts of capital—for example, Mlle. Anne Perin, widow of M. Castel, former procureur des pauvres in the Parlement, who had thousands of livres invested in no less than 24 different rentes on the Charité.[124] Also, there were many women who retained control of their own fortune after marriage, either through express provisions in the marriage contract or due to the fact that no marriage contract had been made. Such women were described, like Mme. Laurence de Lombard, wife of Messire Louis Balthezard de Gantes, écuyer, or Mlle. Anne Therese de Pitton, wife of Dominque Artaud, procureur in the

Parlement, as an "épouse libre de ses actions."[125]   For all women a charity
rente would seem to have been an ideal investment: it brought in a modest
income with no trouble to them, and it was blessed by the Church besides!

Examination of the borrowing practices of Aix's charities has disclosed
a hitherto unexplored chapter in the financial history of Old Regime France.
It has focused attention on two neglected classes of investors, women and the
menu peuple. Whether these findings necessitate a major revision in the
standard economic picture of the French investor is, however, another issue.
Economic historians are inclined to blame France's relative economic back-
wardness on the French investor, who, they say, preferred the modest but
safe and respectable income of the rentier or the social prestige of office-
holding to speculative but often highly profitable investments in business ventures.[126]   The history of the charity rente would seem to bear this out. The
charity rente, with its low income, certainly appealed to the unadventurous.
Further, the charity rente was the perfect choice for those who had lingering
scruples about the capitalist ethic of profit maximization: it was an investment thoroughly approved by the Church. Yet in making these sorts of
generalizations, we must keep in mind the types of people whom the charity
rente attracted. The wealthy did not invest in them; they preferred other uses
for their money, uses producing greater benefits in either profit or prestige.
Those who invested in charity rentes were rather those who, had such a thing
not existed, might not have invested their money at all. It is hard to see what
other alternatives were open to the small investor in a town like Aix, an
administrative rather than a commercial center. Thus the charities, through
their policy of selling *rentes*, performed a definite financial service to the
community, tapping for circulation resources which might otherwise have lain
dormant.

My examination of the administration and financing of Aix's charities has
highlighted the many and diverse roles these institutions played in town life.
For the poor they were charities, but for their rectors they were social clubs
and status symbols, and they functioned as employers, consumers and
bankers for townsmen in all walks of life. It is not surprising that the charities
were deeply imbedded in many phases of life in Aix. In early modern society,
where both the economic and administrative super-structures were still under-
developed, what social organizations there were, of necessity, played multiple
roles. Since the work of Olwen Hufton and John McManners, Old Regime
historians have come to regard the Church as an institution performing many
social functions beyond its nominal religious ones. They should view charities
in a similar light.

In what has been perhaps the single most influential interpretation of
seventeenth-century attitudes toward the poor, Michel Foucault, in his *His-*

toire de la folie (1961), stressed the *separateness* of the charities. Their main raison d'être was to keep the poor separate, apart from the rest of society. But if we examine the many functions of the charities in Old Regime society, we see that their keynote was not separateness but rather integration. They were an important part of the community, and because of this they made the poor a part of the community too. The appearance in the town processions of the poor of the charities, dressed in their uniforms and marching behind the banners of their institutions, exemplifies this. The poor had a place in town life; a humble place, by no means attractive, but a place nonetheless. The charities made them a part of a "famille," a part of the family of man.

The charities could perform their integrating function successfully because they were both the product and the reflection of a shared consensus of attitudes about the nature of poverty and its proper cure. The high level of public support (as I have said, approximately 70 percent of the wills registered in Aix in the first half of the eighteenth century contained charitable legacies) testifies to this shared consensus. But how closely did popular perceptions come to the reality of the problem? Just how effective were Aix's charities against poverty? To answer these questions we must probe deeply into the lives of the poor.

PART TWO

The Poor

CHAPTER IV

The Poor of the Charities

How effective were the municipal charities in relieving the problem of poverty in seventeenth- and eighteenth-century Aix? To answer this question, we must examine the dimensions of poverty in the Old Regime. And when we do this, the gap between the reality of the problem and contemporary conceptions of it becomes apparent. To those who founded and supported the charities, there were basically two types of poverty: a man might be poor either because he could not work, or because he did not choose to (see Chapter II). Those who could not work because of age or illness were the "good poor." And those who did not choose to, but who instead elected to spend their days in idleness and debauchery, were the "bad poor." In reality, of course, the problem was far more complex.

There were indeed two types of poverty in Old Regime France. The French student of poverty in Lyon, Jean-Pierre Gutton, has described them as "structural and "conjunctural" poverty.[1] Structural poverty corresponds to the "good poor" of Old Regime stereotypes. Its victims were the aged, the ill, the very young—those who could not support themselves under even the best of circumstances, and had to depend on outside aid to survive. But conjunctural poverty was something different—something no one in the Old Regime clearly understood. The term "conjunctural poverty" refers to those of the poor who could usually earn enough to subsist on, and who were therefore ordinarily found in the ranks of the respectable poor, but who, because they never could earn enough to accumulate a backlog of savings, could be thrust by sudden crisis down into the ranks of the destitute. Such crises could be the product of either unfavorable circumstances — unexpected illness, the birth of a new baby—or of what the French would call an unfavorable "conjuncture" of the economy—a rise in bread prices, or unemployment. But in both cases the effect was the same: the family was suddenly reduced to utter penury.

Thus the dimensions of poverty in the Old Regime were infinitely expansible. A relatively small hard core of the structurally poor were joined by a much larger contingent of the conjuncturally poor, whose exact numbers varied with circumstances. This does not mean that all the menu peuple should be automatically classified as "the poor," although to the rich parlementaire, to the charity administrator, and, all too often to the modern historian, the two groups looked alike. Actually there were infinite variations in income level and life style among the crowds of travailleurs, servants, innkeepers and candlemakers who formed the ranks of Aix's menu peuple, and the social distinctions between masters and apprentices, between respectable tailors and old-clothes sellers, between ladies' maids and washerwomen, were as carefully observed as those in the upper levels of society. But cutting across all these fine distinctions of status was one major dividing line. At the upper level of the menu peuple were those, perhaps 10 to 20 percent of the whole class, who had managed to accummulate some property—a house, a country plot, or even some hard cash—and therefore had a cushion against disaster. Typical of this group of people was Jean Coutard, a stonecutter, who left when he died in 1733 an estate which included a bit of vineyard and an olive grove in Aix's terroir, (bringing a rent of 40 livres per year), 406 livres worth of household goods, and another 50 livres in stores of wheat, beans, and olive oil. Another of this fortunate group was Etienne Silvestre, who had in his possession at his death over 100 livres worth of jewelry, a sack of money, and three promissory notes, each worth over 100 livres. And Mathieu Latil, a servant in the household of the Baron de Très, left an estate of over 1,150 livres, which consisted of jewelry, linen, china, silver, and an immense number of clothes. This was in contrast to people like Anne Michel, whose total estate when she died consisted of 11 livres of back wages owed to her by her employer, and Jeanne Landine, whose only worldly possessions were six livres, which she wanted spent on masses for her soul.[2]

Thus some managed to accumulate substantial estates, estates which brought them not only the respect of their fellows, but also, and more importantly, security against time of crisis. Yet for the other 80 percent destitution was a very real threat. Most of them managed, by heaven knows what expedients, to keep bread on the table day after day and therefore avoid charity. But the threat was always there.

Life for these people, for the travailleurs, stonecutters, wage laborers of all sorts, was precarious even at the best of times, because wages were so low. Even semiskilled workers like stonecutters rarely earned more than 18 sous per day.[3] Women earned still less. A woman who did agricultural labor rarely received a daily wage of more than eight sous, although salaries for washerwomen could rise as high as 12. Considering that one could not work every day—allowing for Sundays and holidays, some 290 days of work were usual—these wages provided barely enough to live on.

Take the situation of a family of three—husband, wife and small child. If both parents worked the combined family income probably totaled about 380 livres. Out of this must come the money for food, clothing, shelter, light, heat, for medicine for illness—for all the daily necessities. Charity accounts give us some clues for the cost of living among the very poor. Each inmate of the Charité cost the institution approximately 120 livres per year for his food and clothing (Chapter III); this figure, of course, is based on the cost of foodstuffs which the hospital bought wholesale, and does not include the cost of shelter. If prices are converted to retail, and some 10 to 15 livres per year is added as rent for the humblest sort of dwelling, it is apparent that 170 livres is about the minimum necessary for one person to survive. A wife would probably cost a further 100 livres per year. As for the child, the hôtel-Dieu estimated that each newborn baby represented a cost of 5 livres 10 sous per month, or 66 livres per year.[4] Thus the total income necessary for a family of three was 336 livres. This left a margin of only about 50 livres to cope with extra expenses. It is obvious that a prolonged period of illness or unemployment, or a price rise, or another child to feed, could upset this delicate family budget.

Thus most of the poor lived their lives precariously balanced on the thin edge between bare survival and utter penury. The most important distinction among the poor was between those who had some sort of surplus, and those who simply lived from hand to mouth, day to day. As for the latter, most of the time, by dint of endless expedients, they managed to keep food on the table. But an unexpected disaster would push them over the line and leave them penniless. Then they might get a loan from a wealthier neighbor, or pawn their few household goods at the Mont-de-Piété. But most commonly they would resort to charity.

Approximately 20 percent of Aix's population, that is about 5,000 people, received some sort of charity.[5] This percentage seems quite large; actually, given the present state of research on the subject of poverty and charity, it is impossible to tell whether this is indeed unusual. Few such estimates exist for other similar towns in France during either the seventeenth or the eighteenth century. Perhaps the best of these is Jean-Pierre Gutton's calculation that in Lyon in these years between eight and 16 percent of the city's population was aided by charitable institutions.[6] Pierre Deyon had shown that in Amiens in the early years of the eighteenth century at least three percent of the population received some sort of aid.[7] In the latter years of the century approximately one-sixth of the population of Bayeux was dependent upon outside help in order to survive.[8] But until further work has been done in this area, we simply will not know how many people of ancien régime France owed their survival to the availability of charity.

My calculation that 20 percent of the population of Aix received some sort of charity is at most an approximation. The difficulties involved in such calculations are formidable. For only one of Aix's charities, the hôtel-Dieu, were complete records of entries preserved.[9] The records of the other organizations of public assistance show astonishing gaps. For example, the Oeuvre des Enfants Abandonnées, which provided food and shelter for children from the surrounding countryside who flocked to the city to look for work, was founded in 1733, but its sole surviving register covers the period 1770-92.[10] One of the town's most important charities, the Miséricorde, left no records at all of those who received its gifts. This organization, which ministered to the pauvres honteux, those for whom the acceptance of charity was "shameful," ceremoniously burned its records at every year's end, to protect the identities of the people it helped.[11]

Taking every scrap of information available, it is possible to construct the estimates of the number of people aided by each of Aix's charitable organizations, as shown in Table 4.1. These results give no more than an approximation which is more accurate for the period after 1760. Unfortunately we cannot know if these figures are relevant for earlier periods. We also cannot tell how much these totals changed year by year, although the variations were doubtless great. For some charities the population figures never changed, because the number of people they could accommodate was fixed by their endowment. New inmates could enter only when someone in the institution left, or died. Thus the number of unemployed servant girls sheltered by the Oeuvre de Ste. Marcelle was perpetually fixed at 12; the Oeuvre de la Propagande de Foi cared for a constant population of 15 Protestant children.[12] But for most of Aix's institutions of assistance the population fluctuated wildly year by year, and even month by month. At the Enfants Abandonnées the number of children admitted for each year between 1771 and 1789 varied between a low of 13 and a high of 63.[13] Behind these fluctuations lay two factors: a varying demand for admission, and changes in the financial resources available to the institutions.

What sort of people made up this 20 percent of the population who depended upon charity? Most of them shared two characteristics: they were born in Aix or had lived there many years, and they were Catholics. Charity in Aix, as in all towns of France during the ancien régime, was strictly municipal in scope. All but two of Aix's charities stipulated that those who received aid must be natives of the town. Thus the poor agricultural laborers who poured in from the countryside when the harvests were bad were ineligible for Aix's organized charity. They were forced to turn to beggary and will be discussed in the next chapter.

Most of Aix's charities required some evidence that a would-be recipient of their aid had recently attended communion. This provision was designed specifically to exclude Protestants. Until the revocation of the Edict of Nantes needy Protestants were cared for by their own churches, by means of certain properties whose incomes were set aside for the maintenance of the

Table 4.1. Numbers of People Aided by Charitable Organizations*

Institution	1776	1782	Other Years
For the ill			
St. Jacques	212	. . .	. . .⁺
Insensés	. . .	130	. . .
St. Joachim	. . .	6	. . .
St. Eutrope	. . .	. . .	6
Incurables	32	. . .	. . .
Miséricorde			2,800 (?)
For children			
Propagande	. . .	15	. . .
Orphelines	. . .	46	. . .
Enfants abandonnées	. . .	. . .	36
Pureté	. . .	. . .	45
For women			
Refuge	30	. . .	. . .
Ste. Marcelle	12	. . .	. . .
For unemployed			
Charité (internes)	. . .	. . .	151
Charité (externes)	. . .	. . .	1,600 (?)
Bureau de Charité	. . .	. . .	. . .

*The figures below represent available surviving records, or are derived from incomplete information in the sources listed.

⁺Not available.

Sources:
Figures for 1766: A.D., C 3214, Hôpitaux, "Enquête," 1766.
Figures for 1782: A.D., IG 235 bis, "Etat du diocèse d'Aix."

Other years:

St. Eutrope: A.M., GG 519," Mémoire a ms. les consuls et assesseurs de la ville d'Aix, 1766, Hôpital St. Eutrope."

Miséricorde: Bib. Mej., Res. D 349, Miséricorde, *Règlements* 1688, p. 21, states that more than 700 families were aided by the Miséricorde each year. This was multiplied by 4, the average size of Provençal urban households in this period (Edouard Baratier, *La Demographie provençale du XVIIe au XVIe sièle avec chiffres de comparison pour le XVIIIe siècle* [Paris, 1961], p. 58).

Enfants Abandonnées: A.D. (Aix), XX H, E 1, "Registre." Admissions from 1771 to 1792 averaged yearly.

Pureté: A.D. (Aix), XXVII H, E 1, "Livre des deliberations du Bureau. . . . de la pureté, commance le 5 janvier 1711." The figure is for 1781.

Charité: (Internes) A.D., C 3220, "Etat de la maison. . . . de la Charité," 1767. (Externes) A.D. (Aix), XXI H, II E 229-II E 238, "Registres de la distribution du pain," 1692-1705 averaged.

poor. In 1687 the royal government gave these properties to the hospital-general, and after this the remaining Protestants of Aix were without organized assistance until the end of the Old Regime.[14]

Apart from these shared characteristics, the 5,000 - odd people in Table 4.1 helped by the charities were a diverse lot. Perhaps the best way to determine who they were and why they found charity necessary is to examine their socioeconomic positions, by analysis of their occupations as listed in the charities' entry registers. Table 4.2 lists the occupations of the people who entered the Charité during a number of sample years.

This table shows the proportions of the different occupational categories among the entrants compared with their proportion of the population of the menu peuple of the town. Admittedly such a comparison has its

Table 4.2. Occupations of People Entering Charité, or of Parents
of Children Entering, During Sample Years 1745-47,
1755-63, 1767-70, 1780-89

Occupation	Number entering Charité		Percent of total entries		Menu peuple of Aix, 1695: Occupations (%)	
Agricultural laborers						
Travailleurs	105		33.9*		22.5	
Other	18		5.8		3.1	
Total		123		39.7		25.6
Craftsmen						
Building trades	27		8.7		8.1	
Textiles and leather	67		21.6		12.8	
Transportation and lodging	16		5.2		4.2	
Food	13		4.2		3.4	
Other	4		1.3		1.6	
Total		127		40.9		30.2
Servants	36		11.6		31.3	
Soldiers, sailors, public servants	17		5.5		8.0	
Hospital inmates and beggars	7		2.3		5.0	
Grand Total	310†		100.0		101.1	

*Percentages have been rounded
†Ten merchants or bourgeois were also admitted to the Charité in the sample years.

Source: A.D. (Aix), XXI H, II F 9, Charité, "Procès-Verbaux d'amissions des pauvres," 1743-1812; Coste, La Ville d'Aix, Vol. 2, passim.

problems: the figures for the entrants to the Charité date from the middle and late eighteenth century, while those for the town's population are taken from the *Capitation* of 1695. It is possible that the occupational patterns for the town as a whole changed radically between the end of the seventeenth and the middle of the eighteenth century. But, given the slow-moving nature of Aix's economic life, I doubt this very much. I think that a comparison between these figures is valid, and that such a comparison will show that some occupational categories were disproportionately represented among the recipients of charity; that is, that people in some occupations were worse off than in others, and therefore had to rely more on charity to survive.

Foremost among these categories is that of the agricultural laborer. Aix's rural sector was notoriously impoverished. Especially bad was the situation of the occupational group which formed the majority of this category: the simple day laborer or travailleur. These were the people who left the town at sunrise each day to labor in the fields of the terroir. A few were hired by the year, but for most employment was chancy: they stood in the hiring area in the marketplace, hoping to be engaged for a few days or weeks at a time. And when they did find work their wages were very low: 12 sous per day was the rule in 1750, 18 sous in 1780.[15] On such wages the travailleurs could barely support their families even if they possessed another skill. It is little wonder that the travailleurs and their families were always in the forefront of any lists of recipients of public assistance. Pierre-Joseph de Haitze noted that during the hard winter of 1678-79 public and private alms aided more than "six thousand persons, of whom the greatest part were travailleurs."[16] And travailleurs invariably bulked large in the lists of people arrested for beggary (see Table 5.2). As a modern historian of Aix has observed, "The condition of the travailleurs is the last step of socioprofessional degradation before mendicity, the boundary of which they often crossed."[17] The travailleurs constituted probably the one single social group most in need of charity.

Another social group which contributed a disproportionately large number of those who depended on charity was that of Aix's petty artisans. Artisanal trades in the city often suffered from overcrowding (see Chapter I). Not all of Aix's craftsmen could earn enough to support their families.[18] Some trades were overcrowded and depressed—shoemaking is an example. Also, many artisans were poor apprentices who because of the exclusiveness of the gilds could never hope for the prestige and financial security of a mastership. And finally, many of the people classified as artisans were in reality day laborers, who worked for a money wage, usually quite low. Those in the building trades, and textile workers, fall into this category. The latter, the innumerable *tisseurs à toile* and *cardeurs à laine,* who worked for a piecework wage, could earn enough to support a family only by superhuman exertions. It is therefore not surprising that textile workers too contribute a disproportionately large number to the recipients of charity.

Still another social group which contributed a substantial number to the public assistance rolls is that of soldiers, sailors, and public servants. In this case it was not so much the men as their families who suffered. This was especially so if the family breadwinner joined the army. The term of enlistment was long, the pay was low, and probably little of this was ever sent home to needy families. The plight of families whose major breadwinner was forced to join the army or militia was recognized by the royal government when, in the latter half of the eighteenth century, it passed a series of laws exempting from services men with large dependent families.

There was one social group which was found among the recipients of charity far less often than their numbers warranted—the domestic servants. This was probably not because servants as a group were much better off than the artisans or the travailleurs. High-ranking servants in large households might be quite well-to-do (one left an estate worth almost 2,000 livres), but the lowly maids of all work and female textile workers who formed the majority of the servant-class were among the most miserably paid of all the city's working people.[19] Instead, the explanation probably lies in the fact that the old idea of the household still prevailed; it was still customary for an employer to care for his servants, especially those lodged in his own house, in times of distress. One evidence of the prevalence of this old idea dates from the Great Plague of 1720. During that time of troubles, a master surgeon was fined 200 livres by Parlement for putting two of his stricken "garçons de boutique" out of his household and onto the streets to die.[20] When a household servant became too ill or too old to work he was usually cared for, however grudgingly, by his master. The servants who appear in charity registers were most probably either the lowest type or servant girls who did not "live in," or else women who worked in the textile industry.

In time of crisis, what sort of help could the needy artisan or travailleur expect? Aix's charities were many and diverse, and they offered a wide variety of aid. But they were more useful in helping with some problems than with others. In keeping with the stereotype of the "good poor," structural poverty got more sympathetic attention than the conjunctural type, although cases involving the latter were far more numerous. Aix's charities did little for the working man who was temporarily unemployed or whose wages were too low to support a family. But there were a wide variety of charities to help children, the aged, and the sick.

CARE OF THE ILL

Aix had six institutions which provided care for the ill: the hôtel-Dieu, the Incurables, the Insénsés, St. Eutrope, St. Joachim and the Miséricorde (discussed at length in Chapter II). Of these the largest and most important was the hôtel-Dieu, the hospital St. Jacques. It is this institution which most nearly corresponds to our hospitals today.

On the basis of admittance figures from 1780-83, St. Jacques admitted an average of 758 patients each year. All the patients were drawn from the poor or the menu peuple, for in the seventeenth and eighteenth centuries only such people entered public hospitals. Anyone who could possibly afford it preferred to be treated by a private physician at home, where he did not run the risk of additional infection. According to its rule the hôtel-Dieu cared for all types of illness except insanity, venereal diseases, leprosy, the plague and smallpox, and the so-called "incurable" diseases (mostly various forms of paralysis). In practice this boiled down to the "ill who have a fever or are wounded." The vast majority of those admitted were described in the hospital register simply as "having a fever."[21] From the point of view of the social historian such vagueness, characteristic of medical nomenclature in this era, is most unfortunate. More complete and accurate descriptions of the patients' illnesses would tell us much about the effects of undernourishment and unsanitary living conditions on the health of the poor. But the existing descriptions are too imprecise to form a basis for such speculation.

The medical treatment available in Aix's hôtel-Dieu probably compared favorably with that available in other similar hospitals in France. Four doctors, two surgeons, an apothecary, and some 36 nurses provided medical care for the patients. This was a large staff by the standard of the time: Aix had one-third more nurses for the same number of people than did the hôtel-Dieu in Paris.[22] There were both male and female nurses. It is not clear whether they were members of religious orders, as was usual at this time, or laymen.[23]

Although no worse than those of most hospitals of the time, the physical conditions of Aix's hôtel-Dieu were definitely not conducive to quick recovery. The rooms were overcrowded and poorly ventilated. There was little understanding of the infectious nature of diseases: often two patients with different illnesses shared a bed, and convalescents were rarely isolated from the rest of the ill. Here is a description of the hôtel-Dieu, dating from 1780:

The ward for women is situated directly under the roof, and since it is not insulated, it is very cold in winter and very warm in summer. The windows are low, and the air doesn't circulate easily; there are often odors and infection. What a difference can be seen in the ward for men! ... The men are distributed in three rooms, one for the wounded, one for the fever victims, and one for convalescents ....

Should not the number of beds be doubled? Must the ill share a bed with a corpse? Must it happen that someone who enters the hospital with a minor illness immediately becomes infected with a grave disease? [24]

With such conditions it is little wonder that from 10 to 17 percent of all patients who entered died in the hospital.[25]

Conditions in the smaller and more specialized hospitals were somewhat better. At the Incurables, for example, each patient had a bed to himself. This hospital enjoyed a large endowment, and could provide excellent care for its patients, who were required to be "native of Aix, or resident for ten years, Catholic, poor, paralyzed, or attacked by another incurable disease."[26] Its population usually numbered around 32 (see Table 4.1).

One other specialized hospital deserves mention: the Insensés, or insane asylum. This was the only hospital which drew its patients from all classes of society, the nobility and the official class as well as the poor and the menu peuple. Of the 119 patients who entered the Insensés from June 1786 to December 1789, indications of social classes are recorded for 72 (see Table 4.3).

Table 4.3. Social Class of the Insensés' Inmates, June 1786 – December 1789

Army and naval officers (noble)	4
Bourgeois, merchants, professional men	15
Clerics	4
Soldiers, sailors, public employees	12
Servants	5
Artisans	13
Agricultural workers	19
Total	72

Source: A.D. (Aix), XXIII H, IV E 6, Insensés, "Registre, 1786- an 9."

It was customary for families, both rich and poor, to care for the insane at home as long as possible. Only when a patient became too violent to be cared for at home was he put in the Insensés. This tendency toward violence was the major criterion of insanity in the Old Regime, if the rules of the institution are indicative: they specify that the Insensés was designed to treat "insane people who could cause public disorders if they are not shut up."[27] The purpose of the Insensés was far more to protect the public than to help the insane. The rules repeatedly emphasized the need to guard the people of Aix against the insane:

Nothing is more dangerous to the public than this illness; for how many scandals does this sort of person cause in churches, in the streets, and in public places, and even how many murders do they commit if they are not shut away?

Yet the attitudes toward the insane were not as unfeeling as it might appear. The insane were considered to be objects of pity because they could not know God:

Of all the disgraces by which man may be afflicted there is without doubt none more deplorable than that of insanity . . . because . . . through the loss of their reason, they are deprived of knowledge of the Sovereign God, and this renders them unable to gain through their suffering eternal recompense.

The employees of the Insensés were enjoined to treat their charges with kindness, and the guard was ordered not to allow the insane to become a spectacle for the entertainment of the public, but rather to "let enter only a very few people . . . to see the poor, except for persons of piety who wish to exercise their charity." But any real understanding of the problem of insanity would come only in the very last years of the eighteenth century.[28]

CARE OF THE CHILDREN

Children who were abandoned, or whose parents could not afford to care for them, were eligible for an impressive range of charitable care in Aix. The hôtel-Dieu would nurse them while they were babies, the Charité would care for them as they grew older. On reaching maturity they might receive a dowry or an apprenticeship from one of the five lesser charities endowed for that purpose. Charity for children was perhaps the most widespread and popular type of charity in Aix. Yet, despite this concern, the care of children is one of the saddest episodes of Old Regime charity, for the children aided by Aix's institutions of assistance faced lives of hardship and, often, early death.

Newborn babies were nursed at the hôtel-Dieu, which cared for a yearly average of 108. These babies were both illegitimate, abandoned by their mothers, often at the door of a church, hospital, or convent (the so-called *enfants trouvés*), and legitimate children whose parents could not afford to care for them, but did not wish to abandon them. The legitimate children were registered at the Charité, which sent them to the hôtel-Dieu to be nursed. They differed from the enfants trouvés in that they might return home when their parents' fortunes improved.[29] Most of the babies cared for in the hospitals were illegitimate. To calculate the rate of illegitimacy for any period in the Old Regime is impossible, because most illegitimate births were not registered, and thus do not show up in any statistics. To give an example: of the 1,284 births registered in Aix in 1695 there were only 13 recorded illegitimacies. Yet there were doubtless many more illegitimate births, for in 1696 the hôtel-Dieu cared for 135 bastard children.[30] Thus the vast majority of bastard births went unrecorded.

Despite the difficulties in getting valid statistics, it seems incontestable that the rate of illegitimate births in Aix rose sharply from the 1770's on (see Chapter V). At least the number of illegitimate children cared for in the hôtel-Dieu showed an increase. In 1770, for example, the bastard babies in the institution totalled 266, in contrast to the 135 in 1696.[31]

Very few of the babies who entered the hôtel-Dieu survived their first year. This was true especially during the last years of the ancien régime, when infant mortality figures at the hospital showed a steep rise. From the beginning of 1722 to the end of 1767, 4,844 babies were cared for at the hôtel-Dieu. Of these, 2,224, or 46 percent, died during their first year of life. This was bad enough, but of the 1,827 babies who entered from 1768 to 1775, 71 percent, or 1,301, died in their first year.[32] This latter death rate was far higher than that which prevailed in comparable hospitals at Marseille and Lyon.[33] Such an exceptionally high rate of infant mortality had two basic causes: a shortage of nurses, and the unhealthy conditions of the *entrepôt*.

The dangers which the hospitals held for newborn babies helped popularize the widespread practice of sending children to the countryside to be nursed; country nurses and country life were considered healthier for children. A little over one-third of the babies who entered the hôtel-Dieu were boarded out to nurses scattered throughout the surrounding parishes. But most of the children who entered the entrepôt did not get a chance to leave before they died. Conditions in the entrepôt were remarkably unhealthy. There were not enough nurses to care for all the children. From 1774 to 1777, 896 children passed through the entrepôt, but there were only 463 nurses available. Often a nurse breast-fed four infants at a time. This shortage of nurses was directly due to two factors: first of all, salaries were too low to attract potential nurses, and secondly, the nurses feared they might catch venereal disease from their charges. The hospital was fully aware of the latter problem; in 1775 the rectors of the hospital wrote to their confreres in Dijon and Montpellier, asking for suggestions to cope with this difficulty.[34]

Salaries for nurses at the hospital at Aix were considerably lower than those at other hospitals in the province. The nurses earned 3 livres, 10 sous per month, until the child reached the age of eighteen months, when the salary dropped to 3 livres. Comparable figures for Marseille were 5 livres and 4 livres, while some hospitals paid as high as 6 or 8 livres. Furthermore, the level of salaries had not kept pace with the rise of the cost of living: in order to maintain their "real wages" of 1743, the nurses would have had to receive an extra 2 livres per month by 1775. The hospital lacked the resources to raise salaries, however, so the children continued to suffer. Autopsies performed on 12 babies who died in 1775 revealed that in each case the cause of death was lack of nourishment.[35]

Lack of nurses was not the only cause of the high mortality rates which prevailed in the entrepôt. The ward of the enfants trouvés had once been a separate building, but in the second half of the eighteenth century the babies were housed in a few small, low, airless rooms in the attic of the hôtel-Dieu. A contemporary description reveals one of the horrors of the place:

Placed under the roof and exposed to the setting sun . . .infected at one end by the latrines used by the sick, shut up in such a narrow place, how is it possible that it is not perpetually infected? How can one hope to save the children who never breathe pure air, who sleep four in a crib and thirty in a room? [36]

The children died because they were exposed to the diseases of the sick. They died because they were forced to live in their own filth; lack of nurses meant that their diapers were often unchanged for weeks at a time, although each baby was given a new diaper once a month. "The exhalations of their excrement, the vicious odors of those who are the least healthy, perpetuate infections." Even attempts to purify the air by exploding gunpowder were only partially successful. The children died, too, simply because of the heat in the summer months. One can easily imagine how hot it was with the summer sun of Provence beating down on the roof directly overhead. "The months of July and August are those when fewer children are abandoned, but when double the number die as in other months. Thus, for example, we have lost 320 in July and 308 in August, while only 154 died in March, 166 in April."[37]

All in all, the care of the enfant trouvé is one of the saddest chapters in the history of Aix's charitable institutions.

Older children were cared for at the hospital-general, which combined with its functions of workhouse and home for the aged that of an orphanage. Children had always been accepted at the Charité; the earliest version of the institution's rules specified merely that they be at least nine or ten so that "they would be capable of receiving instructions and of working."[38] Later sets of rules elaborated on this requirement. The *Règlements* of 1779 decreed that the charity would receive "poor" children above the age of four, if they were born of legitimate marriage, and if their father, or both parents, were dead. Children who had one living parent would also be accepted if that parent were ill or otherwise incapable of supporting the child. Finally, the Charité would take one child of families in which there were four children under the age of fourteen, or in which there were more than six children.[39]

Most of the children entering the Charité were not orphans, but rather came from families which could no longer support them. Of 395 children admitted during my sample years, 1745-56, 1755-63, 1767-70, and 1780-89, only 30 percent (118) were marked as having lost their fathers. That absolute inability of the child's family to care for it was the criterion for the admission of the rest is indicated by the careful investigations of the families' economic circumstances undertaken by the rectors. There are innumerable cases of children rejected for entrance because "the father earns a considerable amount," "because they have property," "because the parents aren't burdened with more children and are well," "because the mother is charged with only this boy and because she is in a state to support herself."[40] Conversely, a girl was accepted when it was discovered that "the father of this girl was dead and the mother responsible for five other children living in much misery."[41]

The budgetary calculations made earlier in this chapter show that the normal salary of a man and wife could comfortably support only one child. Each new baby was therefore an enormous strain on the family resources. Yet the babies kept coming. It was because it was often impossible for parents to support their children that they sent them to the Charité. It is little wonder that the rectors of the Charité noted as a common phenomenon that "fathers and mothers in order to facilitate the entry of their children into this hospital pretend to disappear and leave them, so that they can be presented (for entry) by other relatives or by neighbors."[42]

Putting one or more of their children in a charity was probably most often envisioned only as a temporary expedient to help tide the family over bad times. The child, it was hoped, might return home again as soon as the family's economic situation improved. About 30 percent of the children above the age of four who entered the Charité did return home before they reached maturity.[43]

Typical is the case of a five-year-old girl who joined the Charité's "family" in June 1770. She was accepted because her father had died and her mother was unable to support her. But when in 1773 the mother was married again, this time to a master shoemaker from Marseille, she took her daughter from the institution to live with her.[44] Often children were in and out of the orphanage several times, according to the fluctuations of the family's fortunes. For example, a girl who entered the Charité in 1746 rejoined her family briefly in 1747, then returned to the Charité, later left again, and finally re-entered the Charité in 1755. This time she remained until 1760, when she received her "trousseau" and left to get married. Frequently, too, if one child from a family were taken home a sibling might enter the institution in his place. A girl who entered in 1745 returned to her mother seven years later, at which time her brother entered the Charité in her place. A year later the girl was back, for the mother had abandoned her whole family.[45]

How such disruptions affected family life is difficult to assess. Philippe Ariès has suggested that in this period in working-class families children were not cherished as individual personalities in the same way that they are today. The high rates of infant mortality prevented such close family ties. A family would expect to lose at least a few of its children before they reached adulthood; therefore it did not pay to invest one's time and love in cherishing them.[46] Similarly, poor parents might apparently expect to "lose" one or more children to an institution. The practices of taking children in and out of the charities, of substituting one child for another, would seem further evidence of this apparent laxity of family ties. Yet this should not be overstressed: the parents, after all, did in many cases try to bring their children back home. There is evidence, too, that siblings stuck together when they entered the institutions: often they ran away together.[47]

What is even more difficult to assess is how these ins and outs affected a child's psyche. To be torn from the security of the family circle and warmth of parental love—however problematic these might be—and thrust into the bleak, regimented life of the Charité, where all ties of human affection were firmly discouraged, must have had severely disorienting effects on the children. Unfortunately there is no evidence which might help the historian trace this.

One fact which must be kept in mind in any evaluation of family attitudes in this connection is the unpalatable truth that putting a child into a charity could be tantamount to sentencing him to death. As was noted, children under the age of four were sent to the hôtel-Dieu to be nursed; the frightfully high rate of infant mortality which prevailed there had been already discussed. But mortality rates for the older children cared for at the Charité also reached substantial levels. About 30 percent of these older children died in the institution before they reached maturity; often they were stricken during their first year of residence. This rate of mortality is probably higher than for children of the same age and from similar socioprofessional groups outside such institutions.[48] It is possible that these children would have died anyway, had they not entered the Charité. Poor diet and debilitating labor would have been their lot in either case. Perhaps even more would have died—from starvation—without the Charité's aid. But one cannot ignore the possibility that the poor diet and crowded living conditions encouraged the spread of disease and therefore pushed the death toll higher than it normally need have been.

That 63 percent of the young inmates returned home or died before they turned twenty-one indicates that only a minority of those entering the Charité reached maturity in the institution. In fact this group numbered only 20 percent. The other 17 percent of the children who entered ran away before their term was up. The motives which prompted such attempts are easy to guess: dislike of the long hours and hard labor, the harsh discipline and regimented life and above all, homesickness. A typical case is that of a young man, named Cabasse, assigned to work in the shoemaking shop. Cabasse ran away on October 26, 1749, "following ill treatment by the master shoemaker." Such young men were apparently especially tempted to run away; if they had acquired the rudiments of a skill they could often find work in town. Joseph Clapiers, who escaped from the Charité in 1757, worked for a master shoemaker in Aix for over a year before he was discovered.[49] These situations were so common that in 1742 the Charité asked the Parlement for an arrêt forbidding anyone to shelter the runaways; but even this was ineffective.[50] Young men were not the only runaways—girls and very young children also attempted to escape. There were even certain recognized escape routes: for example, the aqueduct which led from the girls' quarters to the garden of the monastery of the Recollets next door. The rectors discovered this and ordered bars placed at both ends.[51] Children also used any trips outside the Charité as opportunities to run away: the practice of hiring young boys out to serve in religious processions was cancelled when Jerôme Ray and Joseph Bas fled while employed by the abbess of St. Barthelemy, and it was decided to hire a barber to come to the Charité when too many escapes occurred during the infrequent trips to his shop in town. The rectors feared the escapes as bad examples to others, and punished those who were caught severely: a period in the *cachot*, a small, cramped, underground cell, followed by a session in the refectory in which the culprit got down on his knees to beg forgiveness. Those who made repeated attempts to escape were often punished by being sent away from the institution.[52] Despite the prospect of harsh punishments the escapes went on—indicating, I think, a desire for freedom of movement, even at the risk of material insecurity, and a discontent with the regimented life of the Charité.

Those children who remained in the institution found unremitting hard labor their lot.

Children placed in the hospital because they are orphans or because their families are in extreme misery should be given an education which would make them useful to the public but without changing their status *(état)* in society.[53]

This statement of the Parlement of Aix made in 1742 sums up the philosophy behind the child care practices of the Charité and other charitable institutions for children. Such a goal reveals a great deal about elite attitudes toward the social mobility of the lower classes under the Old Regime. Rendering these children useful to the public consisted primarily of teaching them a trade, preferably the same trade as their fathers'. The Charité attempted "to engage the sons of *labourers* and peasants to follow the occupation of their father" by teaching them the methods of agricultural labor through work in the hospital garden; similarly, sons of artisans were taught "trades which conformed as much as possible to their *état*."[54] Only children of artisans were to be put in an apprenticeship; never children of peasants or ménagers. In this scheme formal education had little place—it would, in the eyes of the local administrators, have had a most unsettling effect on social stability. According to the rules, all the children, both boys and girls, were taught to read and write, "at least those who have the inclination to learn." Also, in theory, the Charité would pay the tuition of four to six of the brightest boys at the local *collège*.[55] In practice these provisions were not carried out. One boy, named Durand, who showed exceptional "talent for studies," was tutored in Latin by a priest of the Cathedral, but there is no evidence that anyone ever attended the collège.[56] In 1741 the school for girls at the Charité was ended; lessons henceforth were to be given in the workshops while the children labored at their looms, and the schoolroom was converted into a store-room.[57]

Far more important than formal education in the training of children was religious instruction. The charities were concerned primarily with saving the souls of the poor. For this, the method followed was constant religious instruction, drummed in by rote. The inmates of the Charité prayed as a body at five A.M. and again before going to bed. Religion was bound up in the normal routine of work in the fabriques. In the morning the boys chanted the Veni Creator and the litanies of the Holy Name of Jesus, in Provençal, as they worked, while the girls recited the Veni Creator and the Veni Exultemus. After this there were readings from the Bible or the lives of the saints. Later in the morning the children were drilled in their catechism. At noon the Angelus was chanted, at 2:30 P.M. the Vespers, and at four the laborers recited the rosary. This was merely the routine on normal working days; on Sundays and feast days almost the whole day was devoted to prayer.[58]

Part and parcel of the religious atmosphere in which the children were raised was an obsessive concern for sexual morality. In the Charité the sexes were kept rigidly separated. They ate, slept, and worked apart. As the rules stated, "no girl will enter the men's quarters; no boy, those of the women, without express orders."[59] Persons of the opposite sex could converse together only in the presence of a supervisory official. The minutes of the governing bureau of the Charité reveal on the part of the rectors an obsession with problems of sexual morality which bordered on prurience. Transgressions of the sexual code, especially the presence of men in the women's quarters, were constantly recorded and commented upon.[60] When it was discovered that a window of the girls' section overlooked the bakery, where because of the heat the baker's helpers worked in the nude, the rectors' shock and concern knew no bounds:

the natural curiosity of the girls about sex makes them often go to look at these boys . . . this is liable to dirty their conscience and corrupt their hearts; . . . it is very important to prevent without delay the dangerous consequences which this curiosity might have and the knowledge of evil which it carries.[61]

This attitude on the part of the rectors contrasts to the permissive attitude toward the acquisition of sexual knowledge by children which prevailed in their own families, at least in those of the high nobility, if the records of Hérouard's journal are any indication.[62]

Almost as important for the children's future welfare as instruction in religion and morality was teaching them a love of labor, an "amour du travail." It was, after all, this quality which separated the *true poor* from the *false poor*, the industrious poor from the idle, vicious, and depraved. Learning to work, and to like working, thus had moral overtones, and was almost as vital for the child's welfare as learning the tenets of religion. As the rules of the institution noted, "Since the Charité is a religious house, a seminary, and a factory, the exercise of piety must not be lessened to favor the workshops, and the workshops must not be weakened under the pretext of furthering piety."[63]

This desired love of labor was to be inculcated by putting the children to work as soon as they were able: that is, from the age of four. When it was discovered that some toddlers were "remaining all day in the courtyard with nothing to do" but play, the rectors decided they must "keep them busy to accustom them to a labor which was within their capabilities." Therefore they were set to work threading the looms in the shop where stockings were made.[64] Children of both sexes worked in the various textile workshops: the *tisseranderie*, in which wool was woven, and the *fabrique de bas*, where stockings were knitted, the *fabrique de soie*, which produced silk cloth, or the workshop which produced the lightweight, printed wool called Cadiz so fashionable in the early eighteenth century. Girls might also be put to cooking, or washing linen; while tailoring, shoemaking, cement-making, gardening, or shepherding provided alternative employment for the boys. Hours of labor were long. The inmates of the Charité rose at five in summer and six in winter. They worked from six to eleven A.M., at which time they stopped for the midday meal, *le dîner,* and worked again until six P.M., when they had supper and went to bed. The only opportunity for relaxation came during the so-called "recreation hour" held after the dîner. During this period inmates were allowed to talk—while they continued their work. At all other times silence reigned in the fabriques.[65] The work discipline was harshly enforced: corporal punishment, or imprisonment in the cachot, were the lot of the laggards. Working conditions, especially in the textile manufactures, were grim. In winter the fabriques were unheated; in summer the heat and fetid air combined with the unvarying tasks to produce in the children "an air of stupidity, an insupportable slowness in all their actions."[66]

Historians have scarcely begun to explore the psychic effects of the inculcation of the harsh work discipline required by factory labor. This change from the easy rhythms and self-paced activity of the agricultural cycle to the strict, disciplined use of time and the repetitive tasks of industrial activities is one of the greatest changes which ever overtook mankind, yet only the English experience has been studied in detail, and even in this case the work is sparse.[67] In France the workshops of the hospitals-general often pioneered the introduction of the work discipline in an area such as Aix, yet this aspect of the role of the charities has never been analyzed.[68] But the effects of such a hard work discipline, combined with the generally repressive atmosphere of these institutions, probably had drastic psychic consequences.

If the children survived these rigors, they were allowed to leave the institution at age sixteen. Young men were apprenticed to masters in the town; the girls entered domestic service. Here are the examples of two young brothers, born on the island of Santo Domingo, who entered the Charité in 1774, and left to be apprenticed to tailors in town in 1777 and 1780, respectively. Another example is the eight-year-old girl who joined the Charité on the death of her mother in 1781, and who left in 1789 to enter service in the household of Mme. Arnaud.[69] The rectors carefully investigated the piety and morals of the households into which the inmates would enter before they permitted them to leave. Upon departure the inmates received a "trousseau": for the young men, two shirts, two cravats, one hat, one pair of stockings, two pairs of shoes (one old and one new), one suit, one vest, and two pairs of pants, one winter-weight and one for summer. The girls received three chemises, three palatines (a sort of neckerchief) three caps, two new pairs of stockings, two pairs of shoes (one old and one new), an apron, two sets of underclothes, and two skirts, one old and one new.[70]

Occasionally a girl of the Charité would marry rather than enter domestic service. The Charité had a few foundations which gave dowries to such young women. The bride also received a trousseau, slightly more extensive than that for girls who entered domestic service.[71] The characters of the girl and her future husband were carefully investigated before the rectors approved the match. Consider this entry of the minutes of the Charité for June 7, 1764:

Anne Duc, former *pauvre fille* of this house, presented herself for admission to one of the foundations which are at the nomination of Ms. les Recteurs of the Charité, having announced her marriage with Guilleaume Ribe, a cobbler of this city. Mlle de Bruelle, abbess of St. Barthelemy, has given a favorable testimony of the conduct and morals of this girl since she left this house to go into service at the convent of Ste. Claire and St. Barthelemy.[72]

La Charité was not the only charitable institution to provide for the care of children. Four others were devoted to this end: the Oeuvre de la Propagande de la Foi, the Filles Orphelines, la Pureté, and the Corpus Domini de St. Sauveur. The Oeuvre de la Propagande was a small institution, founded in 1655, which fed and housed 15 Protestant children in the open intent of converting them to Catholicism. The Filles Orphelines, dating from 1762, cared for 46 orphan girls who might otherwise have had to go to the Charité.[73] The purpose of the Pureté, founded by Archbishop Grimaldi in 1680, was to care for girls between the ages of eight and sixteen who, either "through the bad conduct of their parents, or . . . because of their poverty, might lose their virtue and innocence." In actual fact, however, the Pureté functioned merely as a seminary for upper-class young ladies; daughters of avocats, merchants, and bourgeois predominated.[74]

Of more importance to the poor of Aix was the Corpus Domini de St. Sauveur, a religious confraternity founded in 1680. The Corpus Domini gave dowries to any poor and unmarried girl of Aix, although preference was given to the inmates of the Charité. Similarly the Oeuvre would pay for the apprenticeship for boys over the age of thirteen, provided that they were the sons of artisans or "others of a similar état."[75]

With its provision of apprenticeships and dowries, the Corpus Domini de St. Sauveur served a useful purpose for the poor of Aix. A young man who could not inherit his father's land or shop, and did not have a salable skill, would be doomed to a life of wandering in search of work from village to village, from harvest to harvest. And, although it would be too dramatic to say that lack of a dowry doomed a girl to prostitution, it is nonetheless true that at best dowerless girls could look forward only to working as harvest hands or washerwomen, lives of drudgery for which they received a low subsistence wage.

Care for children thus occupied a great number of Aix's charities. Perhaps the popularity of this sort of charity depended on the nature of its beneficiaries; in a period which, according to Ariès at least, was starting to sentimentalize over the innocence and purity of childhood, young victims' need and want would be especially appealing to the charitably inclined. Unspoiled children were guaranteed to be a part of the "good poor" who deserved help, and the chance to mold a life in the direction of righteousness was also tempting.

How well did the charities which cared for children succeed in their task of turning out devout, respectable, and hardworking adults? There is little evidence to help answer this question. But what evidence there is suggests that the Charité's attempts at socialization ended in failure. This was, at least, a charge often brought against the hospitals-general by those interested in the reform of public assistance in the last years of the ancien régime. It was often stated that children emerged from the institutions completely unfit for life in the outside world, and that, unable to earn their own living or to direct their own existence, they drifted into beggary, debauchery and crime. In 1787, M. Achard, a physician and philosophe from Marseille, accused the hospitals-general of giving the children entrusted to their care an education "without method and without praiseworthy end," which produced adults of "low, crude souls," who lived "lazily, uselessly, idly, knavishly; several end their days on a scaffold."[76] The presence of former inmates of the hospitals-general on lists of those arrested for beggary and for various crimes indicates that this assessment was at least partially correct.

We know the life story of only one of the countless children cared for in Aix's charities. This was a girl named Catherine Tempier. Born in 1676, the seventh of nine children of an agricultural day-laborer, Catherine entered the hospital-general on her parents' death in 1684. She lived in the institution for 19 years. In 1709 the confessor of the Charité, who had known her through most of her residence there, wrote a 164-page manuscript recounting her life.[77]

When Catherine first entered the Charité she lived a normal life, although she was apparently much persecuted by the other children. As a girl, she worked in the kitchens and in the *fabrique de bas*. In her adolescence she suffered some sort of sexual attack.[78] Shortly after this Catherine began to be possessed by demons. They held back her skirts when she tried to go to confession, and put dirty words in her mouth. They tortured her with "iron instruments of the Devil" which drew blood from her teeth and breasts.[79] They flooded her room with ice water, and drowned her New Testament in a bucket. Catherine levitated several feet above her bed; she passed through locked doors. She could repeat the psalms in Latin, though she scarcely knew French and spoke primarily Provençal. When she prayed for relief from the demons who tormented her, she had visions of the Jesus, of John the Evangelist, and of the Virgin Mary accompanied by Saint Catherine. Many doubted the reality of these events; " 'they said that she scarcely ate and that she slept still less and that what she called her 'transports' were only an effect of her imagination! ' "[80] But her confessor believed Catherine to be truly inspired by God.

To the chaplain and rectors of the Charité, Catherine's religious transports were doubtless proof of her devout nature, and a sign that they were succeeding in raising the young people under their care in a properly religious atmosphere. To the modern historian, however, Catherine's experiences seem evidence of the tremendous psychic costs of the immensely harsh, disciplined, and regimented life which the charities of Aix inflicted on their children. Catherine's religious transports might be evidence of a sort of internalized escape from all the pressures of her life. And if her escape was more spectacular than most, nevertheless the fact remains that many children did literally escape from the institutions. On the whole the care of children, the most widespread form of charity in Aix, must be judged a failure.

THE AGED

Less widespread was a concern for the problems of the aged. For one reason, there were simply fewer of them: very few people survived to old age in ancien régime France. For another reason, care of the old was traditionally a family duty. But there were of course some who had no family, or whose relatives could not or would not care for them, and who no longer could work to support themselves. Such people could find a refuge in the Charité.

During my sample years some 317 elderly people entered the Charité; 150 were male and 167 female.[81] Most of the women were widows. These people were in their late sixties and seventies; many suffered from some physical disability; they were described as "blind," "paralyzed," or severely "infirm." Obviously they were people who could no longer work to support themselves. Most of them were poor travailleurs or petty artisans. Very few had any property or savings—indeed any possessions but the clothes they stood up in—when they entered the institution.[82] If they did own anything valuable, it was sold at their deaths for the benefit of the hospital. For the elderly inmates of the Charité life was the same as that of the children—an unrelenting round of disciplined hard work. And like the children, the elderly often ran away.

How successful were the municipal charities in solving the problem of poverty in Aix? This question is difficult to answer with any precision. But it is important to remember that in the Old Regime aid for the poor was designed not to eradicate the causes of poverty, but only to alleviate certain effects. That is, Aix's charities cared for the victims of illness and old age. But little was done for those who formed the bulk of the problem of poverty in the city—the able-bodied unemployed. .

There was one form of charity which catered to such people. This was the so-called *secours à domicile*—aid, usually bread, given to the poor in their homes. An examination of those who received such aid would shed great light on the problem of poverty. Unfortunately the records for such an examination do not exist. The institutions which provided secours à domicile, unlike those institutions which actually housed the poor, had no need of an elaborate bureaucratic structure. Therefore the records they kept—and the records which survive—are minimal.

There is evidence that the hospital-general La Charité distributed approximately 4,000 loaves of bread to an average of 410 people every week during the years 1692-1706 and 1719-1720.[83] Such distributions probably took place during the rest of the eighteenth century as well.[84] These distributions were held on Sunday after services in the chapel of the Charité; the poor were required to attend these services in order to qualify. The bread distributed was "of wheat and of good quality." A single person received 7 one-pound loaves, a week's ration; and families might receive 12 or 14 loaves. Unfortunately it is not possible to tell who received such gifts. Most of the surviving records give only the total amount of bread distributed. One record, covering the years 1705-6 and 1719-2, does have a list of recipients but this gives only their names.[85] This shows that more women than men received secours à domicile (in 1705 the figures are 256 men and 289 women), which suggests that one of its primary functions was to help women whose husbands had died, or abandoned them, and who had families to care for. This sort of charity probably also aided the infirm, and perhaps the unemployed. It is possible too that the bread distribution of the Charité provided a major supplement to the diet of many of the "respectable poor"—artisans and day-laborers—who were able to work but who simply did not earn enough to support their families.

Even less is known about the work of the other agencies which distributed secours à domicile, the bureaux de charité. These were charitable organizations which functioned at the parish level; in theory one was attached to each of Aix's five parishes. These organizations were founded in 1702, under the influence of the Jesuit, Père Guevarre, who played such a vital role in insuring the success of the hospital-general.[86] Due to the almost complete lack of documentation we cannot tell how long they continued to function; they most probably disappeared some time before 1778.[87] These bureaux distributed bread to the needy of the parish every Sunday in much the same way as did the Charité. Those who received such alms had to be poor—but not beggars—and had to have a demonstrable knowledge of the catechism.[88] Besides carrying out such distributions, the bureaux also attempted to find work for the unemployed.[89]

Because no records of the bureaux de charité survive, there is no information on how many people benefitted from their aid, or on their occupations, and the circumstances of their lives. The best clue to the type of people who probably sought the aid of the bureaux can be found in the sample entries which are set out in the rules to aid the charities' record-keepers. These provided a selection of problems deemed typical by the administrators of the charity:

Pierre N., surnamed La Rose, shoemaker, aged 70, almost blind, his wife the same age, without children. Poor beggars. They are given twelve pounds of bread each week.

Jacques Notre, *journalier*, widower, aged 30, ill for a week with a continuous fever, two children who are under six, and very poor. During his illness . . . for the children 12 pounds of bread.

Jean N., surnamed "le petit Jean," journalier, aged 45; his wife of the same age, having five children, the eldest is in service, a girl of twelve who is blind, another of ten, the others two and four, 12 pounds of bread.

Yves N., aged 12, blind and paralyzed in one leg, cannot walk, carried to the parish from four leagues away to beg; (sent back, but with 8 pounds of bread).

Joseph N., orphan, age 15 . . . who has left his job, and does not look for another, preferring to beg. M. Le Directeur is asked to find a job for him, and if he does not take it, he will be sent away.

Françoise N., orphan, age 12, employed at putting cows to graze, had neither linen nor clothes, almost nude, and has no means to cover herself, because those who employ her out of charity are almost as poor as she is. (The bureau will try to find her some clothes.)[90]

Secours à domicile was doubtless the most attractive sort of charity available to the poor of Aix: it answered their most basic need, keeping bread on the family table, yet it carried less shame than entrance into a hospital, and it had fewer strings attached. Because of its popularity among the poor—and also because of its relative cheapness when compared to institutionalized care—secours à domicile appealed increasingly to those who thought and wrote about the problems of poverty as the eighteenth century progressed, and it would appear to the Revolutionary reformers of the Committee on Mendicity as an ideal solution. But despite its attractions this type of aid still did not solve the problem of poverty in Aix. The bread distributions were on too small a scale to reach all the needy. And this points up one of the basic drawbacks of charity in the Old Regime: the amount available was so small that it did not even begin to make a dent in the problem of poverty.

Another basic difficulty of charitable assistance in the Old Regime was its inflexibility. The dimensions of the problem of poverty—the numbers of the poor who needed help to stay alive—varied greatly from time to time. As we have seen, almost all of the menu peuple lived poised precariously on a thin line between poverty and utter destitution. Something like a rise in the price of bread could push hundreds over the line into destitution and starvation in a moment. Yet charity as it was organized in the Old Regime could expand little to meet this new demand. There were, to be sure, often special distributions of bread organized by the municipality or the archbishop in times of trouble. But charitable institutions themselves did little to meet the changing circumstances. This is illustrated by Table 4.4, which shows the

Table 4.4. Yearly Admissions to Charité, 1755-64, 1780-89

	Yearly admissions to Charité	Price of bread	
		White	Rye
1755	50	25	20
1756	66	25	20
1757	39	28	22
1758	66	27	21
1759	48	31	25
1760	35	28	23
1761	26	24	19
1762	38	23	18
1763	51	25	20
1764	68	28 .	23
1780	32	32	25
1781	29	33	26
1782	30	35	27
1783	64	37	29
1784	70	38	29
1785	56	*	*
1786	43	35	27
1787	31	34	26
1788	46	34	27
1789	43	38	30

*Not Available.

Sources: Admissions to Charité: A.D. (Aix), XXI H, II F 9, "Procès-Verbaux d'admissions des pauvres," 1743-1812.

Price of a pound loaf (15 ozs.) in deniers and centimes, for months of October-November, taken from Baehrel, *Une Croissance*, pp. 547-33, Table 4, Le prix du pain de boulangerie à Aix.

number of yearly admissions to the Charité. Rises in the price of bread, always a useful indicator of hard times for the poor, are not reflected in changes in the number of people admitted to the charity, which seem to follow no discernable pattern. The years 1751, 1759, 1766, 1789 saw insufficient harvests, high prices and dearth, but these left little trace in the records of the charities. The only clues to the great social dislocations of these years are the mentions in the deliberations of the charities' rectors of the presence of "a considerable number of poor of the town, increased still more by crowds of foreign beggars who want to continue to enter."[91] Such remarks give tantalizing indications of crisis, but, as René Baehrel has said, "A curve is not constructed with adverbs."[92] The number of people cared for by charity did not fluctuate according to need. This is true not only of yearly but also of monthly variations in admissions. For Aix's poor the most dangerous months, the times when the chances of death was greatest, were January and February, the months of cold and winter unemployment, and July to September, the end of the summer, when the last year's harvest was running short, and the great heat brought epidemics in its train.[93] Yet admissions to the charities were greatest in the relatively benign months of May and June (see Table 4.5).

Table 4.5. Admissions to Charité for 1756-63, Averaged Monthly

January	39	July	23
February	28	August	24
March	32	September	19
April	26	October	32
May	42	November	24
June	43	December	35

Source: A.D. (Aix), XXI H, II F 9, Charité, "Procès-Verbaux."

These facts suggest that the amount of charity available varied little according to need. Far more important as a determinant of the amount of assistance given was the financial condition of the charitable institution. The charities gave only the aid they could afford. In the aftermath of the financial cirsis experienced by the hospital-general in 1760, the admission of new inmates was cut for months at a time, regardless of need, until the number of inmates was low enough to be "adequately accommodated" by the charity's diminished resources.[94] Thus the financial health of the various institutions was the main factor which determined the amount of charity available. This meant that it was precisely in times of crisis, when the poor had the greatest need of outside aid, that the least amount of assistance was available. For, as one of the charity's rectors put it, "The alms of the faithful . . . dry up in the times when the need increases."[95] In periods of financial crisis people tended to hold on to their money, rather than give it to charity.

Finally, in assessing the effectiveness of Aix's charitable institutions still another factor must be taken into account: the apparent reluctance of many of the poor to resort to charity, however great their need may have been. The unpleasantness of institutional life was doubtless a major factor behind this attitude, but perhaps even more influential was the feeling that entering a charity was a personal defeat, a failure of a lifetime of struggle against poverty. The poor's reluctance to resort to charity should not be exaggerated. It is easy for the modern historian, both sympathetic to the unfortunate and horrified by the regimentation of the charitable institutions, to project back onto the poor of the Old Regime his own extreme distaste for the institutions, and to see signs of disaffection where there were none. Doubtless if you are starving you are grateful for any sort of help, no matter how many demeaning conditions are attached. But nevertheless there were what seem to me to be definite signs of distaste for charitable institutions among the poor. The immense number of runaways is one. Another is the testimony of the curé of Lançon, a small village in Aix's terroir. The Charité of Aix had a special foundation, started by the Baron de Très in the seventeenth century, to care for a number of needy children from Lançon. In 1779 there were openings available, and Curé Roubaud of Lançon undertook to approach needy parents. The curé reported to the Charité that he had asked numerous "fathers and mothers, poor and burdened with many children," to put their child in the Charité, but "all answer that they love their children too much to deprive themselves of them." Castigating what he termed their "sottish vanity," the curé commented that "they have so little zeal for the good education of these children that they prefer them to grow up in a village and live the way they do."[96]

Also there is the story told by Jean Joseph Esmieu. As Esmieu, a young *marchand colporteur*, was walking along the road to Marseille, peddling his wares, he met an old man who fell into step with him, and who told him the story of his life. He had been, said the man, a servant in one noble household for forty-four years, until he was struck by illness. Since he was no longer able to work the noble put him out. He now lived with his brother. "It is hard for me to eat the bread of his children; but without my brother, I would have to go to die in a hospital."[97]

The parents of Lançon who preferred to keep their children at home and the old servant who told Esmieu he dreaded dying in a hospital may be only isolated cases, but they seem to indicate that at least some of the poor would rather do anything than enter a hospital. For such people, in times of trouble, few alternatives existed. They will form the subject of the next chapter.

CHAPTER V

The Poor outside
the Charities

What little evidence there is suggests that a poor man would do anything he could to avoid entering a charity. Entrance to a charity was a last resort, a step to be taken only when the situation was desperate. The unpleasantness of institutional life doubtless was a major factor behind this attitude, but perhaps even more influential was the conviction that entering a charity was somehow a personal defeat, a confession of failure of a whole lifetime of struggle to keep the family together, to keep bread on the table, to keep on the right side of that almost invisible line which separated grinding poverty from utter destitution. It is little wonder then that many who needed help avoided any contact with the hospital-general or other charitable institutions. For such people there were two major alternatives: beggary and crime.

BEGGARY

Beggars infested the city of Aix throughout the Old Regime. They squatted on street corners, swarmed near the city gates, and crowded the churches, disrupting services with their piteous pleas for alms. Once in the troubled days of the 1620's more than 2,000 beggars crowded the courtyard of the Hôtel-de-Ville; when they tried to climb a staircase to beg outside the chamber of the municipal council it collapsed under their weight and several unfortunates were injured.[1] Almost a century later, the town's chronicler, Joseph de Haitze, still would write of the "infinite number of mendicants" infesting the city.[2] This despite the fact that demanding alms was illegal in Aix, and had been so since 1555.[3]

In the latter half of the sixteenth century advanced opinion on the problem of poverty began to find beggary unacceptable, both because of the problems of public order it created and also because of its supposedly demoralizing effect on the poor. Indeed, the charitable impulse of the early seventeenth century, with its institutionalization of charity and its enfermement of the poor, had as its major motivation a desire to wipe out beggary (see

Chapter II). To make the new institutions like the hospital-general effective, the municipality passed numerous ordinances against beggary. The town's *gardes de police* and the archers of the Charité made daily patrols to sweep the beggars off the streets and out of the churches.[4] Those caught begging were incarcerated in the hôtel-Dieu, or, after its foundation in 1640, in the hospital-general.[5] To give money to a mendicant was illegal, and carried a 100-livre fine.[6] The town repeatedly required that all those who came from outside the town to beg in Aix return to their place of origin, and decreed that the guards at the city gates were not to let "poor strangers" enter the town.[7] These efforts by the municipality of Aix were supplemented by innumerable royal ordinances against mendicity, and by great nationwide roundups of beggars undertaken by the royal government in the 1720's and 1760's. But mere legislation against beggary, fitfully enforced, did not wipe out the evil. In Aix, as elsewhere in France, mendicity persisted throughout the Old Regime. Aix's last municipal ordinance against beggary dates from May 1789.[8]

Beggary persisted for two reasons. First of all, despite the propaganda efforts of the proponents of the new-style institutionalized charities, public opinion continued to accept begging as a legitimate means of survival for the poor. As late as the 1740's, a full century after the founding of the hospital-general, it was still necessary to pass new laws reasserting that giving alms to beggars was illegal.[9] The people of Aix, especially the *bas peuple*, who might one day have to resort to beggary themselves, simply would not accept the arguments against mendicity. The records of the Charité show numerous instances of such people preventing the enforcement of the laws against beggary. In July 1749, for example, the archers of the Charité, while engaged in a roundup of beggars, were set upon by an angry crowd and forced to free their captives.[10]

The other reason that beggary persisted was even more simple: the poor needed to beg to survive. Organized, institutionalized charity simply did not go far enough to meet the needs of the poor. In times of dearth or personal disaster, the alternative for the poor was simple and stark—beg or die.

Who were the beggars of Aix? We are fortunate in having one document which will throw a great deal of light on this, for one point in time, at least: the register of all those people arrested and incarcerated in the Charité of Aix under the provisions of the royal ordinance against beggary of July 18, 1724.[11]

This ordinance was the product of one of the royal government's periodic attempts to crack down on beggary, and to confine all potential beggars in institutions. The provisions of the ordinance, like others before and after it, were quite complex (perhaps this was a factor in their lack of success). The ordinance decreed that all people who needed aid had voluntarily to enter the nearest hospital-general within two weeks of publication of the edict. Those who were genuinely unable to work—the very old, the very young, the ill—would be housed and fed in the hospitals-general, and set to work at "tasks proportioned to their age and their strength." Profits from their work would be divided between the hospital and the inmate. Able-bodied men and women who were genuinely unable to find employment were also invited to enter the hospital during the period of grace. They would be employed, in gangs of 20, on bridges and roads and other "public works" projects. They would receive at least one-sixth of their wages; the rest would go to the hospitals for their expenses. Such inmates could leave the hospital when they found legitimate employment.

The framers of the declaration assumed that all who were genuinely in need of aid would flock to the hospitals with the publication of the edict. Anyone without a legitimate occupation found in the towns or on the road after the period of grace expired was assumed to be a beggar. Such people were to be sentenced to two month's confinement in the hospitals, during which time they would be fed on bread and water, and made to work for the profit of the institution. Special punishments were decreed for runaways, and also for those deemed exceptionally dangerous: those who carried arms, or traveled in groups larger than four, or who feigned illness or infirmity, those who demanded alms "with insolence," or those who were discovered to have been branded as thieves.

In Aix 1,277 people entered the town's hospital-general under the provisions of the ordinance of July 18, 1724, during the eight years in which the law operated—an average of 151 per year. Of the 1,277 beggars, 83 were repeated offenders, people known to the officials of the charity to have been arrested for begging before.[12] These "repeaters" have been omitted from the calculations which follow in order not to distort the sample. Elimination of these frequent offenders leaves a total of 1,194. Of the latter, 56 percent (663) entered the Charité voluntarily under the provisions of the ordinance of 1724, while 39 percent (470) were involuntary detainees, arrested as beggars.[13]

Of course, it cannot be assumed that these 1,194 constitute all the people who begged their bread in Aix and its environs during these years. It is impossible to tell how many beggars escaped the net of the mounted police (the maréchaussée), and the archers des pauvres. Probably there were many, for the maréchaussée, understaffed and underpaid, was notoriously inefficient.[14]

Whether all these 1,194 people were actually beggars presents another difficulty. The maréchaussée had a tendency to arrest anyone who aroused their suspicions—and their suspicions were remarkably easy to arouse.

Peculiarity of dress, lack of a hat, a "suspicious" bearing—all these could prompt arrest.[15] Nine percent of those arrested later managed to obtain testimonials to their character and honest employment from their families or their local priest sufficiently convincing to prompt the officials of the hospital-general to release them. Many more unfortunates were doubtless wrongly arrested and *not* released; precisely how many, it is impossible to calculate. Despite these drawbacks, this sample provides the most authentic evidence we are likely to get concerning beggary in Aix. Who were these people arrested as beggars? First of all, very few were natives of the town. Aix's municipal council was correct when it blamed "poor strangers" for the mendicity in the city. Information about their geographical origins is available for 878 of the 1,194 beggars. This information is summarized in Table 5.1.

Of the total only approximately one-fourth (227) were from Aix itself. These natives doubtless included many scions of dynasties of professional beggars. For some of the poor in the town mendicity was indeed their profession: on the Capitation roll of 1695, 350 citizens of Aix gave "beggars" as their professional designation.[16] The métier was apparently profitable. In the early eighteenth century Haitze, our town chronicler, estimated that anyone who begged could easily take in, in a day, 10 or 12 sous, the equivalent of the daily wages of an agricultural laborer, while those especially skilled at begging might gain as much as 30 or 40 sous.[17] Often the professional beggars of a town formed a caste; the skills of beggary were handed down from generation to generation.[18]

But such native dynasties formed only a small percentage of Aix's beggars. Most of the town's citizens who found themselves in need turned to the municipal charities rather than beggary. The vast majority of Aix's beggars were not natives. Some had come to Aix from very long distances. Seventeen percent of the total for whom the geographical origins are known came from outside of Provence—from Paris and northern France, from Italy and other foreign countries. (see Table 5.1). The presence of such well-traveled beggars on the list is not surprising, when one considers Aix's geographic position. Aix was situated on the major roads from Marseille and Toulon, which meant that those who came from maritime Provence or up the coast from Italy passed through the town on their way to the heart of France. Italians were quite numerous among the beggars arrested near Aix; the "Genoese beggar" (a term applied indiscriminately to all Italians) was a familiar bogey in the folklore of Provence.[19]

Aix was also an obvious point of attraction for those who came down the Rhône valley from Lyon. The Rhône valley route was the easiest road to the southeast and the Mediterranean, not only for those from the region around Lyon, but also for those who had come from the Paris area and northwestern France. This easy route doubtless accounts for the relatively

Table 5.1. Geographic Origins of Beggars and Itinerant Laborers

Origin	Beggars 1725-33		Inmates of Enfants Abandonnées 1771-89
Italy	21		27
Other foreign countries	21		7
Paris and environs	18		7
Other regions of France			
Northwest	38		31
Northeast	32		23
Southwest	23		15
Southeast (excluding Provence)	37		104
Subtotal		190 (17%)	214 (33%)
Areas contiguous to Provence	88		117
Provence	331		233
Diocese of Aix	232		49
Aix	227		13
Subtotal		878 (79%)	412 (63%)
Place of origin unidentifiable	49		32
Total		1,117	658
Place of origin not listed	77		96
Total no. of beggars arrested*		1,194	754
Urban		395 (35%)	224 (34%)
Rural		722 (65%)	434 (66%)

*Adjusted to remove duplicate entries.

Sources:
Beggars: A.D. (Aix), XXI H, II F 11, Charité, "Livre d'entrée des mendiants enfermés en vertu de l'ordonnance royale de Juillet 1724."

Enfants Abandonnées: A.D. (Aix), XXX H, E 1, "Registre ou Sont inscrits tous les Enfans qui passent dans L'Oeuvre depuis 1771 Jusqu' En [1792]."

large number of those from Brittany, Normandy, and other depressed areas of the northwest in our sample.[20] The Lyonnais themselves also provided many of Aix's beggars. Of the sample of those arrested, 13 were from Lyon. This was the largest total for any single city in France, except, of course, for Aix. The almost constant depression of the city's silk industry largely explains this exodus from Lyon; the majority of the beggars from that city described their trade as "ouvrier en soye." Apart from Lyon, the small towns of the Rhône valley—for example, Vienne, St. Etienne, Montelimar, Tarascon—also supplied many of the beggars who came to Aix from the area roughly labelled the southeast. Others were from the notoriously poverty-stricken Auvergne.

Only southwestern France was relatively underrepresented in the sample. The cause for this was probably not a greater prosperity in the region. The clue lies rather in different patterns of migration: the routes of this region tended to run north and south, rather than east and west, and the beggars tended to move north toward Paris or south toward Spain. Even many in the southwestern corner of Auvergne went to Spain rather than to the Mediterranean.[21]

Most of the beggars who came to Aix from such long distances were of two types. They were either the sort of beggars who later inspired the Great Fear, the kind who traveled in large bands, robbing farms and terrorizing the countryside, or else they were urban artisans looking for work. Because of their threat to public order, the royal government greatly feared the outlaw beggar bands, and tended to consider all mendicants under this stereotype. This standard government conception of the beggar is perhaps best illustrated in the *Mémoire Sur Les Vagabonds et Sur Les Mendiants*, distributed by the controller-general to all the royal intendants in 1764. According to the *Mémoire*, the beggar was a man who lived in a "veritable state of war with society," who traveled in bands of 15 or 30 strong, terrorizing the countryside, and robbing and killing the lonely farmer who would not give in to their demands.[22] But in our sample, at least, only a very few beggars actually fitted this stereotype. Only 27 percent (129) of the people arrested on the roads had been traveling in a group, and of these the vast majority (82 of 129) were in groups of only two people.[23] Such groups were most often familial relationships (husband-wife, parent-child, brother-sister) and frequently included a young child. They were not, therefore, necessarily dangerous. Of the larger bands, there were four groups of three, three groups of four, one group of five, and three groups of six. None were larger than six. This would suggest that the cliché of the dangerous beggar band was true for only a small percentage of Aix's beggars.

More usual was the urban artisan who left his native town to look for work. Occupations were given for 361 of our 1,194 beggars (see Table 5.2). Of these the largest group, 41 percent (149), were artisans, and the greatest number of these in turn were textile and leather workers. Most of these artisans were young, unmarried, salaried workers. Such men had few ties to keep them at home, and when they could not find work in one town, they left in hopes of better opportunities elsewhere. They wandered the roads from town to town, following rumors of jobs.[24] Between spells of employment, they begged. But beggary was not their primary occupation. That they

Table 5.2. Occupations of Beggars Confined by the
Ordinance of July 1724

Occupation		Total	%
Arts and métiers			
Building trades & metal work	25		6.9
Textiles & leather	101		27.9
Food	13		3.6
Transport & lodging	4		1.1
The arts	6		1.7
		149	41.3
Agricultural workers			
travailleurs	71		20.0
other	50		13.5
		121	33.5
Soldiers, sailors, public servants		42	11.6
Servants		23	6.4
Professions		11	3.0
Bourgeois, merchants, etc.		4	1.1
Wandering peddlers		6	1.7
Inmates of charities		1	0.3
Unidentifiable		4	1.1
Total whose occupations are given		361	100.0
Total sample of beggars	1,194		

Source: A.D. (Aix), XXI H, II F 11, "Livre d'entrée des mendiants enfermés
en vertu de l'ordonnance royal de Juillet 1724."

came to Aix to look for work is suggested by the fact that their patterns of
migration closely parallel those of legitimate job-seekers. Information about
the latter can be found in the register of the Oeuvre des Enfants Abandonnées. Founded in 1733, this charity gave shelter to young men, mostly in
their teens, who came to Aix looking for work.[25] A register of the 754 young
men who found shelter in the institution from 1771 to 1789 has survived.
Table 5.1 summarizes their geographical origins. The similarities with those of
the people arrested for beggary are striking.[26]

Thus many men who begged on Aix's street corners were artisans who
had come long distances looking for work. But not all of the town's mendicants fell into this category. Seventy-nine percent of our beggars came from
Aix or its immediate area: from the city's terroir (the farmland directly
surrounding it), or from other areas of Provence. Although some people from
cities such as Marseille and Toulon show up in these statistics,[27] the vast
majority of those who came to Aix from other areas in Provence were coun-
trymen, that is, travailleurs or petty craftsmen who lived in small peasant

villages of 50 to 200 inhabitants. Of the beggars in our sample whose occupations are known, 34 percent were agricultural laborers (see Table 5.2). Why did such people leave their land and village and come to Aix to beg?

The answer lies in the economic difficulties of the Provençal countryside in the 1720's. The seventeenth century had been a period of relative prosperity for the peasants of Provence. Large harvests of grain brought low prices in their train, but the harvests were usually large enough to compensate the seller for the lower unit prices, while the low prices helped the peasant whose plot was too small to provide all the grain his family needed and who therefore had to buy on the market. But in Old Regime France such prosperity could not last—the prosperity itself bred the forces which would destroy it. The relative prosperity encouraged population growth (the population of Provence reached its peak during these years near the end of the seventeenth century), and this in turn encouraged the extreme subdivision of property.[28] This subdivision of property ultimately reached a point at which production was inadequate to feed a family.[29] Therefore from 1690 to 1730 the situation in the countryside deteriorated. The harvests shrank, and prices rose. While the larger landowners could profit from the higher prices, such prices hurt many peasants with very small plots who had to buy grain on the market. Moreover, the small size of the harvest meant that the seigneurial dues, and the church tithe paid in kind, were relatively more burdensome, while the taxes borne by the peasantry of course increased in these years of war. The decline in population provided some relief, in that it caused salaries to rise; indeed, they rose so much in 1722 that many towns in Provence set salary maximums.[30] But this salary rise hardly compensated for the rise in prices, and the population decline meant a small tax base, and this in turn meant even higher taxes on those who remained. Thus for the countryside this was a time of crisis. It was in this period that what René Baehrel has termed the relative "inequality of fortunes," that is, the position of the peasant vis-à-vis the rich landowner, which he pictures as almost constant throughout the Old Regime, tipped slightly in favor of the landowner.[31]

Contemporary evidence shows what this meant for the life of the peasant. In 1730 the archbishop of Aix ordered an inquiry into the state of his diocese, one of the largest in Provence, which included 108 country parishes as well as the five parishes of Aix. Each parish priest was to report not only on the spiritual state of his flock (such matters as the average number of communicants, and problems of immorality or laxness of faith), but also on their temporal condition. The curés were to describe the economic situation of the peasantry, and to note the charity available. Their replies are striking testimony to the grinding poverty of the countryside. In village after village, the inhabitants are described as desperately poor, "especially in winter when they cannot work."[32] It is true that in 72 of the 113 parishes of the Diocese of Aix, some sort of organized and institutionalized aid for the poor existed. But only in the case of seven of these parishes, major *bourgs* such as Puyricard, Pertius, and Lambesc, could the available charity be considered adequate. As for the others, most had only a small donation made by the seigneur—perhaps the 54 livres distributed in Ollières every Christmas by the seigneur with the aid of the curé—or the product of the collections taken for the poor, like those in Beaumont, a village of about 600 whose lord was the Marquis de Mirabeau. The curé of Beaumont reported that "every year the town consuls take a collection and give the curé the product, which is usually five or six livres."[33] Some of the towns had charitable establishments, but most of these hospitals lacked sufficient revenue, and they were often mismanaged by the curé or the village consuls. Typical was the case of Meyaurgues, a village of about 220 communicants, where, it was reported, "there is a very dilapidated building called the hospital, which has neither rectors nor revenue."[34]

It is of course possible that this survey underestimates the extent of help available to the rural poor. Michel Vovelle argues that personal alms-giving persisted longer in the countryside, with its traditional piety and close social ties, than it did in the more depersonalized towns. Indeed, he has found that in rural areas of Provence about one-fifth of the wills registered in the eighteenth century made provision for some sort of traditional donation to the poor, usually in the form of the distribution of money at the funeral of the deceased.[35] But such gifts were both small and erratic, and did little to alleviate the chronic poverty of the countryside.

Thus when times were hard, as they were during the 1720's and 1730's, a travailleur could get little relief from local charity. His only recourse was to go to the nearest city to beg. Apparently many did. Some 232 of our 1,194 beggars came from the diocese of Aix. I have been able to trace 96 of these to their native villages. Of the latter number, 34 came from villages cited as poverty-stricken by their curés, and 86 came from villages where the charity available was either nonexistent or at least inadequate. Doubtless if such information was available for the other rural areas from which Aix's beggars came, it would reflect a similar state of poverty and lack of charitable resources. For the most part the beggars of Aix were country people driven to beg in the city by hard times on the land. And Aix was not at all unusual in this. Every French city was flooded with beggars escaping the poverty of the countryside.[36] The misery of the peasantry was the single most important factor in the problem of poverty in Old Regime France.

This misery followed a rhythm of its own, ebbing and flowing according to the harvests and even the seasons. Certain times of the year were especially dangerous for the peasant—the winter months of agricultural unemployment, and the period in spring and early summer before harvest time, when supplies from the previous year were running out, and the new crops were not yet gathered in. The curés are almost unanimous in citing these times as difficult ones for their flocks. As the priest of Tourves reported, in his village "there are many poor, principally in winter when the peasants cannot work."[37] That during these periods many peasants left home to go to the city to beg is borne out by analysis of the monthly variations in the number of beggars arrested. As Table 5.3, shows, the months when the most arrests occurred were January and February, the months of winter unemployment, and April and May, in the spring before the harvests.

Table 5.3. Number of Arrests Per Month, 1725-32

Month	1725	1726	1727	1728	1729	1730	1731	1732	Total
Jan.	14	43	12	41	6	16	13	8	153
Feb.	26	27	6	30	9	20	19	6	143
Mar.	19	8	3	22	10	16	13	0	91
Apr.	20	4	19	19	27	10	6	3	108
May	17	11	4	24	21	2	18	10	107
June	24	7	14	8	24	3	10	5	95
July	17	6	17	5	9	7	12	4	77
Aug.	12	5	14	29	11	8	7	10	96
Sept.	3	4	17	15	9	3	5	2	58
Oct.	0	8	10	10	14	4	8	5	59
Nov.	4	5	31	17	13	15	14	4	103
Dec.	9	5	19	1	22	13	10	6	85
Total	165	133	166	221	175	117	135	63	1,175*

*If the 19 arrests for the year 1733 for which only partial information is available are added, the total is 1, 194.

Source: A.D. (Aix), XXI H, II F 11, "Livre d'entrée des mendiants enfermés en vertu de l'ordonnance royale de Juillet 1724."

Our sample of beggars comes from the 1720's, a period of agricultural crisis. It might be thought that when the situation in the countryside improved in the mid-eighteenth century the number of poor travailleurs who left their land in the winter and the spring to beg in Aix might decrease. But this is not necessarily true. The gains from the improved harvests of mid-century were constantly threatened by population growth which put a new squeeze on the land, a development intensified by the conversion of much acreage to olive-growing and viticulture. And if the situation in agriculture did not really improve for the travailleur in these years, neither did the amount of charity available in the countryside. This is shown by the Etat of the diocese of Aix, similar to that of 1730, which was made in 1782.[38] From this État it would appear that in only twelve of the parishes of the diocese were new charities founded in the years between 1730 and 1782–a gain almost balanced by a probable decrease in aid in seven of the parishes. Thus at the end of the eighteenth century, as at the beginning, the agricultural laborer in the countryside had little alternative but begging when faced with disaster.

Many of the beggars who infested the street corners of Aix and roamed the roads of the surrounding countryside were thus either urban artisans who had traveled long distances in search of work, or agricultural laborers forced to leave home by hard times. There was, however, one other major category to be found among Aix's beggars. These people were the unemployables, the structural poor–those who could not find work because of age or infirmity. Their presence shows up in an analysis of the age and sexual distribution of our beggars, and also in the large number of beggars who suffered some sort of illness or injury.

The age and sexual distribution of the 1,194 people who entered the Charité under the declaration of 1724 are illustrated in Figs. 5.1 and 5.2. Many more beggars were male than female. Men form almost 70 percent (834) of the total, while only 30 percent (360) were women. That there were more male than female beggars was common throughout Old Regime France. A sample taken by P. Crépillon of all those sentenced by the prevotal court for beggary in Basse-Normandie between 1768 and 1788 shows that 80 percent were male and 20 percent female.[39] Similarly an American student, Thomas M. Adams, has found that of the 204 individuals arrested in the vicinity of Rennes for begging in 1777, 66 percent were men and only 34 percent were women.[40]

That more men than women were likely to become beggars is easily explained. Traditionally the young man has always left home at an early age to find employment, and being footloose and adventurous (in theory at least) he liked to wander far afield. In eighteenth-century France the young artisan who found the gild of his own town closed to him, or the silk worker who faced unemployment in Lyon, might take to the road, and end up begging his way. A young girl, by contrast, was far more apt to remain at home supported by her parents until marriage. If she did leave home to find work, she usually did not go any great distance, but instead became a servant girl or washerwoman in the nearest town. Even at a more advanced age, a man was far more likely than a woman to take to the roads and beg. In an established household, it was the husband who would leave when disaster struck, the husband who set out on the road to find work, and who often turned this temporary leave into a permanent disappearance. The wife had to stay at home and care for the children.[41]

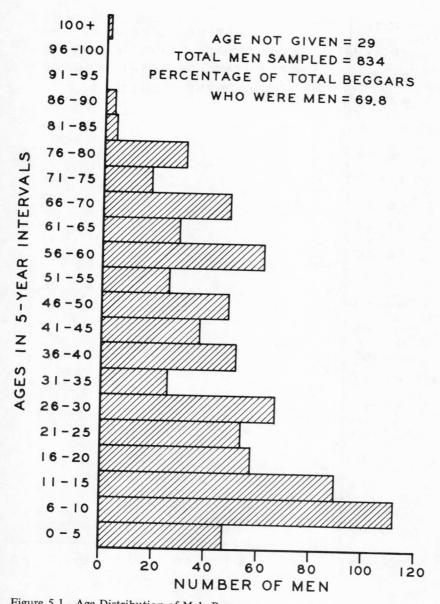

Figure 5.1. Age Distribution of Male Beggars.

Source: A.D. (Aix), XXI H, II F 11, "Livre d'entrée des mendiants enfermés en vertu de l'ordonnance royal de Juillet 1724."

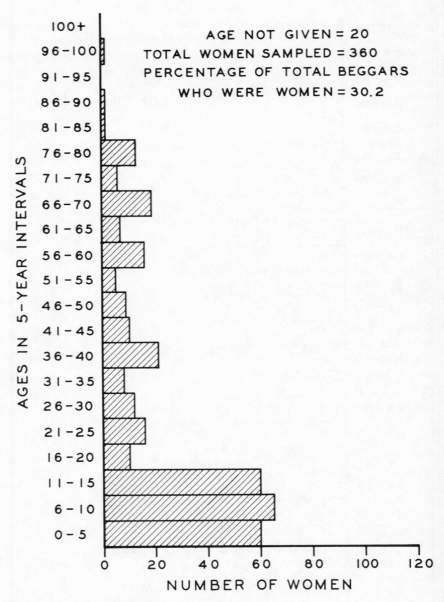

Figure 5.2. Age Distribution of Female Beggars.

Source: A.D. (Aix), XXI H, II F 11, "Livre d'entrée des mendiants enfermés en vertu de l'ordonnance royal de Juillet 1724."

Even more striking in these charts than the prevalence of men over women is the age distribution of the beggars, especially the large number of young people. Of the total sample, 42 percent were under the age of twenty. This again was a common characteristic of beggars in eighteenth-century France. For example, in Rennes in 1777 the largest concentration of those arrested clustered in the age group of fifteen- and nineteen-year-olds.[42] It is with these young people that the problem of unemployability comes to the fore. Some of these children, especially the very young ones, doubtless show up in our sample because their parents brought them along when they set out on the road. But many more probably begged because they were left on their own and could not find employment. If a very young child was left orphaned and homeless (as many were in our sample, due to the plague of 1720), he found few chances of employment. If his home town or village was not large enough to have a charitable organization to care for him, he had little choice but to beg. Often whole gangs of homeless children roamed the roads, finding protection and fellowship in numbers. For the slightly older child, the teen-ager, the situation was somewhat different. Even if he had a family, such a young person might be forced to leave home at a very early age to look for work. But his youth and lack of training and skills often made it hard for him to find employment. In this case, again, beggary or charity were the only alternatives. This points up the usefulness of such charities as Aix's Corpus Domini de St. Sauveur, with its program of apprenticeships for poor boys, and the Enfants Abandonnées, which provided both food and lodging for unemployed young men. If his town lacked such charities a young man could do little else except beg. Thus those made unemployable by their youth often turned to beggary, and form a large portion of our sample.

Similar problems of unemployability faced the very old. A relatively large number of elderly men and women show up in our sample. The age configuration for the sample does not show the same steep decline in the upper age brackets as does the normal population configuration in the ancien régime. Other statistics of beggary usually show a similarly large portion of older people.[43] The reasons for this are obvious. Few were willing to hire the very old, who were often too feeble to work anyway. If their families could not care for them, or if their town lacked a hospital-general, there was little else they could do but beg.

Unemployability also explains the large number of the physically handi-capped who appear in our sample of beggars. Some 411 of the 694 adults over twenty-one arrested, or almost 60 percent, were noted in the entry register as "invalid." This number seems quite large. Beggars of course often faked injuries or illness to gain sympathy. The more horrifying the injury, the more sympathetic passers-by were likely to be. Hospital administrators were of course alert to the possibility of feigned illness, but in Aix in 1724-32 they unmasked only two such cases. Doubtless a few more escaped their scrutiny, but most of the physical disabilities reported were probably genuine.

As Table 5.4, which classifies the specific illnesses cited in the register, illustrates, the maladies which affected the poor were many and varied. Many of these disabilities are testimony to the disastrous inroads of poor diet and unsanitary living conditions on the health of generations of the poor. Congenital blindness and feeblemindedness especially often resulted from malnutrition. People with such afflictions could rarely find employment, and thus were forced to beg to survive. It was a miserable existence, especially for the poor simpleminded "imbecilles" who were such a standard feature of life in the French countryside. These village halfwits wandered from place to place, clothed in rags, sleeping in haystacks or ditches, and surviving on what little food they could beg or steal. These unfortunates met with little but cruelty from the farmers on whose land they trespassed, and from the casual passer-

Table 5.4. Physical Disabilities of Those Interned under the
Declaration of July 18, 1724

"Imbecille"	20
Blindness & other vision problems	24
Deafness	1
Dumbness	2
Epilepsy	3 (1 doubtful)
Paralysis of limbs	41 ⎤
Missing limbs	12 ⎟
Difficulties in walking	32 ⎬ 90
Burns	3 ⎟
Injuries from falls	2 ⎦
Unspecified illness in:	
Arms	3
Stomach	2
Chest	2
Gunshot wounds	1
Venereal disease	1
Lump in cheek	1
Extremely fat	1
"demy invalid"	1
Unspecified or untranslatable maladies	13
Faked injuries	2
Total	167

Source: A.D. (Aix), XXI H, II F 11, "Livre d'entrée des mendiants enfermés en vertu de l'ordonnance royale de Juillet 1724."

by. A distressing case in point is that of a twenty-year-old girl, blind and halfwitted, who did not even know her own name. She wandered the countryside near Aix, with a little girl to guide her, and was raped one night by a "man unknown" as she slept in a ditch.[44] For such souls arrest and incarceration often meant an improvement in their lot.

Accidental injuries incurred at work were another common affliction. If a carpenter fell from a ladder, or a travailleur had a tendon cut by a scythe, they had little chance for medical attention, which probably would do little good anyway. Such accidental injuries might maim a man for life, and thus make him unemployable. In our table there are 90 beggars who possibly suffered such injuries. For these people as for the other unemployables, if they could find no charity, begging was the only answer.

Aix's beggars were thus a varied lot. Some were natives of the town who were more or less professional beggars. Others were Aixois who for various reasons preferred the independent life of a beggar to entering a charity. But many more were strangers to the city, travailleurs driven from the countryside by hard times, out-of-work artisans tramping long distances looking for a job, and unemployables of every description. This points up an important fact about poverty in eighteenth-century France: the immense dimensions of the problem. The founders of Aix's charities took as their purpose the eradication of beggary. But the type of institutions they founded, municipal charities, simply could not do this. Such institutions might keep the needy of Aix from beggary, although some would prefer the freedom of that life to the regimentation of charities. But municipal organizations were ineffective against the flood of foreign beggars which inundated the city. For such people beggary was often not deliberately chosen alternative—it was the only way to stay alive. Municipal charities alone could not solve the problem of poverty in eighteenth-century France.

CRIME

For the needy of Aix, one other alternative to charity and beggary existed. This was, of course, crime, especially theft. In the latter half of the eighteenth century the city was plagued by a wave of petty thievery. A glance at criminal statistics shows this. Of the 157 sentences handed down by Aix's sénéchaussée court from February 1773 to December 1779, 113, or 72 percent, concerned thefts. Similarly, thievery figures in 141, or 67 percent, of the 212 sentences passed by the court from May 1780 to June 1790. Most of these crimes were "country thievery," usually thefts of food, either from the gardens and orchards within the city limits, or from the small terres of the surrounding countryside.[45] Examples of this sort of crime abound. In 1776

Table 5.5. Criminal Sentences, February 1773-December 1779,
and May 1780-June 1790, in the Sénéchaussée Court, Aix

Offense	1773-79	1780-90
Theft	113	141
Murder	13	13
Minor violence	13	30
Vagabondage	5	14
Morals offenses	3	4
Other	10	10
Total	157	212
Acquitted	15	21
Discharged without trial	3	7
Multiple indictments*	16	15

*Some defendants acquitted, some convicted.

Source: A.D. (Aix), B, IV B 988, Sénéchaussée d'Aix, "Sentences criminelles,"
1773-79; IV B 989, "Sentences criminelles," 1780-90.

thieves stole some pigeons belonging to Sr. Estienne Aubert, bourgeois, of
Aix. In Puyricard ripe apples and apricots were pilfered from the orchard of
Jean Michel Aillard, ménager. Srs. Joseph Bossy and Simenon Ribaud, owners
of the right to collect the Cathedral's *dîme,* were robbed of newly harvested
wheat.[46] Deserted country homes whose absentee owners remained in the
city made another tempting target for thieves. There are numerous cases of
country houses being broken into. The complaint voiced by Jean Rastin,
master scalemaker, could stand for many. Sr. Rastin stated that he owned a
small house in the countryside near Aix. When he visited it in January 1776,
after a month's absence, he found the door ajar. Further examination
revealed that a basket, a napkin, a knife, and a few raisins had been stolen.[47]
Doubtless the thief pawned the basket, napkin, and knife, and ate the raisins.

Most of these petty thefts were probably not the work of professional
criminals. It was hungry men, men who did not know where their next meal
was coming from, who were tempted by fat pigeons and ripe fruit. That this
was so is suggested by information about the types of people arrested for
theft (see Table 5.6). This configuration shows that those who turned to theft
came from the neediest sectors of Aix's society. The bulk of them were poor
travailleurs and textile workers, the same sort of people, as we have seen, who
provided most of Aix's beggars and received most of the city's charity.

This does not mean that there was no criminal class in Aix, that there
were no professional criminals among its population. A rich parlementaire

Table 5.6. Occupations of People Sentenced for Theft, 1773-90

Agricultural laborers (81 travailleurs)	92
Artisans and craftsmen (24 textile workers)	46
Soldiers and sailors	6
Servants	8
Bourgeois, merchants, clergy	4
Wandering peddlers	5
Beggars	3
Unidentified	1
Total	165

Source: A.D. (Aix), B, IV B 988, Sénéchaussée d'Aix, "Sentences criminelles," 1773-79; IV B 989, "Sentences criminelles," 1780-90.

had to guard his purse and watch as he walked the city streets, and he faced the perils of highway robbers when he rode out to his country home. Such criminals made their headquarters in the city's shadier cafés, where they could be sure not only of protection from the police, but also of a market for their stolen goods. The most prestigious of these criminals was the highwayman. This romantic figure roamed the countryside, alone or with a band, swooping down, armed with pistol or sabre, to rob the lonely traveler, then retreating to his hideout. Typical of the highway robbers was the unknown man who victimized Sr. Jean Gaspard Cars, écuyer, as he was coming in his carriage from Marseille with his brother, a priest. Sr. Cars reported that near Albertas, a man, armed with a pistol, came from hiding in a "small hill covered with pine," and cried in Provençal, "Stop, stop." The robber got away with 33 livres. It was Sr. Cars' opinion that "he had a soft and flexible voice which did not appear to be that of a peasant." The next day the same man apparently robbed Antoine Copié, a courier who traveled from Lyon to Marseille, at the same place. Copié described his assailant as a "peasant, armed with a pistol, who cried in a French patois, 'Your purse or your life.' " The thief robbed Copié of three louis d'or, two small écus, and one 24-sou piece.[48]

Some of these dashing highwaymen became legendary figures. One such was Gaspard de Besse, who roamed the forests of the Esterel, on the frontier of Nice.[49] De Besse combined highway robbery with a profitable trade in salt-smuggling. His daring exploits, together with his rough attempts at social justice, made him a hero among the peasants of Provence. But such "social bandits" were in the eighteenth century the exception rather than the rule. The real heyday of the social bandit would come later, with the rise of the counterrevolutionary brigands of the White Terror.[50] Social brigandage would continue to plague Provence throughout the Napoleonic era and even into the Restoration.[51] But in the eighteenth century the heyday of the "social bandit" lay in the future.

Less daring but equally enterprising were the pickpockets who haunted the crowds at the fairs and made the streets of Aix unsafe for the rich. Perhaps typical of this type of professional thief was Dominique Benoit, a seventeen-year-old marchand colporteur, who shows up in the police records as accused of stealing a purse containing three louis d'ors at the fair at Pertius. Dominique, who traveled from fair to fair with his mistress, twenty-two-year-old Antoinette Boudon, denied having stolen the purse but admitted that he had been arrested twice before for picking pockets, the first time at the age of fourteen and a half.[52]

Despite the efforts of such professional thieves, the crime rate in eighteenth-century Aix was surprisingly low—in the vicinity of 30 crimes per 100,000 people.[53] Apart from the innumerable petty thefts and the less widespread activities of professional criminals, there was extraordinarily little crime in Aix. There were very few murders. A total of 19 occurred between the years of 1780 and 1790, a rate of far less than one per 100,000 people. [54] Six of these murders occurred during the course of attempted robberies. The rest were the typical sort of "private" crimes which take place within the family circle, husbands killing wives, sons killing their fathers. Such were the cases of the man from Allauch who killed his brother, and of the travailleur who committed parricide "in a fit of madness." There were also a few murders for gain, such as the elaborate poison plot discovered at Rians in 1774. [55] Such crimes were usually the work of social classes more elevated than the menu peuple; the poison plot, for example, involved four members of a bourgeois family.

"Bourgeois" crime also accounted for the remainder of Aix's criminal activity—a miscellany of gambling, swindling, perjury, etc. Table 5.7, which lists the traceable "bourgeois" crimes for the period 1780 to 1790, suggests that such crime was rather a different matter than the theft and violence of the artisan and travailleur.

All in all, eighteenth-century Aix was quite law-abiding. The biggest single cause of crime was the poverty which drove many of the poor to petty theft. But most of the poor chose in the desperate situation other alternatives—beggary or charity. On the whole, despite the firm conviction of the founders and administrators of Aix's charities, the town's poor were not criminals.

What of the lives of the respectable poor, of the people who managed to stay on the right side of that thin line between poverty and utter destitution, who somehow kept food on the table for their families, who never had

Table 5.7. Bourgeois Crimes, 1773-90

Accused	Crime
Bourgeois family	Poisoning
Innkeeper	Helping soldiers desert
Lazarite monk	Theft
Former army officer	Demanding alms with indecencies and threats
Schoolmaster	Breaking into a church
Commissaire, lawyer	Beating up two Jews
Two surgeons, abbé, priest	Murder
Innkeeper (2)	Breaking gambling ordinances
Doctor	Theft
Curé, former army officer	Perjury, subornation of witnesses

Source: A.D. (Aix), B, IV B 988, Sénéchaussée d'Aix, "Sentences criminelles," 1773-79; IV B 989, "Sentences criminelles," 1780-90.

to resort to charity or beggary or crime? These people present the greatest problem of all for the historian, since they leave no trace on the surviving records, not even on the criminal dockets and charity registers which memorialize their more feckless fellows. Yet such documents allow us a few glimpses into the lives of this least known group of the menu peuple.

The center of their lives was of course their home and family. Despite the tirades of the charity officials about the debauchery of the poor, there are few signs that many of Aix's poor departed far from the strict moral standards of the Church. Although prostitution might flourish among the poor in a sink of iniquity like Paris, it was relatively rare in a quiet and respectable provincial city like Aix. There were only four cases of prostitution recorded in the years from 1773 to 1790 (Table 5.5). And the Refuge, a prison for prostitutes from all over Provence, usually had a population of only between 65 and 70, a surprisingly low number.[56] Admittedly the town had a large number of illegitimate births, and, as Chapter IV pointed out, the rate of illegitimacy was increasing in the last years of the Old Regime. Some modern historians have taken these rising rates of illegitimacy, common in Europe in this period, as evidence of a loosening of the bonds of traditional morality. Edward Shorter, for example, has argued that this increase in illegitimacy is a result of the spread of a market economy. That is, as young people of the lower classes left the countryside and found jobs in town which made them economically self-sufficient, they experienced a "desire to be free" of their families, and of traditional social conventions, which expressed itself in increased sexual permissiveness and thus was reflected in rising rates of illegitimacy.[57]

But it is doubtful whether this hypothesis adequately explains the situation in a town like Aix. Aix did have its share of servant girls, fresh from the country and free from their families for the first time, who allowed themselves to be seduced by the apprentice or shop clerk they met in the big city. Such was the case of Julienne Berne, age twenty-two, the daughter of a peasant from St. Jullien Le Montagnier. She came to Aix in 1787 to work in a dress-shop and was seduced by a domestic servant.[58] But not all the cases of illegitimacy fell into this obvious category. Proof of this lies in an analysis of the surviving *déclarations de grossesse*, statements about the circumstances of pregnancy made by the unfortunate young women when they entered the hospital to give birth. A sample of 75 of these declarations, dating from 1787 to 1788, shows that in only one-half of the cases were the girls independent of their families and self-supporting. And even these supposedly emancipated girls show little signs of any sort of permissive morality. Only two, Anne Rubi, a butcher's daughter, and Elizabeth Audibert, servant girl, recount their experiences with any gusto. In nine of the cases forcible rape was alleged. And in most of the other incidents the women involved were deluded by some sort of promise of marriage. Typical is the story of Marie Sauzé, twenty-two years old. Marie, the daughter of a butcher, had been courted for a year by a *faiseur de chaise*. He constantly followed her, "he continually brought her flowers," and he frequently offered marriage. One day he came to her house while she was alone, and "threw himself on her." After the incident, she went to his shop and begged him to marry her. He promised to do so, and told her to tell her father to arrange the marriage. She never saw him again. A similar story is told by Elizabeth Martel, the daughter of a travailleur from Pertius:

> She asserts that she had known for one year François Pellegrin, originally of the town of Lambesc, resident in the terroir of Aix in the *bastide* of Sr. Parmentier. She says that this young man courted her for six months without having obtained her favors, but one day when she found herself walking with him he assured her in all sincerity that his wish was to marry her, that he did not have any other women than her, and she succumbed to his pressing solicitations and accorded him the last favors. That having been done, she continued to live with him until she discovered she was pregnant.[59]

Pellegrin repeatedly promised to marry her, but finally said that his financial situation didn't permit him to support a wife.

This story points up an important fact of life among the poor. Most illegitimacies occurred as a result of premarital sex by couples who considered themselves betrothed. Because of the precarious financial situation of young men like François Pellegrin, it was often impossible for young couples to marry. The courtship period of waiting and saving often took years. It is not surprising that many couples jumped the gun a bit. But most did intend eventually to legitimatize their union in the eyes of the Church. This was not the promiscuous concubinage which the moralistic charity administrators saw as rife among the lower classes. Marriage and family life remained all-important for the poor of eighteenth-century Aix.

Mainstay and center of the family was of course the wife and mother. She cared for the home, bore the children who came year after year, and usually worked as well to help support the family, taking in washing or spinning cotton in the moments she could spare from all her other responsibilities. The fact that she worked to help support the family does not, however, seemed to have improved her status in the eyes of her husband or of the male-dominated society at large. Police reports abound in cases of wife-beating, of "mauvais traitements envers la femme." Here is one example. Magdelaine Vidal, wife of Claude Girard, an artisan who made the combs used by wool-carders, deserted her husband in 1774 after five years of marriage, "in which there was no sort of ill treatment that she did not experience." Her husband followed her to her parents' house where she was staying, climbed in through a window and began beating her, in the process "seizing her neck to strangle her."[60] Such violence could easily result from the continual pressures—the endless arguments about money, the countless expedients necessary to get bread on the table—which poverty puts on fragile human relationships. When the situation became insupportable, a husband could leave and take to the road, but a wife, bound to her home and children, could not.

Home for such families might be a small house. Even some of the poor who eventually ended their lives in the hospital-general occasionally owned a bit of property. Marguerite Gerin, widow of M. Morel, a *huissier en la siege*, (a minor court official and therefore among the most well-off of the poor) owned a "house within the walls of this town" which the hospital administrators estimated might bring in a rent of 60 livres per year. Esprit Fillol owned one and one-half *journaux* of vineyard in Puyricard in Aix's terroir.[61] But more often property-owning was something to which the poor, especially the very poor, could not aspire. Typically, they lived in rented rooms, in dilapidated houses which might contain as many as nine families. The meanest of these dwellings cost 10-15 livres a year; more usual among the respectable poor was an expense of 15-20 livres, which might bring the relative luxury of two or three rooms, on the upper floors of a respectable house or shop. Thus Louis Gautier, a travailleur, rented for 18 livres a year three rooms on the second floor of the house of Marguerite Rimbaud, across the street from the *chapel des dames*.[62]

Household furnishings were meagre, and, like clothing, were confined to only the basic necessities. They were of poor quality, often purchased secondhand, and used until the breaking point (when they were not being pawned at the Mont-de-Piété during periodic crises in the family's fortunes). Of the estates of the poor who died in the Charité, only a few apparently had household goods worth over 100 livres. Most of them were considerably less. The estate left by Marie Roux, widow of Louis Teste, a travailleur, who entered the Charité on November 10, 1782, is typical:

	livres	sous
1 bad table	4	4
3 bad planks of wood for a bed-frame	1	2
2 other bad planks		6
1 bad mattress	1	12
2 bad warming pans		14
2 rush & 1 wooden chair, all very bad		15
1 grill, 1 tripod, 1 frying pan, all broken		6
1 bad woman's corset		10
1 bad cap & 1 kerchief		12
2 pottery pots		3
12 plates, 1 platter of pottery		8
12 bottles, 1 bad flask		8
1 bedspread of Indian cotton in a bad state	2	
1 bad sheet & 2 napkins in shreds		18
1 woman's chemise, bad	1	10
1 cloak, & 1 apron, for a woman	1	2
1 woolen coverlet, ripped		18
3 other sheets, 3 chemises all in shreds	2	
Other bad goods	1	2
Total	20	10[63]

More appalling, perhaps, even than the meagreness of material comforts in these households was their lack of privacy. With so many families crowded together in one building, privacy was a luxury unknown to the poor. The neighbors saw your comings and goings on the stairs, and heard your quarrels from across the courtyard. Given such conditions, it is not surprising that arguments and vendettas among neighbors were frequent and virulent. Here is another illustration of the corrosive effect of poverty on human relationships. A slighting remark or even a contemptuous glance became a grievance nourished for months, to break out eventually into the bitter yelling and fighting matches which abound in the records of Aix's police courts. Here is one such complaint, lodged by Georges Aguillon, a teamster:

Georges Aguillon, *portefaix*, of this city of Aix, in the quality of father and legitimate administrator for Thérèse Aguillon, his daughter, and Marie Curet, his wife, remonstrates that they live in the house of Sieur Lauther, master wigmaker of this city, on the road to Marseille, in which house also lives Marie Clavel with her husband; for three or four years the aforesaid Dlle. Clavel has conceived a hatred and dislike for the Suppliant, his wife and daughter. . . . Today, September 29, 1774, at around eleven A.M. the daughter of the Suppliant was in her apartment, and the aforesaid Dlle. Clavel did not hesitate to enter and threw herself on the daughter of the Suppliant, calling her a slut, a bitch, a whore, and adding that she was just like her mother who had never been anything but a public whore and that she was actually the whore of Sr. Clavel her husband. . . . She slapped the face of the daughter of the Suppliant several times and punched her.[64]

The corroding effects of poverty were equally evident in employee-employer relationships. Modern-style struggles over wages and hours of work were apparently infrequent, although further investigation of this subject is necessary. But numerous other evidences of friction exist. It was not at all unusual for a servant or apprentice to pay back an employer's fancied meanness by petty pilferage. The servant girl who stole her mistress's handkerchief, the printer's apprentice who made off with a ream of paper, the draper's assistant found with his hand in the till are common figures on Aix's police blotters. Often the tensions inherent in these relationships went beyond such petty pilfering to violence and assault. In August 1789, for example, Laurens Bresson, a mason's apprentice, attacked his master, Joseph Marguerit, and Marguerit's pregnant wife, with a "large stick three feet long" and beat them into insensibility.[65] Police records of course present to the historian only the worst side of human relationships. But the abundance of these cases of violence among the poor, violence toward their employers, their neighbors, even their wives, does suggest that for at least some of the poor, the pressures of their poverty were enormous, and that these pressures most often found their outlet in violence.

For the poor there were few other escapes from the narrowness and sordidness of their lives. One possible source of consolation was religion. Aix's poor were still most probably believers in a faith of saints and sacraments, thickly overlaid with superstition. Admittedly parish priests often complained about the laxity of religious devotion among their flocks. The curé of St. Esprit noted indignantly in 1730 that not only did the poor frequently miss Sunday services, but also that "many people did not take communion at Easter," the basic minimum religious duty the Church considered necessary for practicing Christians.[66] But the lack of attendance at church services need not be a sign of a spread of disbelief. For the poor man it probably signified only an understandable preference to spend his precious holiday time relaxing in a cabaret. Freethinking was not unknown in Aix, but the criminal sentences of the sénéchaussée court show only two cases of sacrilege in the period from 1773 to 1790.[67] Two instances hardly suggest that unbelief was rampant. Many of the poor numbered among their meagre possessions religious pictures and icons. The estate of Nicholas and Marguerite Mayon, who died in 1772, included "a plaster Christ" among the one plate, the three napkins, and the "two bad chairs" which formed the bulk of their household possessions. Anne Agnel, widow of a porteur, left an estate valued at over 100 livres; included among her possessions were "a painting representing our Lord on the Cross," value six livres, and three pictures representing "the Holy Virgin, St. Magne and St. Elizabeth," respectively, together worth five livres, plus a small Limoges plaque of the Disciples, cost twelve livres. [68] Mere possession of religious pictures is of course no guarantee of faith. But it does, I think, suggest that religion was still an important part of the lives of the poor. Although the father might be more often found at the cabaret than in the chapel, and although the daughter might have conceived a child without benefit of clergy, most families probably considered themselves good Catholics, and religion was doubtless one of the major consolations for the misery of their lives.[69]

Even more consoling, perhaps, than religion were the holidays and popular celebrations which punctuated their working year. The city's three fairs were occasions for drinking, dancing, and wenching, and despite their dangers—pickpockets combed the crowds, and many illegitimate children were conceived at fair time—they were a delight for all. Throughout the year other holidays and feast days also brought their own festivities. There were even popular recreation clubs organized among the menu peuple. In 1730 the parish priest of the faubourg of St. Jean complained to his ecclesiastical superiors about a "kind of *confrerie*" organized by the bas peuple, which planned the celebration for the day after Easter, and devoted itself to "making noise, flirting and dancing, often very indecently, from noon until night." "These dances are initiated in numerous Parishes, and cause church services to be deserted during all this period".[70] Apart from these special celebrations, the poor also had a daily focus for relaxation and recreation in the cabaret. The local cabaret was the center of life in each neighborhood; it was to *La Mule Blanche, La Mule Noire,* The Golden Claw, and the *Pomme de L'Amour* that the weary travailleur or apprentice repaired after his day of labor, to meet his cronies, drink watered red wine, and perhaps play a few friendly hands of cards. Some cabarets were criminal haunts, especially those near the city gates and therefore convenient to smugglers who brought goods into town without paying the *droits d'entrance*. Such establishments also served as fences for stolen goods and hideouts for criminals on the run. Gambling, the "jeux prohibées," against which the city police struggled so often and so vainly, flourished in their back rooms. Soldiers who innocently stumbled into these establishments were made drunk, robbed, and urged to desert.[71]

Most cabarets, however, were far more respectable places, centers of life for the whole neighborhood. This is not to say that things never got rough. In even the most respectable of cabarets a friendly game of cards might suddenly turn ugly. Drunken brawls and knife fights were common occurrences. Here is one as described by Sr. Mitre Lamour, patronne of the *Pomme de L'Amour*. The fight began when a ropemaker named Bonnet tried to take his winnings from a game of piquet and leave. One of the players, Carles, a master baker, assaulted him. When Sr. Lamour tried to stop the fight, Carles attacked him too:

He threw himself on the Suppliant with the greatest violence, he seized him by the hair, he pulled the left side of his beard and a great portion of the hair on the back of his head . . . he kicked him, he hit him, so many blows in so many parts of the body that the Suppliant was almost killed, and without doubt he would have been murdered by the aforesaid Carles, if three men who were present had not with the greatest effort stopped the effects of the furor and of the rage of the aforesaid Carles.[72]

With such occurrences almost nightly, it is little wonder that the town decreed a 10 P.M. curfew for its cabarets, and that the city's police patrols gave them most of their attention.

The violence manifested in these cabaret brawls was always close under the surface of the lives of the poor. We have evidence of this violence in the frequent fights between neighbors, and in the physical abuse of women, who bore the brunt of their men's frustrations and the poverty and emptiness of their lives. Almost any incident, a jostling in the street, an argument in the marketplace, might trigger a fight. Here is the statement of Joseph Dubarry, a travailleur, concerning one such occurrence in 1789:

(He) remonstrates that on the fourth of this month at about nine A.M. he was at the marketplace with his wife who sent there to sell fruit; Catherine Aubert who was also a fruitseller addressed herself to the Suppliant asking him angrily to leave his place and overturning his stall, saying that the place belonged to her, which was false . . . (She) threw a bucket of herrings on the ground, and then Aubert raised her hands to his face, and scratched him considerably, and she would have scratched his eyes, if he had not stopped her.[73]

Violence provided for the poor an outlet for the frustrations built up by the narrowness, the barrenness, the hopelessness of their lives.

Surprisingly enough, such violence was only rarely directed against the "natural enemies" of the poor—against the state, against the police, against the rich. Authorities on criminality in Old Regime France have noted that such occurences—attacks on police officers, on tax collectors, on custom officials—were fairly common in the seventeenth century, but showed a marked decrease as the eighteenth century progressed.[74] I could find no statistics on criminality for Aix in the seventeenth century, but I suspect that it followed a similar pattern—that the number of violent assaults against hated authority symbols declined precipitiously, while the number of petty thefts showed a startling rise. At any rate, theft was the most common crime in eighteenth-century Aix, as we have seen (Table 5.5). Stealing a rich man's pigeons or fruit is of course in its own way a form of social protest, but it seems to me to be a qualitatively different one than violent assault, attractive to a different sort of person.[75] At any rate, cases of assault against figures of authority were few in eighteenth-century Aix. Even bread riots, a standard feature of urban life in Old Regime France, were infrequent, doubtless because of the municipality's care to import bread from abroad in times of scarcity.[76] Also, for the poor of eighteenth-century Aix, the police do not seem to have been the "natural enemy" that they constitute for the "culture of poverty" in more modern times. At least the poor showed no reluctance to involve the police in their frequent quarrels. Reading records of complaints to police in a town like Aix gives one the impression that the menu peuple ran to the police over every petty upset and argument.[77] And if the poor seem not to have hated the police, neither do they seem to have hated the rest of the apparatus of the royal government, including the king. The poor of eighteenth-century Aix seem curiously apolitical. If they showed little compunction about robbing their masters or otherwise attacking the people who oppressed them, they seem not to have made the connection between the personal oppressions they suffered and the system which permitted such oppressions to exist. In the last fifteen years of the Old Regime the court records of Aix show only two crimes which might be termed political agitation. In 1780 a baker from Rians was accused of pasting up inflammatory placards; what they said was not reported. He was acquitted. In 1782, four men were prosecuted for promoting "sedition and popular uprising" in an army camp. One was sentenced to banishment, and the rest were acquitted.[78] There is in eighteenth-century Aix little sign of what would become in Revolutionary years the political mob. The poor of the Old Regime were too preoccupied with their daily struggle for existence to give much thought to politics.

Generalizations like those above about the lives of "the poor" are about all that the historian can manage. More so with the poor than with other social groups, the inner reality of their individual lives eludes him. Their "mentality," their day-to-day preoccupations, remain a mystery; historians must reconstruct them as best they can from statistics on the geographical mobility of beggars and rises in the price of bread. The poor do not as a rule leave behind them diaries, memoirs, or autobiographies.

There exists, however, one autobiography written by a poor man in this period.[79] His name was Jean Joseph Esmieu: he was a traveling peddlar, a marchand colporteur, who wandered the roads in Basse Provence. He was not, strictly speaking, one of the poor of Old Regime Aix, since he lived mostly in the Var, and his life spanned the period of the Revolution and the Napoleonic Wars. But doubtless his life was similar to those of many of the poor of Aix. Like Catherine Tempier, the one other figure from among the poor for whom we have firsthand information, Esmieu can be made to stand as a symbol for the many poor people who died unknown. If Catherine with her meekness and her piety typifies the "good poor" of the charities, Esmieu, the independent and self-reliant wanderer, symbolizes the "respectable" poor who manage to keep their heads above water in their struggle with poverty, without having to rely on public assistance. The mentality of such people can be glimpsed in Esmieu's autobiography. He was apparently uninterested in politics; although he lived through exciting incidents of the Revolution like the siege of Toulon, he said little about them. He rarely mentioned religion, or even his family. What he does discuss are his recreations—his drinking and card-playing with the fellow-travelers he meets in inns and cabarets—and, above all, money-making. Esmieu seems to have remembered and set down for the edification of his family the circumstances surrounding every franc he ever earned. Esmieu's obsession with money-making is eloquent testimony to the immense importance of the struggle to earn a living—to survive—in the lives of the menu peuple. It was a struggle in which charity was of little help.

Charity by itself could not alleviate the poverty of Old Regime France. This exploration of the lives of the poor of Aix has given at least some idea of the immense complexities of this problem. Its dimensions alone were staggering. The underemployment and low wages of the urban population combined with an underproductive agriculture to keep the vast majority of the population mired in misery. If the example of Aix is typical, perhaps 20 percent of the population were so poor that they survived only with charity, while perhaps another 40 to 50 percent, better off, nonetheless lived in the constant shadow of destitution, their lives so dominated by the struggle for survival that all their human relationships were corroded by the poison of poverty. Among the menu peuple, only servants escaped this fate to some extent; their masters guaranteed them at least food and shelter. Worst off were the petty artisans and day-laborers of the towns, and the travailleurs of the countryside.

Charity in its traditonal form scarcely made a dent in this enormous problem. Inspired by religious stereotypes rather than economic realities, the municipal charities were most helpful in the case of the unemployables — the aged, the young, the ill. Yet even in these cases the unattractiveness of institutional life limited their effectiveness. And in the case of the able-bodied unemployed, who formed the core of the problem of poverty in Old Regime France, the institutions' inflexibility, plus their limited resources, made them almost useless. Further, the fact that most charity was urban-centered meant that aid for the rural poor was almost completely lacking. This gave rise to the hordes of beggars which infested city and countryside alike. Therefore the verdict on the charity of the Old Regime must be that it was ineffective. Doubtless only an industrial revolution combined with an agricultural revolution could have really "solved" the problem of poverty in seventeenth- and eighteenth-century France. But charity in its traditional form was almost useless. To make any substantial inroad upon the problem, a new departure was necessary.

PART THREE

The Crisis of Traditional Charity

CHAPTER VI

The Financial Crisis

Until now the picture presented has been a static one. I have examined the charities of the Old Regime, and described the attitudes behind them. And I have tried to assess their effectiveness in relieving poverty, and their role in the lives of the poor. The picture I have presented holds true for the heyday of the traditional charity, from approximately 1680 to 1760. But after 1760 the situation changes. The years from 1760 to the outbreak of the Revolution in 1789 were years of crisis for the traditional charity. In this period both the realities of the problem of poverty, and popular perceptions of it and attitudes toward it, changed. Because of these changes, the traditional charity became increasingly repudiated by public opinion as the proper means of caring for the poor.

Behind these changes in the functioning of the charities lay the major economic and intellectual changes which were transforming Old Regime society on the eve of the Revolution. The economic and social changes—the growth of population, the increase in illegitimate births, the price rise, and the decline of Aix's traditional industries—changed the dimensions of poverty in Aix, in a way which spelled increasing hardship for the poor. But just when the need for charity increased, the amount of aid available declined. For in these years the charities experienced grave financial problems, problems which brought them to the brink of bankruptcy. The cause of their financial woes lay mostly in the declining level of popular charitable donations. Underlying this change was a basic shift in mentalities, best characterized as a spread of deChristianization. People ceased to give to charities because they ceased to worry about the salvation of their souls. And, whatever the cause, the financial problems of the charities not only increased their ineffectiveness, but also increased public dissatisfaction with them. Thus it was a vicious circle: changing public opinion about charity caused the financial crisis, but the crisis itself also contributed to creating an adverse public opinion. These complex and interrelated phenomena form the subject of this chapter.

CHANGING DIMENSIONS OF POVERTY

There is no absolute statistical proof that the demand for charity increased greatly in Aix in the years after 1760. As I showed in Chapter IV, the records of numbers of people aided by charitable institutions did not fluctuate according to need. But all available economic and demographic indicators seem to suggest that poverty worsened in these years, both in the town itself and in the surrounding countryside. This meant both that there were more people who could be properly classified as poor, and that living conditions worsened, although when dealing with destitution it is hard to measure it by degrees.

A major factor behind the worsening condition of the poor in this period was the rise in population which Provence, in common with the rest of Europe, experienced after 1740.[1] But the pattern of population growth in Provence differed slightly from that elsewhere in France. In Provence, unlike the rest of the country, the population reached its peak for the Old Regime in the last years of the seventeenth century. But this growth was cut off abruptly by the plague of 1720. Marseille lost half of its 100,000 people, and in Aix the population dropped from 29,000 to approximately 16,000.[2] While recovery was quick in most areas, Aix's population never returned to its pre-1720 level. But after 1740 the population started to grow; it was 25,000 in both 1765 and 1793. This stable figure suggests that the birth rate did not rise in Aix as it did elsewhere after 1740. But that is not true. The level of births did rise in Aix; the population figures remained stable because of the large number of people who left the city to try their luck in Marseille.[3] That in itself is an indication of economic hardship among Aix's menu peuple.

But there are also other indications that the changes in population patterns created a greater demand for charity in Aix. For one thing, the rising birth rate meant that a larger proportion of the population was under fifteen, and such young people, as we have seen, formed the bulk of the charities' clientele. Further, the increasing rate of illegitimate children created a new problem for the charities, the *enfant trouvé*. As was mentioned in Chapter IV, the number of illegitimate children cared for in the hôtel-Dieu increased sharply after the 1770's.

Yet another fact to bear in mind is that the growth in population after 1740 was greatest in the countryside. If in Aix itself the population remained stable in our period, in the city's viguerie the population rose dramatically. Taking the population of 1716 as a base of 100, by 1765 it had increased proportionately to 153. And it continued to rise thereafter.[4] This population growth deepened the already desperate rural poverty. There were now more men competing for the scarce resources: for land, for work, for bread. In the wake of this increased poverty, as more and more men were forced to leave their homes and families to look for work and food, the rural beggar became increasingly common. When the ordinance of 1724 was in effect, an average of 151 beggars per year were arrested in Aix and its environs.[5] But in 1773 the number of beggars arrested under the provisions of the royal declaration of August 3, 1764, stood at 2,631.[6] Thus the population growth in rural Provence meant for Aix an increase in the number of beggars which flooded its churches and street corners. And beggary was a problem which the charities had never handled adequately.

Another factor which made life more precarious for the poor after 1760 was the notorious price rise of the last decades of the Old Regime. C. E. Labrousse has shown that prices of clothing, shelter and above all, food—the necessities of life—rose 65 percent in this period, while wages rose only 22 percent.[7] Surviving wage and price series for Aix show that the cost of living in the town followed Labrousse's general trend. For example, the price of the "dark" bread of the poor rose from 18 deniers per loaf in 1750 to 29 deniers in 1783. But the average daily wage of a carter rose only from 15 sous to 18 sous.[8] This rising cost of living hit the salaried workers and agricultural laborers of Aix extremely hard—and these groups, which found it difficult enough to make ends meet in the best of times, had always been in the forefront of the recipients of charity.

Finally, Aix's artisans, another major group of the charities' clientele, also experienced increasing hardship in the last thirty years of the Old Regime. The city's artisanal trades had always been overcrowded. From 1760 on, however, they entered a period of deepening crisis. The textile industry, Aix's largest, was adversely affected by the changing fashion which encouraged milady to favor the lighter and more attractive cottons and muslins instead of the heavier cloths which Aix's artisans had traditionally produced. And the city's second largest industry, tanning, also declined during this period.[9] Also trades like carting and hotel-keeping, which owed their prosperity to Aix's role as a local regional market, suffered greatly in the last decades of the eighteenth century. For one of the major characteristics of the economy of Provence during this period was the eclipse of such local markets by the great commercial center of Marseille.[10]

Thus all the available economic indicators seem to suggest that the condition of the poor gravely worsened in the last decades of the Old Regime. Yet it was precisely in this period, when the need for charity so greatly increased, that the charitable institutions in towns like Aix were least able to fulfill their functions. For during this period Aix's charities were paralyzed by their financial problems.

THE DECLINE OF TRADITIONAL ALMSGIVING

In 1760 Aix's two largest and most important charitable institutions, the hôtel-Dieu and the hospital-general, threatened to close their doors because of financial problems. Both charities were on the verge of bankruptcy. And one major cause of their financial difficulties was the drying up of their most important financial resource, the charitable donation. For private donations to charitable institutions declined markedly in the course of the eighteenth century.

Fig. 6.1, which shows the receipts of the annual fundraising quête of the hospital-general, La Charité, from 1706 to 1794, illustrates this process. In the first decades of the century the charity could expect to take in between 4,000 and 5,000 livres a year. But by the 1730's the typical yearly yield was only around 2,500 livres, and by the 1750's the figure had dropped to between 1,000 and 2,000 livres. In the late seventies an even more abrupt drop occurred, and by the eighties the yield was a paltry few hundred livres. The hôtel-Dieu, the only other of Aix's charities for which full accounts remain, experienced a similar decline.[11]

This suggests that fewer and fewer people made charitable donations as the century progressed. And there is other evidence to bear this out. A gift to the quête was not the only form a charitable donation might take: people

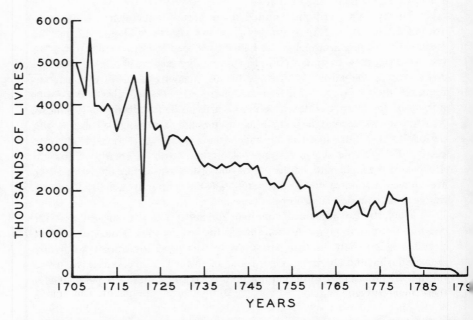

Figure 6.1. Donations, in Livres, Given in the Annual Quêtes of La Charité, 1706-90.

Source: A.D. (Aix), XXI H, II E 204, Charité, "Livre des Quêtes des mois commancé premier janvier 1706," and II E 205, "Quêtes . . . commancé 1736."

might also leave the institutions legacies in their wills. But the number of people eager to make such donations also declined markedly in the eighteenth century. In 1710, 80 percent of the wills registered in Aix included some sort of charitable donation; by 1770 the figure was 30 percent.[12]

Since charitable donations came from people in all walks of life, they are perhaps the most accurate barometer we have of truly "popular" public opinion about poverty and charity. They are at least more genuinely popular than the royal ordinances and writings of intellectuals which historians usually cite as evidence of "popular opinion" about poverty. Our evidence therefore suggests that gradually during the eighteenth century a major shift in popular attitudes toward poverty and charity occurred. What underlay this shift? Was it caused by popular dissatisfaction with some particular policies of these specific institutions? Or was it the result of something more general? Was it a reflection of a new and harsher climate of opinion toward the poor? Or was it simply a repudiation of the traditional conception of charity, with all its Christian connotations?

What evidence there is suggests that the latter is the answer. The shift in popular attitudes toward charity was tied to a major shift in what the French would call "mentalities"—specifically, the gradual spread of deChristianization in eighteenth-century France. Michel Vovelle has in *Piété baroque et déchristianisation en Provence au XVIIIe siècle* traced this process in Provence with intricate and imaginative statistics. Vovelle argues that the form which deChristianization most often took was a changing attitude toward death. In the eighteenth century death lost its terror for the average Provençal. The intense concern with the fate of the soul after death, the obsession with the perils of Purgatory and the torments of Hell characteristic of earlier religious beliefs, faded from popular consciousness. Vovelle has traced this shift through a statistical analysis of the provisions of wills through the eighteenth century. The early testaments specified elaborate funeral processions and rites; they contained careful formulations of invocation to heavenly intercessors, and careful provision for the saying of masses for the repose of the soul. But in wills from the later years of the century, especially after 1760, all this was absent. The elaborate funeral procession had almost disappeared; fewer and fewer wills invoked heavenly intercessors or asked for requiem masses. Vovelle argues that this is evidence of a major shift in popular religious mentality.

But what caused this shift Vovelle never really says. He does suggest that it was probably not due to the spread of the Enlightenment. The timing of the shift, which began, Vovelle suggests, in the years from 1710 to 1740, as well as the generally low level of literacy in Provence, argue against the influence of the Enlightenment. Vovelle implies that more likely causes can be found in the economic and social changes of the century: the economic growth and internal peace, the increased life expectancy and mobility of society. Such factors gave an increased confidence in the possibilities of life on earth.

Whatever its causes, this basic shift in popular mentalities did occur. And it is important to note that it was indeed a shift in *popular* mentalities, which affected not just an educated elite but rather all levels of society. Vovelle found the same pattern in peasant villages as in big cities, and among artisans and salaried workers as well as nobles. Indeed, nobles apparently clung to the old traditions longest; bourgeois merchants and urban artisans were the first to abandon them.

The connection between this shift in popular mentalities and the decline in charitable almsgiving should be obvious. For the major motivation for charitable giving had always been the notion that a donation to a charity could purchase salvation for the donor. With decline in popular concern over the fate of the soul after death, the charities lost their major selling point. Other factors also doubtless played a role in the popular repudiation of the charities. The financial crises of the charities probably did not endear the institutions to the townspeople of Aix, many of whom had invested their savings in charity rentes. And the worsening of the problem of poverty no doubt made the shortcomings of the traditional charities painfully obvious. But the major factor remains, I think, this change in popular religious attitudes. Whatever its cause, the decline in traditional almsgiving was financially disastrous for Aix's charities.

THE CRISIS AND ITS AFTERMATH

Important as it was, the decline in almsgiving was not the only factor which brought the charities to the brink of financial disaster after 1760. Financial mismanagement, especially an overextension of borrowing, also played a role. When the return from the annual legacies and quêtes began declining in the early years of the eighteenth century, the charities made up the deficit by borrowing funds through the selling of rentes (see Chapter III). And as the deficits continued to grow, larger and larger sums were borrowed. But this borrowing only made the financial situation of the charities worse, for they were now liable for increasing amounts of interest on their loans. In 1722 the yearly interest on their rentes sold cost the Charité 11,955 livres. By 1755 the amount had risen to 32,439 livres, an increase of 171 percent. Further, the capital of some rentes had to be reimbursed by the Charité when it could not meet the interest payments. The Charité's outlay for these, too, showed a substantial increase over the years, from 5,864 livres in 1723 to 38,298 livres in 1754, a 550-percent rise.[13] Thus the charities were caught in a vicious circle: they had to keep borrowing ever-increasing sums to pay off the interest, and principal, on money they had already borrowed.

It was thus this pyramiding of loans which led the charities to financial disaster. The rectors were not unaware of the folly of this unlimited borrowing. As long ago as 1751 there had been talk of calling a bureau-général which might legislate against the contracting of new debts. But this was not done. The constant borrowing continued unchecked until finally, in 1760, the institution could no longer meet its obligations, that is, pay the interest due on its rentes. At this point the indebtedness of the institution totalled some 824,118 livres, with an interest of 40,118 livres due each year. On January 24, 1760, the long-delayed meeting of the bureau-général was at last called to consider ways to deal with the crisis.[14] Unless the charity could raise over 50,000 livres, it was faced with the prospect of having to declare bankruptcy, default on its debts, and turn its inmates out to starve.

When they realized the seriousness of their plight, the rectors' first thought was to call for aid from these people and institutions which traditionally had "watching briefs" over the care of the poor: the royal government, the municipal government, and the archbishop. Since the fifteenth century the state and Church had duelled over who should have ultimate control over charity (see Chapter II). Although in theory the state won, the Church never surrendered its pretensions in this area. Depending on their zeal, the local archbishops could exercise a great deal of leverage over the charities, For one thing, they were important donors—for example, Archbishop Cardinal Grimaldi left at his death, in 1684, 30,000 livres to seven different charities.[15] And they could also, with a timely suggestion, influence rich laymen to favor the charities in their wills. Thus, in 1762, the Charité received a bequest of well over 40,000 livres from Dlle. Catherine Chambon, younger daughter and heir of Sieur Randolphe Chambon, seigneur of Velaux. It is recorded that Catherine made the Charité her heir "under the direction of Mgr. the Archbishop."[16] The archbishop could also influence the charities through a judicious use of his privilege of selecting priests for the institutions, and his position as arbiter in their many disputes over quêtes.[17]

The royal government, too, had many means of exercising influence over the charities. Like the archibishop, the king was an important donor. The king was "the father of the poor"; it was his duty to protect and succor his least powerful subjects. Further, it was the duty of the king to present to his subjects an example of Christian virtues—and the greatest of these was, of course, charity. Aix's hospitals benefitted from this royal largesse. Anne of Austria was "founder and chief benefactress" of the hospital La Charité of Aix. In 1643 the institution received a royal gift of ten émines or minots of salt, weighing 170 pounds each, from the greniers à sel of Marseille or

Berre.[18] Anne's generosity to the Charité was continued by her son: in 1660, when Louis XIV visited Aix to quell a rebellion against his rule, he donated to the hospital-general the proceeds from a new tax of fifteen deniers on each pack of playing cards and dice, two sous six deniers on tarot cards, and twenty sous on each pound of tobacco sold in Provence.[19]

Apart from his position as an important donor, the king could also exercise control over the charities through his right to issue letters patent, which gave the charities legal existence, and therefore the all-important right to inherit property.[20] And the royal government had other legal means to influence the charities through the "king's men" of the Parlement. The Parlement had the right to register the rules, or *Règlements*, of the charities which regulated the admission of inmates, the hours of work, and all the other details of the functioning of the institutions. The Parlement was also the court of the first instance for cases involving the charities. In judging such cases the Parlement invariably invoked the "droit des pauvres," a doctrine, surviving from the customary law of Provence, that the charities had an interest which overrode that of private individuals.[21]

One other outside body also had pretensions to influence over the charities. This was the municipality. Members of the municipal council were considered *recteurs nés* of the charities; they sat by right on the grands bureaux which supervised the institutions' finances.[22] The municipality was also a source of financial support; for example, it gave the Charité wheat during the plague of 1720, and similarly during a shortage in 1749.[23] It also allotted to the charities the *amendes de police*, small fines collected for the infraction of various town ordinances.[24]

Thus three outside agencies, the archbishop, the royal government, and the municipality, had a tradition of interest in and support for the charities. It is therefore not surprising that when the extent of the financial crisis became known, the first step of the rectors was to lay bare the situation before the royal intendant, Gaulois de la Tour, and to ask that he put pressure on the royal government to pay promptly the 4,000-livre pension due from the Cinq Grosses Fermes, the tax farm, now two years in arrears. The Charité's previous pleas to the government had been unavailing. But a series of letters from de la Tour to Trudaine, the controller-general, explaining the situation and threatening that, if the Charité went bankrupt, its inmates would be turned out to starve and to terrorize the province, elicited at least partial payment.[25]

Meanwhile the rectors also turned to that other traditional "father of the poor," the archbishop of Aix. When informed of the problem, the prelate, "whose attentions and gifts knew no bounds," offered to donate the sum of two hundred louis d'or (4,800 livres) to help the Charité meet its current expenses. This gift also stimulated further largesse. For not to be outdone by its traditional clerical rival for control of charitable relief, the municipal council voted to match the archbishop's gift, and to add a donation of 90 charges of wheat besides.[26] But these and other gifts, totalling some 16,000 livres, were sufficient only to cover operating expenses and thus allow the stricken institution to keep its doors open. The Charité still had no money to make the 40,118-livre payment due on its rentes. Only by selling some of its assets could the Charité raise that much ready money. The institution therefore began to cash in some of its own rentes. In theory and law such a course was impossible; once a rente was purchased the capital was permanently lost to the buyer. This was especially true of the best-known "blue chip" rentes, those on the Hôtel de Ville of Paris and the Clergé de France, for example. Nevertheless, exceptions might be made even by these august institutions when the need of the rente-holder was truly great. But redeeming a rente was far from an ideal solution to the crisis. Legally a rente could be redeemed only for less than its face value.[27] Further, once a rente was reimbursed, it was lost to the institution as a source of income for the future. In the long run such a policy could bring only disaster. But in the short run such actions allowed the rectors to offer to pay at least a part of their obligations: in 1760 they paid about 18,000 of the 40,000 livres due.[28]

This course did not satisfy all the Charité's creditors. Most feared that further alienations of capital by the Charité would destroy any prospect of future income. Therefore many banded together and consulted two prominent avocats, who obtained from the Parlement in November 1760 an *acte interpellatif*, or injunction, against any more such actions. The lawyers based their argument on the fact that under French law a bankrupt could not sell or in any way alienate his assets, since in reality they no longer belonged to him, but rather to his creditors. Since the Charité was known to be bankrupt, its rectors were forbidden to cash in any more rentes.[29]

The Charité's creditors also demanded that a delegation of 12 of their number be allowed to examine the institution's books and records. This examination took place on November 24, 1760. The examiners found many irregularities. Some were relatively minor; for example, failure of the recteur semainière and the secretary to sign the minutes of the bureau, and omission of the annual inventory of linen belonging to the institution. The other charges, however, were more serious. The rectors were accused of making themselves perpetual, in direct violation of the *Règlements,* which limited their service to three years. Further, it was alleged that some rectors may have profited from the purchases of wheat and other supplies, receiving kickbacks from suppliers. The rectors were also charged with deliberately bypassing the bureau-général, supposedly the watchdog of the institution's financial affairs. The creditors noted that bureaux-généraux had been held only three times in the last 40 years, although the Charité's regulations stipulated annual meetings. Finally, the creditors complained of the alienations of rentes, which, again according to the regulations, could be undertaken only with the permission of the bureau-général. Such flagrant violations of the *Règlements,* the creditors argued, constituted mismanagement; they stated the rectors could be held personally liable. The creditors admitted that the *Règlements* exempted the rectors from personal liability for the debts of the institution, but argued that the failure of the rectors to fulfill their duties properly cancelled such immunity. The rectors, they added, were the "tutors of the poor and were, like the tutors of minors, responsible to the law for the manner in which they administered the property of their charges."[30]

In their arguments the creditors revealed a thoroughly hardheaded approach. For them a charity rente was an investment like any other. They expected the charities to conduct their financial affairs according to the same rules and with the same standard of efficiency as other businesses. As they noted, if a private merchant had acted as they had done, he would have been considered not only "bankrupt" but "fraudulent." If laws governing bankruptcy could not be bent for the "merchants, for whom life is a continual round of vicissitudes," still less could they give way for institutions such as charities. The creditors were completely unsympathetic to arguments that the charities were a special case, in which leniency was necessary because of hardships which might be created for the poor. "It is certain," they stated, "that it has never been permitted that the directors of the hôpital de la Charité nourish the poor at the expense of the creditors."

The poor must live off of the donations of the faithful, and these donations must be voluntary. The father of the poor, the Almighty, rejects involuntary sacrifice. Justice (and not charity) is the first of all virtues.[31]

The creditors cited the case of the hospital for enfants trouvés in Paris, which was forced to close in 1709 for lack of funds. The infants cared for in the institution were put out on the street to die. Such action was unfortunate, but it was also necessary: "it is never permitted to increase the number of the poor (by robbing the creditors of their due), in order to ease the misery of those already in such a state."[32] Such hardheadedness, such "businesslike" attitudes, seem to show a great change from the days when profitmaking was scorned as sordid and unChristian. This new hardheadedness, when accompanied by the acceptance of mercantile values and, further, the sympathetic portrayal of the problems of the merchant which the memorandum of the Charité's creditors shows, seems to indicate a triumph of values which might be termed "bourgeois." This is in one sense a misnomer, for those who held these attitudes, the rentiers of the Charité, were not primarily people whom we would today classify as bourgeois, that is, businessmen and professional people. They were not even in a majority those who were bourgeois by their own, eighteenth-century definition. Rather they came from all social classes, from the noble to the servant, and most were from the menu peuple (see Chapter III). Does this indicate a diffusion of "bourgeois" values throughout much of society? Perhaps what the mémoire of the creditors indicates is less a diffusion of bourgeois values than simply a changing attitude toward charity, a loss of sympathy for the poor, part and parcel with the decline in charitable donations. With this mémoire we are obviously far from the days of the late seventeenth century, when all the people of Aix rallied to aid the grand enfermement (see Chapter II).

In any event, the creditors' threatened suit aroused the rectors to take positive steps to settle the crisis. In a meeting of the bureau-général on December 14, 1760, the policy of alienation of rentes was abandoned. Instead a comprehensive program designed to put the finances of the institution back on an even keel was adopted. In its final version the program was given a royal patent in May 1762. Under this program, the first step was the splitting of the Charité's reserves into two separate parts, the *caisse des créanciers* and the *caisse des pauvres*. It was hoped that the poor could "live off their own." Only the donations of the pious, and the proceeds from the labor of the inmates, went into the caisse des pauvres, from which the internal administrative expenses of the charity were paid. The receipts from the rentes held by the institution, as well as the funds from royal donations, went straight into the caisse des créanciers, and were to be used solely to pay off the Charité's creditors. Thus money to cover the Charité's debts was guaranteed. Those creditors holding rentes viagères were to be paid, but at reduced rates of interest. Rentes with interest at ten percent were reduced to seven percent; those at nine to six and one-half. When a holder of a rente viagère died the principal from his rente was to be divided among the remaining rente-holders, at the rate of one sou for every livre. The rentes perpetuelles (and most of the Charité's rentes took this form) were, by contrast, to be paid their full interest. If, however, the holder wished his capital refunded, he would receive only two-thirds of its original value. This plan was formulated with the help of the royal government, which was prepared to donate 30,000 livres a year in each of the next three years, 1762, 1763, and 1764.[33]

It was doubtless too much to hope that such unprecedented royal largesse would come with no strings attached. And in that era of royal initiative in the field of public assistance the price the royal government exacted for its aid was increased control over the administration of the Charité. Its instrument for the accomplishment of this end was the Commission Générale des Hôpitaux, created by royal letters patent in September 1761, to oversee the functioning of all hospitals and oeuvres de charité in Provence. This commission was composed of the intendant, two présidents and six conseillers of the Parlement, plus the former avocat-général and present procureur-général.[34] Its duty was to oversee the financial administration of the charities, to prevent recurrence of those financial expedients which had brought the charities to their present crises. A charity had to have the approval of this commission before it could alienate any of its property worth over 500 livres. The commission also had to approve any borrowing undertaken by a charity, and a limit of 30,000 livres per year was set for such financial initiatives. The commission also was required to inspect the charities' accounts each year, and it had a veto over any settlement between the charities and their creditors. Thus agents of the royal government could exercise almost complete control over the finances of the charities.

Such an increase in royal power in the field of charitable endeavor did not go unchallenged by others with similar pretensions. The archbishop, especially, was incensed by the creation of the commission, since by tradition he had the right to oversee the financial affairs of the hospitals within his diocese. In April 1765, we find the mayor and consuls of Aix informing the royal government that the archbishop had recently given an ultimatum: either the commission be abolished or he would stop his yearly gift of 4,800 livres, which formed an important financial resource for the Charité.[35] The intendant, De La Tour, joined the municipal government in pleading that the commission be abolished, arguing that "utilité publique" should take precedence over a concern for royal prerogative.[36] But the royal government was reluctant to surrender its initiative. It proposed a compromise solution, by which the commission would continue as before, but with the Charité no longer subject to its control.[37] Apparently it was not necessary to put this into effect, for the archbishop was somehow persuaded to back down. At any rate, the records of the Charité reveal that the commission continued to oversee its financial affairs throughout the 1760's and 1770's.[38]

Under the supervision of the commission, the Charité slowly but steadily climbed from the depths of near bankruptcy. Careful supervision of the caisse des pauvres, the budget for internal administration, gradually lessened the threat that the institution would be forced to turn its inmates out on the streets to die. The budget was balanced, however, only by the most stringent economies, which often entailed very real hardships for the poor. Given the propensity of the rectors for "good and holy economy" in internal administration, there was little slack which could be taken up in this area (see Chapter III). Some of the economies were relatively harmless. For example, the profitability of the various fabriques was investigated carefully, and those not sufficiently lucrative, the wool-spinning and wool-carding, were dismantled.[39] But the main burden of the economy drive was borne by the poor. When resources seemed insufficient, the Charité simply suspended admissions. On July 4, 1767, the Charité deliberated that:

since the hard times has caused daily increasing numbers of the poor to present themselves for reception in this hospital, and since the excessive cost of supplies causes expenses to increase, . . . it does not seem possible to furnish subsistence even for the poor who are actually in the institution, let alone those who have presented themselves. . . . Therefore it is agreed to suspend all reception until the beginning of next winter, with the exception of children deprived of both parents.[40]

Thus just when "hard times" struck and conditions were most difficult for the poor, their one resource, the Charité, was taken from them. Further suspensions of admissions were noted in November 1767, May 1768, June 1769, May 1770, June 1771, May 1779, and October and November 1779.[41] This meant that new admissions, which had averaged 50 per year in the ten years before the financial crisis, fell to approximately 20.[42] And the total number of poor cared for in the institution, which had run as high as 800 in the last years of the seventeenth century, dwindled from an average of 350 in the 1740's and 1750's, to a low, after the financial crisis, of 106, in 1780.[43] The Charité was not alone in limiting admission; most other institutions of public assistance, similarly suffering from financial difficulties, did likewise. This grave setback in the amount of aid available occurred, it should be remembered, in a period of rising bread prices, and must have caused untold hardships for the poor.

Such economy measures enabled the Charité to hold the line on internal expenditures. The institution was for the most part similarly successful in meeting its obligations to its creditors. Problems, of course, occasionally arose. The royal government was, as usual, slow in paying its promised 90,000 livres.[44] Occasionally the creditors' demands for reimbursement of their capital outran the resources available.[45] But by and large the process of liquidating the gigantic load of debt went steadily onwards. By 1766 the Charité reported that it had reimbursed a total of 172,357 livres, 13 sous, 4 deniers worth of rentes, saving the institution some 2,596 livres in interest payments each year. A further 4,806 livres of rentes viagères were extinguished when their owners died.[46] In 1765 the yearly payments made by the caisse des créanciers totalled 56,206 livres; with the policy of extinction of rentes by 1777 this figure was reduced to 13,038 livres.[47] In their policy of debt liquidation, the rectors of the Charité were apparently concerned to keep the sufferings of their creditors to a minimum. As has been noted, a majority of those who owned rentes on the Charité were of the class of menu peuple, who invested in the rentes their life savings, and could ill afford any loss or delay in payment. Such people had the first call on the Charité's resources, and creditors like Catherine Sauvanne, widow of Jean Tornon, a domestique, who had "grave need" of her 400-livre rente, and the garçon cordonnier and his wife who needed a capital sum for the dowry of their daughter, were reimbursed before all other creditors.[48]

During the 1770's the Charité's plan for the gradual liquidation of its debts seemed to be working well. By 1778 the rectors were reporting a surplus in the caisse des créanciers of over 4,000 livres.[49] But as long as any debt remained, a sudden heavy call for reimbursement could upset the budget's still delicate balance. Further, as the gifts and alms of the faithful steadily decreased, it was becoming increasingly difficult to cover internal expenses with the resources available to the caisse des pauvres. For these reasons the rectors of the Charité thought it advisable to seek a final settlement of their debt. In 1780 they proposed to the royal government a plan whereby all their remaining rentes would be liquidated at 50 percent of their face value. Payment to the creditors would be made either in cash or in the Charité's own rentes on the Clergé de France and other institutions. After some hesitation on the part of the government, due to Necker's concern at this point for the rights of creditors, the plan was finally adopted in July 1780.[50] Thus ended the 20 years of financial crisis at the Charité.

The story of these years of crisis at the Charité is important for the historian, less perhaps for its own sake than as an example of what was happening in countless other hospitals throughout France. For the financial difficulties of the Charité were not unique. In these same years three other charities in Aix alone, the hôtel-Dieu, the Miséricorde, and the Insensés, are known to have experienced similar problems.[51] It is probable that other of the town's charities felt the pinch as well, although lack of their records makes it impossible to state this with any certainty. Nor were such financial difficulties peculiar to the charities of Aix. By 1764 the hôtel-Dieu of Marseille was running an annual deficit of 240,049 livres. And innumerable charities in the smaller towns of Provence, like Brignolles, Apt, and Draguignan, were faced with the threat of bankruptcy. The Charité of Lyon had to borrow two million livres in the money market of Genoa to pay off its debts. And financial problems troubled hospitals in Burgundy, Normandy, Brittany, in fact throughout France.[52] The years from approximately 1760 to 1789 were a period of crisis for all the traditional municipal charities of the kingdom.

These years of crises destroyed the traditional charities of France. Not literally, of course, at least in most cases; the vast majority of institutions were, like the Charité of Aix, able to avoid outright bankruptcy and lingered on in a crippled state until they were dealt their final death blow by the Revolution. But these years saw the destruction of the traditional municipal charity as a viable institution. The spreading religious indifference had cost them both their public support and their raison d'être. After 1760 a new spirit reigned in the institutions. Rectors from the old robe families which had long dominated the charities left their administrative boards (see Chapter III); the new men who came in were, if the tone of the minutes of their meetings is any indication, more interested in the financial state of the institution than the welfare of the poor.[53] But this change in spirit of their ruling boards did not really matter, for after 1760 the charities, for all practical purposes, ceased to exist as independent institutions. Most charities survived their financial crisis only by calling on outside institutions—the local bishop or archbishop, the municipality, even the royal government—for help. And these agencies took advantage of the weakness of the charities to reassert their traditional pretensions to control over public assistance.

What happened at the Charité of Aix illustrates this process. The institution stayed afloat only by means of subventions from these three agencies: the yearly 4,800-livre gift from both the archbishop and the municipality, and the generous if tardy 90,000-livre grant from the state. But the charities gained these gifts only at the cost of losing their traditional autonomy. After 1760 both the archbishop and the municipality constantly interfered in the internal administration of the Charité. In November 1762, for example, we find the rectors of the Charité accepting, on the suggestion of the archbishop, two children of an epileptic. In the next month, when an experienced rector wanted to quit his post, the archbishop was the one called in to talk him out of this. And the next year, when it was decided to do away with the fabrique de Cadiz, a special deputation was sent to the archbishop to explain the move. Similarly, in May 1768, the Charité accepted two children sent to them by the municipality, although ordinarily they would not have been admitted since their mother was still alive.[54] The incident which perhaps best epitomizes the charities' loss of autonomy occurred in 1783, when the Miséricorde turned to the municipality for help in its hour of crisis. The town government made its help conditional upon the surrender of the charity's books. The Miséricorde, mindful of protecting the identities of those it aided, refused, but only at the cost of forfeiting possible aid.[55]

In the contest for control over the charities which arose in the aftermath of the financial crises, the real victor was not the municipality or the archbishop, however, but the royal government. Through the instrument of its Commission Générale des Paurvres, the central government gained almost complete control of the financial administration of the charities. This provided support for the government's contention, which gained currency in these years, that the property owned by the charities was in reality a "patrimony of the nation" to be administered by the government in a way to best provide for the public good. The creation of the Commission Générale was thus a foreshadowing of the nationalization of hospital properties first attempted under Necker in 1780 and finally brought to completion during the Revolution.[56]

This assertion of control by the royal government was a significant straw in the wind. Traditional, religiously motivated charity had in the years after 1760 been revealed as both ineffective and intellectually bankrupt. What should take its place? Enlightened public opinion turned increasingly toward the notion of a national, secular, state-supported system of public assistance.

CHAPTER VII

From Charité
to Bienfaisance

In France the period from 1760 to 1789 marked the first hesitant steps toward the birth of a modern, secular, state-supported system of public assistance for the poor. The years of financial crisis had revealed the inadequacies of traditional charity, while the shift in mentalities connected with the spread of religious indifference had robbed the problem of poverty of its religious overtones. The way was open for a new departure. And this was supplied by the thinkers of the Enlightenment. They insisted that the care of the poor was the duty, not of the Church, nor of private individuals, but rather of the state. Thoroughly secularized, they viewed poverty in an economic rather than a religious context. They were concerned not with the saving of souls, either their own or those of the poor, but with putting the idle to work for the greater prosperity of the community as a whole. Because it was a matter so important to the public good, the assistance of the poor could not be safely left to local private initiative. Instead, state action was necessary. Such convictions prompted new government programs in the field of poor relief, for example the *dépôts de mendicité*, and Turgot's *ateliers de charité*. These programs were the precursors of the statewide system of public assistance put into effect by the Revolution.

In this period of transition the change from *charité* to *bienfaisance* was not clearcut. The traditional charities did, after all, linger on, and the new governmental initiatives were, in Provence at least, largely failures. Nonetheless the climate of opinion was definitely shifting, and shifting in favor of a national program of public assistance. For the first time in over a hundred years, since the formation of the traditional system of charity during the Counter-Reformation, assistance to the poor became a matter of public debate. In Provence homegrown philosophes produced innumerable plans to spread bienfaisance to the unfortunate. And all of these plans shared two characteristics: they viewed poverty as an economic, not religious, problem, and they favored some sort of state-financed aid to the poor. It is this development of a program of national public assistance for the poor, on the levels of both theory and practice, which forms the subject of this chapter.

ROYAL INITIATIVES IN PUBLIC ASSISTANCE

By the 1760's, the decade of financial crisis for the hospitals, the old-fashioned municipal charity had already been dismissed as a method of dealing with the problem of poverty by most enlightened opinion. Of the earlier philosophes, both Montesquieu and Voltaire had attacked the traditional charitable foundation as doing the poor more harm than good. The availability of alms, they charged, simply encouraged idleness. Both noted that the countries like Spain and Italy, where traditional religious charities flourished, had the most widespread poverty and most wretched poor in all of Europe.[1] Perhaps the most telling of these early Enlightenment attacks on the traditional charitable foundation is to be found enshrined in that compendium of enlightened attitudes, the *Encyclopédie*. The article "Fondations," written by Turgot, charged that traditional types of charities most usually had an effect opposite to that intended by their founders; that is, instead of lessening the suffering of the poor, they increased it. "Often," the article stated, "private persons give aid against an evil whose cause is general; and sometimes this remedy that, it is hoped, will eradicate the effect, instead increases the influence of the cause." This was especially true of charitable institutions:

The poor man has certain incontestable rights to the abundance of the rich; humanity and religion equally enjoin on us the duty of aiding our fellows in difficulties; it is to accomplish these indispensable duties that so many charitable establishments have been founded in the Christian world, to meet all sorts of needs; that numberless poor are brought together in hospitals. ... What is the result? It is precisely in those countries where charitable resources are most abundant, as in Spain and in some parts of Italy, that misery is more common and more general than elsewhere. The reason is simple. To allow a large number of men to live gratuitously is to underwrite laziness and all the disorders which are its consquences; it is to render the condition of the faineant preferable to that of the man who works. As a result it diminishes for the state the total of work and production from the soil ... from this come frequent famines, the increase of misery, and the depopulation which is its consequence. The caste of industrious citizens is replaced by a vile population, composed of vagabond beggars and delivered to all sorts of crimes ... from which results a void in work and the riches of the state, an increase in the weight of public taxes on the head of the industrious man, and all the disorders that we notice in the present consititution of society.[2]

These early attacks on charitable foundations were strictly destructive in character. While critical of the traditional methods of relieving poverty, they offered only the vaguest suggestions for possible alternatives. This situation changed with the rise of the Physiocratic school in the 1760's. The Physiocrats were not only the first to offer a coherent program for the relief of poverty, but also, because of their influence in government circles in the early 1760's, they were also the first to be in a position to put their program into effect.[3] Inventors of a general model of how an economy functions, the Physiocrats viewed the problem of poverty in a strictly economic context, shorn of the religious concern for the spiritual welfare of the poor which had prompted earlier efforts at public assistance. Interested primarily in increasing the wealth of France through increasing productivity, the Physiocrats wished to eliminate poverty because the poor were unproductive—they were a drain on the country's resources. Since they thought agriculture the source of all wealth, the Physiocrats based their hopes for the eradication of poverty on measures to increase agricultural production: enclosures, tax reform, freedom of the grain trade. In time such measures would increase the prosperity of France as a whole. Meanwhile, the poor had to be helped, but only by means which would encourage their productivity.

Under the physiocratic influence the ministry of Controller-General Bertin in the early 1760's adopted a four-point program for the relief of poverty.[4] The able-bodied poor who were willing to work were to be employed in ateliers de charité. The wilfully idle, the beggars and vagabonds, were to be swept from the roads and confined in galleys and dépôts de mendicité, where they too would be put to work. Those of the poor who were genuinely unable to work because of age or illness were to be helped, but not at the old-fashioned, unhealthy, and expensive hospitals. Instead, they were to receive aid at home, a so-called secours à domicile. As a final measure, the program of public assistance in rural areas was to be greatly expanded, for the Physiocrats, with their concern for agriculture, were mindful that rural poverty was the true cancer eating at the vitals of the French state. Enactment of this program would create a system of government-controlled public assistance which would completely bypass the traditional municipal charities.

Dogged by opposition to its attempt to introduce free commerce in grains, Bertin's ministry fell before its war against poverty could be put into effect. Perhaps unsurprisingly, the part of Bertin's program which survived unscathed into the succeeding ministry of de l'Averdy was the least innovative and controversial: the attempt to suppress beggary through the establishment of the dépôts de mendicité.[5] Such a program had potentially wide support, for the problem of beggary was becoming increasingly grave in the 1760's. The new pace of the population increase, plus the dislocations caused by the Seven Years' War, brought great bands of beggars on to the roads, to harass travelers and pillage and burn isolated farms. The situation was especially grave in the prosperous wheat-growing *pays de grande culture* of northern France.[6] In the face of this situation the royal government acted, passing the Ordinance of August 3, 1764, proposing new and harsher punishments—

confinement in the galleys rather than banishment—for able-bodied male beggars, and setting up a system of dépôts de mendicité to house those who because of age, illness, or sex could not be sent to the floating prisons.[7] The idea of the dépôts de mendicité for the confinement of beggars was not new: it had been tried, with only modest success, from 1724 to 1733 (see Chapter V). But the new program differed in one significant way from its predecessor: in the earlier period the already existing charities had been used as dépôts; the dépôts of the 1760's were to be totally new creations, directly under the control of the royal government. For this program for the suppression of beggary was to be the first step of a nationwide system of public assistance.

But in Provence at least this innovative program met with nothing but opposition and ultimate failure. From its outset the program was harshly criticized by the most responsible opinion in the province, including even the royal intendant himself. The intendant, Gaulois de la Tour, was first informed of the program in a letter from the controller-general, Bertin, written in April of 1763. In his reply de la Tour took the position which he was to hold throughout the ensuing battles over the program: he did not attack the new ordinance itself, rather he simply maintained that it was unsuitable for Provence. De la Tour admitted that "there are in Provence as in all the rest of the kingdom a large enough number of beggars," but he denied that they presented such a threat as the new legislation seemed to imply. "They (the beggars)," de la Tour noted, "have not formed bands, and there have not been any complaints against them."[8] The already existing charities were, he implied, perfectly adequate to handle the problem.

Other criticisms of the new government policy were not so mild. For example, an anonymous mémoire, most probably written by one of de la Tour's subdélégués, contained harsh attacks on the Declaration of August 3, 1764, and on the Résultat sur la Mendicité, the pamphlet in which the government described and justified its new program. The first point of criticism was the problem of expense. The commentary noted that the previous royal efforts to control beggary had cost the province some 1,100,000 livres and brought financial ruin to its hospitals-general—all to no avail. Further, the writer criticized the underlying presupposition of the ordinance that those who begged did so not from necessity but choice. "The Résultat appears to take for its maxim that work is never lacking." This was simply not true. There were occasions when beggary was involuntary: "it is caused by the lack of work, by the illness of some member of the family, by a too large number of children, by bad weather or hard times or unforeseen accidents." Rather than punish the beggar, the state should try to find him work. For example, the commentator suggested the establishment of cotton-spinning workshops.[9]

Criticism of the new legislation was not confined to the official circle of the intendant. This can be seen in the wide varieties of opinions on the new legislation offered, in answer to a royal request, by the bishops of the various dioceses of Provence.[10] None of the eight bishops whose replies have been preserved favored the new legislation. Many, including the archbishop of Aix, criticized its probable cost, citing the financial disasters brought upon the hospitals by the earlier royal legislation. The bishop of Fréjus even recalled his own experiences with the earlier programs in Tours in the 1720's. Most of the bishops felt it their duty to suggest alternatives preferable to the new legislation. Some of these were fairly crackbrained: the bishop of Fréjus, for example, had a plan to train child beggars as cabin boys. But others were more useful and showed a greater understanding of the problems of poverty than did the royal legislation. The bishop of Glandèves, a mountainous area in Haute Provence, where an estimated one-fourth to one-third of the population turned to beggary to stay alive, pointed out the main cause of the region's distress was rural underemployment, especially in the winter months. He suggested that teaching the peasants an alternative trade, for example, wool-carding, which they could practice in the winter, would be of more practical benefit then new punitive legislation against beggary. Similarly, the bishop of Riez, who realized that a major cause of poverty in the French countryside was the fact that once he paid his taxes and seigneurial dues, the peasant often did not have enough to live on, let alone plant for the next harvest, suggested the establishment of a loan bank from which the peasants could borrow grain as needed.[11]

The royal government called on lay as well as clerical opinion, and found it was also unfavorable toward the new royal initiatives in the area of public assistance. The procureurs du pays of Provence, for example, criticized the new legislation and suggested a simple method for curing poverty: dun the Church for the vast wealth which was in theory "the patrimony of the poor."[12] Different as this opinion of the procureurs was from that of the bishops, they both had one thing in common: opposition to the new royal legislation.

Given this apparently universal opposition, it is little wonder that the royal government's attempt to set up a system of dépôts in Provence met with delaying tactics and sabotage at every turn. Provence was well placed to resist the royal program, for it was a pays d'état, and thus had a series of intermediary bodies—a provincial estates and a Parlement—which could effectively block the enforcement of the royal will. These, combined with the fact that the royal intendant himself, who combined his office with that of premier président of the Parlement of Provence, sympathized with the objections of the provincial leaders, allowed the province to wage a successful fight against the new royal legislation.

The first step in the battle was the Parlement's refusal to register the royal edict. The parlementaires gave in only when it was pointed out to them that if Provence was the sole province in which the edict was not enforced, it would be flooded with beggars from all other areas of France, seeking a safe refuge.[13] But although the edict became law in Provence, it was still not enforceable. When the royal administration attempted to set up the dépôts—six were planned for Provence—it ran into innumerable snags and delays, as town after town balked at receiving a dépôt, and site after site was rejected as unsuitable by the intendant.[14]

But the major confrontation between royal and provincial administrations occurred over the delicate problem of how the dépôts were to be financed.[15] In the pays d'élection funds to support the dépôts came from a three denier per livre supplement to the taille. But in the pays d'état like Provence the government could not levy such direct taxation; instead, subventions for the dépôts had to be voted by the provincial estates. After prolonged bargaining, the government eventually pried the necessary funds from the estates of the other pays d'état, Burgundy, Languedoc, and Brittany. But the estates of Provence proved recalcitrant. They argued, with reason, that they had already in effect paid for the dépôts. The argument they put forth was complex, far too much so to be described in detail here.[16] Suffice it to say that the basis of their claim was a fund of some 1,446,109 livres still owed to the province by the royal government for a suppression of various municipal offices back in 1724. Instead of paying the sum owed, the central administration had promised to use it to support the hospitals of Provence. As might be expected, this had not been done. The provincial estates argued that as long as this sum remained in the hands of the royal government, Provence had in effect paid for the dépôts in advance. Apparently the royal government realized the justice of this claim and let the matter drop, for there is no evidence that the provincial estates ever voted necessary sums for the support of the dépôts.[17]

Despite all the efforts of their opponents, dépôts de mendicité functioned in Provence from 1767 to 1776. In 1773, for example, 2,631 people were arrested for beggary, of whom 2,025 were condemned to the dépôts.[18] Unfortunately, no information has been preserved about what sort of people they were and what circumstances forced them to beggary. The only inmates who left traces on the records were ne'erdowells like Nicolas Mellon, runaway son of a bourgeois, whose families made efforts to free them.[19]

From the bits of evidence remaining, the dépôts de mendicité of Provence appear to have been far from ideal advertisements for the efficiency of the royal administration in matters of public assistance. The dépôts were badly organized and administered. The building used for the dépôt in Aix, for example, was singularly ill-suited for that purpose. It was by far "too small" and its site was unhealthy.[20] Overcrowded conditions led to dangerous epidemics:

The mendicants who are imprisoned in the Lazare are lodged crowded together in very small rooms, sleeping on the floor on piles of straw; in these small rooms there are sometimes 25 to 30 people. The wooden trench which serves as a latrine, and the fetid odor it exhales, joined to the unwashed state of these unfortunates, and to the bad food which is given them, make the place thoroughly unhealthy . . . the inmates suffer from intermittent fevers, putrid fevers, and malignant fevers.[21]

When the inmates were brought to the hospital they infected the whole town with their diseases. And in addition to all these faults, the dépôt did not even efficiently perform its function of confining the beggars. For as the intendant reported:

the building serving as a dépôt de mendicité in Aix is in such a bad state that it cannot confine the beggars, and this allows frequent escapes. . . . The walls and floors are so weak that the prisoners don't need tools to breach them.

Twenty-one beggars escaped one night, and 12 the next.[22]

With such conditions, it is only to be expected that opposition to the dépôts continued unabated in Provence throughout their existence. But the abolition of the dépôts in 1776 was the result not of this opposition but of a change of personnel in the royal administration. Their abolition was a part of the sweeping reforms enacted by Turgot during his brief period in power. A convinced Physiocrat, deeply concerned with increasing productivity, Turgot believed that his ateliers de charité were a far more useful solution to the problem of poverty than the inefficient and ill-administered dépôts.[23] Turgot therefore ordered the dépôts dismantled early in 1776. But soon after issuing this order, Turgot fell from power. His successors, Senac de Meilhan, and later Necker, attempted to re-establish the dépôts. They were successful elsewhere in France, but not in Provence. There the opponents of the dépôts trotted out all of their previous arguments.[24] The intendant once again stated that the dépôts were unnecessary:

as far as Provence is concerned the suppression of the dépôts had not occasioned the least inconvenience. There have been no *attroupements*; one does not hear of more thefts or assassinations than in all other circumstances and there reigns throughout Provence the greatest tranquility.[25]

The provincial estates, for its part, prepared to do battle over finances once more.[26] Faced with this opposition, the royal government did not press the issue, and the dépôts were never re-established.[27] And /apparently the royal government, fearing similar opposition, did not even try to found any ateliers de charité in Provence, although this program was quite successful elsewhere in France.[28]

The history of the dépôts de mendicité in Provence is a striking illustration of the difficulties surrounding any attempt to establish a nationwide system of state-controlled and financed public assistance under the Old Regime. So long as France's administrative structure remained unreformed, so long as intermediary bodies like the parlements and the provincial estates continued to exist, local opposition like that which grew up in Provence over the issue of the dépôts could block new governmental initiatives. Only with the Revolution, which swept away these barriers to the powers of the central-izing state, could an effective system of national bienfaisance be established.

Until the Revolution royal reforms could be successfully opposed, as the dépôts were in Provence, on the issue of particularism. Enlightened public opinion in Provence saw the issue of the dépôts as a challenge to provincial prerogatives. But this did not mean that Provençal opinion was opposed to the principle of state responsibility for public assistance per se, or that it clung to traditional Christian charité as the ideal solution to the problem of poverty. For Provence in the latter years of the ancien régime produced a spate of books and pamphlets which challenged traditional assumptions about poverty and sought new solutions for its cure.

PROVENÇAL ATTITUDES TOWARD POVERTY AND PUBLIC ASSISTANCE ON THE EVE OF THE REVOLUTION

First and most famous of Provence's homegrown philosophes who wrote about the problems of poverty was the elder Marquis de Mirabeau, "L'Ami des hommes" and a founding father of Physiocracy. Lauder of agriculture as the ultimate source of all wealth, inventor of the famous slogan, "L'impôt unique sur le produit net," Mirabeau exemplified the tendency, increasing with the spread of secularization and Enlightenment in the latter years of the ancien régime, to view the problem of poverty in an economic rather than a religious and moral context. In his *L'Ami des Hommes, ou traité de la population,* published from 1756 to 1760, Mirabeau dismissed the notion, central to traditional charitable institutions like the hospitals-general, that the poor were poor because of their own laziness. There was no such thing as "oisiveté," Mirabeau declared; "in a word, generally speaking, laziness and misery exist only because they are forced on an industrious people."[29] The true cause of poverty was economic: the roots of France's misery lay in its inefficient and overburdened agriculture. Mirabeau understood as did few others in that era the true nature of the French peasant: his deep devotion to his land, his willingness to endure backbreaking toil to obtain it. The French peasant was not poor because he was lazy, rather his laziness was the result of the hopelessness of his overburdened condition. "Misery brings in its train only discouragement, . . . and discouragement, laziness." The peasant would always work hard in his own interest.[30]

Therefore the solution to the problem of poverty lay in the encourage-ment of the peasant proprietor and in the removal of the burdens which held back the development of French agriculture. This was a purely economic solution to a purely economic problem. In aiding the poor, the traditional charities were worse than useless. "In general, hospitals increase poverty instead of lessening it, and torment rather than aid humanity." Hospitals merely wasted their vast endowments, which could be put to much better use. Mirabeau gives an example of what was for him the ideal evolution of a hospital. He describes a small rural hospital, with four beds for the care of the sick, which stood empty and decaying because its small endowment was not adequate to keep it going. An energetic curé converted the endowment to dowries for the peasant girls, and to a sort of loan bank from which the peasants could draw grain in years of meagre harvest.[31] Such an organization, Mirabeau stated, was infinitely more useful to the poor than the traditional charitable hospital, for "enlightened charity looks less to aiding the poor than to preventing poverty."[32] As a means to this end Mirabeau advocated a system of such loan banks, financed not by private charity but by the government.[33]

Mirabeau's proposal for rural loan banks points up one of the most important changes in attitudes toward poverty and public assistance which took place in this era: the shift in focus from urban to rural poverty. The traditional charities, like those of Aix, had been above all *municipal* institutions, financed by the people of a town and serving, in theory at least, only the local poor. The urban orientation of such institutions is revealed in their training programs for the poor: they trained the children in their care in a métier, so that they could become urban artisans. But in reality the greatest misery in France lay in the countryside; even in large towns like Aix the majority of the poor were rural travailleurs. By the 1760's, men like Mirabeau were beginning to realize this, and to emphasize the need for rural organizations of public assistance. Indeed, Mirabeau perhaps disliked the traditional hospital precisely because it was a municipal organization. For Mirabeau, convinced of the superiority of agriculture over all other forms of wealth, towns were mere economic excrescences, sources of luxury which spread their terrible corruption into the countryside.[34]

Concomitant with this shift in focus from urban to rural poverty was a new emphasis on a hitherto neglected problem: that of the foundling child, or "enfant trouvé." In the seventeenth century writers on charity in Aix barely mentioned the care of foundlings, for they were much more interested in the problems posed by the adult beggar. But a number of factors combined to make this an important issue in the years before the French Revolution. For one thing, the problem increasingly obtruded on public attention, as rates of illegitimacy and abandonment rose to staggering proportions.[35] Another factor was doubtless an increasing interest in the state of childhood, and a new Rousseauist sentimentality over these most unfortunate of children. But for

Mirabeau interest in the problem of the enfant trouvé was connected with his concern for the future of French agriculture. Mirabeau was convinced that the number of cultivators of the soil was declining, as the towns drew more and more people from the countryside. An obvious replacement for these arms lost to agriculture were the enfants trouvés. Mirabeau objected to the traditional religious charities' treatment of the mother of an illegitimate child as a vessel of sin; rather, she should be honored for contributing to the growth of the population. Similarly, Mirabeau deplored the traditional practice of raising foundlings as urban artisans. Instead the state should take over their education, and train them as cultivators of the soil.[36]

Mirabeau's themes, his view of poverty as an economic rather than a religious problem, his criticism of traditional charitable institutions, his emphasis on rural rather than urban misery, and his concern for the problem posed by the enfant trouvé, were repeated endlessly by the Provençal philosophes who wrote about poverty and public assistance in the years before the Revolution. Typical was M. Achard, a médecin from Marseille, who filled his work, ostensibly a "Description Historique, Geographique et Topographique des Villes, Bourgs, Villages et Hameaux de la Provence Ancienne et Moderne," with asides on the proper form of public assistance.[37] In his description of Aix's hospitals he included a scathing commentary on their financial crises, and he suggested that, for greater efficiency and economy, many of the smaller hospitals be united—a reform brought about by the Revolution. Achard also devoted some 21 pages to the problem of the enfant trouvé, advocating, like Mirabeau, that the state distribute the children in the countryside to be raised as cultivators of the soil.

Perhaps the most representative of all those who wrote about public assistance in this period was Jean-Joseph Baptiste Honore Miollis, author of the pamphlets *Réflexions Importantes sur L'État Présent des Communautés de Campagne en Provence* and "Mémoire sur les Enfans Trouvés."[38] In his secular, rational, scientific approach to the problem of poverty Miollis exemplifies enlightened public opinion in the years from 1760 to 1789, just as the religious exaltation of the writings of a man like Pierre Joseph de Haitze exemplifies opinion in the years of the Counter-Reformation, when the traditional charities of Aix had their start. A comparison between the works of the two men who won similar local fame can, therefore, do much to reveal the changes which took place between the years of the beginning of Aix's system of charities and the years of its decline.

Both men came from similar backgrounds, from the office-holding class which so dominated the city of Aix. Haitze, born in 1656, was the son of an *homme de confiance* of the Comte d'Alais, governor of Provence, and of the niece of a président of the Parlement of Provence. Miollis (1743-1809) was the son of a career office-holder, who rose from *lieutenant-criminal* of the sénéchaussée court to the post of *assesseur* of Aix and conseiller in the Cour des Comptes.[39] Miollis followed in his father's footsteps, becoming himself a conseiller in the Cour des Comptes. Haitze, however, did not hold an official position but rather devoted himself to good works. A member of the Company of the Holy Sacrament in its latter years, Haitze was the recteur secrétaire of the Oeuvre des Prisons from 1686 through 1689, and recteur of the Hôpital de la Miséricorde from 1702 to 1709. Haitze wrote fund-raising pamphlets for both of these institutions, and he also produced a multivolume history of the town of Aix in which the foundation of the charities, their quarrels and processions, their fund-raising and their building programs, bulked very large indeed.[40]

Haitze saw assistance to the poor as above all a Christian duty. In giving help to the needy, "the sole motive is to please God."[41] The Christian act of charity was beneficial to both donor and recipient. He who gave gained salvation. He who received gained both a sense of his own worthiness and spiritual comfort, and thus too came closer to God. In Haitze's Oeuvre des Prisons, for example, the rectors gave spiritual as well as material aid: "wrongdoers are corrected, the ignorant are taught, and we try to make the unhappy prisoner understand the enormity of their crimes."[42] But Haitze also understood and wrote about with genuine compassion the material sufferings of the poor.[43] He exemplifies the best of the spirit of those who supported Aix's charities in their heyday.

Miollis, by contrast, betrayed a completely secular viewpoint. Assistance to the poor was for Miollis a responsibility not of the Christian gentleman but rather of the state. Public relief was the duty of "a state regenerated by an improved administration."[44] Miollis' secularism made him uninterested in the traditional religious justification for charity: he was concerned neither with saving his own soul nor those of the poor. Admittedly he did express concern over the morality of the poor, but the method he chose to improve this was totally secular. He proposed a system of moral injunctions enforced by the state, similar to that of ancient Sparta.[45] For Miollis poverty was the result, not of the laziness of the poor, but of economic forces. He was vitally concerned with improving the lot of the Provençal peasant, and suggested tax reforms to ease his burdens, including the abolition of the noble's exemption from the taille.[46] Obsessed with the problem of increasing the number of cultivators of the soil, Miollis turned his attention, as did so many other Provençal pamphleteers in these years, to the lot of the enfant trouvé. His "Mémoire Sur Les Enfans Trouvés," abounding in statistics of every possible kind collected in imitation of Buffon, in reports of new experiments in hospital ventilation, and bottle-feeding for babies, reflects the scientific spirit and the conviction of the possibility of improvement of man's life on earth which typify the Age of Enlightenment. Miollis in his attitudes is as typical of the period from 1760 to 1789 as Haitze was of the period a century earlier, and together they exemplify the change from charité to bienfaisance.

In 1789 the communities of Provence met to draw up *cahiers* which would express their opinions on the great issues confronting the country. One of these was the question of the care of the poor. Only the nobility of Provence ignored this issue completely. The clergy, unsurprisingly, favored traditional charitable organizations. But the cahiers drawn up by the Third Estate reveal how public opinion in the prerevolutionary years had come to accept the necessity of a state-supported system of bienfaisance. The cahiers of 10 of Provence's 113 communities mentioned the problem of the care of the poor. None favored the traditional municipal charity. Many suggested that the rectors of the charities should be elected by municipal councils—a position tantamount to recognition of state responsibility for the administration of poor relief. Indeed, this position was explicitly stated in two of the cahiers, those of the communities of Peypin d'Aygues and St. Martin de la Brasque. These villages maintained that it was the duty of the state to assist all those who were unable to work.[47] Thus when the revolutionary Committee on Mendicity proposed the establishment of a national system of bienfaisance, they were not suggesting something radically new. In the field of public assistance, as in so many other areas, the revolution had been made in the minds of men before it became an actual fact.

The years from 1760 to 1789 were crucial for this development. These years saw the eclipse of traditional municipal charities like those of Aix. Losing the support of their contributors and plagued by financial crisis, they were repudiated as a means of providing assistance to the poor by enlightened public opinion. It was in this period that the principle of state responsibility for public assistance became widely accepted, and these years saw the first fumbling state initiatives in this field. But blocked by the numerous barriers to reform in the administrative structure of the Old Regime, a properly functioning, state-supported system of public assistance would come into being only with the Revolution.

Conclusion

In 1790 the Committee on Mendicity of the Constituant Assembly proclaimed the great principle that assistance for the poor was the responsibility of the nation as a whole. And eventually, under the Jacobins, this principle was implemented in a series of decrees which nationalized and sold hospital properties, made the state responsible for hospital expenses and administration, and provided direct state subventions to hitherto neglected groups of the poor, for example, peasants and artisans too old or infirm to work.[1]

Unfortunately this system of national bienfaisance did not work at all well. The sale of their properties stripped the hospitals of their major financial resource, but the government, obsessed with the war effort, did not allocate sufficient funds to fill the gap. Further, the program of government grants directly to the needy existed only on paper. The consequence of all this was, of course, that the poor suffered terribly.

These events of the Revolution provide the perspective from which historians have usually evaluated the traditional charities of the Old Regime. Ever since Alfred Cobban, in his perverse but very influential *The Social Interpretation of the French Revolution*, attacked the failures of the Revolutionary attempts at public welfare, and stated that whoever won the Revolution, the poor lost, it has been customary to mourn the passing of the traditional charity.[2]

But this perspective is misleading. Admittedly the traditional charities had their attractive aspects. Important to their towns in many ways, as employers, consumers, and bankers, as well as monuments of civic pride, the charities were able to integrate the poor into the community as a whole. The charities made the poor a part of a "famille."

Yet it is wrong to sentimentalize over the passing of these institutions. Even in their heyday they were never effective instruments against the poverty endemic in Old Regime France. Inspired by religious stereotypes, the charities were most effective in caring for the unemployables — the aged, the very young, the ill. But even here their unattractiveness to the poor limited their effectiveness. And the inflexibility of traditional charity, plus of course its lack of resources, made it almost useless against the heart of the problem of poverty in Old Regime France—the plight of the able-bodied unemployed. Further, traditional charity was urban-centered, and therefore did little to relieve the vast misery of the rural population. The Revolutionary legislation, with its direct state grants to the poor, and its emphasis on the eradication of rural poverty, was, in theory at least, both more effective and more humane than traditional charity.

In evaluating the effectiveness of traditional charitable institutions, we must also keep in mind the fact that they were moribund long before the Revolution gave them their final death blow. By 1789 the charities, troubled by financial problems and repudiated by public opinion, were both financially and intellectually bankrupt, and had been so for over two decades. The Revolution did not destroy an effectively functioning system of charity; instead, a new departure was long overdue.

The traditional charities of the Old Regime were the product of a certain set of circumstances and attitudes associated with the France of the early seventeenth century—especially the religious attitudes of the Counter-Reformation, with their emphasis on the Christian duty of charity and their concern for the moral reformation of the poor. The traditional charity was the product of seventeenth-century society, a society which was both stable and rigidly hierarchical, a society where both rich and poor knew their place and their duties. And as long as French society remained stable, the charities functioned relatively well. But in the last decades of the eighteenth century new attitudes, tied to growing religious indifference, undermined the religious raison d'être of the charities. And behind the widespread acceptance of these new attitudes lay the new economic and social forces which were undermining traditional society and changing the face of France: the population growth, increased migration, and economic expansion. Aix, with its backward economy and well-entrenched and old-fashioned elite, seems to have been one place where the old attitudes might linger. But even there the change came. The Revolution did, not, as Cobban claims, produce new attitudes toward poverty; instead both these attitudes and the Revolution itself were products of the new forces which were changing French society.

The national system of bienfaisance introduced by the Revolution, or at least something very like it, was therefore inevitable, and it was more suited to the changing conditions than the traditional charity had been. Admittedly it did not work well in practice. But the recognition that poverty was an economic phenomenon, subject to human cause and therefore to human cure, and the recognition that the state was responsible for the welfare of its citizens, had great humanitarian implications for the future.

PART FOUR

Abbreviations

Notes

Bibliography

Abbreviations

A.D. = Archives Départementales, Bouches-du-Rhône, in the main depository in Marseille.

A.D. (Aix) = Archives Départementales, Bouches-du-Rhône, in the annex in Aix-en-Provence.

A.M. = Archives Municipales, Aix-en-Provence.

Bib. Mej. = Bibliothèque Méjanes, Aix-en-Provence.

Lib. Arb. = Libraire Arbaud, Aix-en-Provence.

Notes

PREFACE

1. Jean-Pierre Gutton, *La Société et les pauvres: L'Exemple de la generalité de Lyon, 1534-1789* (Paris, 1970), p.8. A livre was worth approximately as much as a preinflation dollar of the early 1960's.

2. Olwen Hufton, *Bayeux in the Late Eighteenth Century: A Social Study* (Oxford, 1967); Gutton, *La Société et les pauvres.*

CHAPTER I

1. Arthur Young, *Travels in the Kingdom of France* (Dublin, 1793), 1:369.

2. Quoted in Jean Paul Coste, *La Ville d'Aix en 1695: Structure urbaine et société* (Aix, 1970), 2:1094-95.

3. Bib. Mej., Ms. 1191, Achard, "Description Historique, Geographique et Topographique . . . de la Provence . . . Précédée d'un Discours sur l'état actuel de la Provence, par M. Bouche . . . ." For an example of these accusations, see Coste, *La Ville d'Aix,* 2:771.

4. E. J. Hobsbawm, *The Age of Revolution, 1789-1848* (New York, 1962), p. 28.

5. This figure is only approximate. The population of the town in 1695 has been estimated at 30,600 (Jacqueline Carrière, *La Population d'Aix-en-Provence à la fin du XVIIe siècle: Etude de démographie historique d'après le registre de capitation de 1695* [Aix, 1958], p. 33). The *dénombrement* of 1763 gives a figure of 28,720 (A.M., GG 112, "Dénombrement général de habitans de la ville d'Aix, fait en 1763 par Jean Joseph Perret de cette ville . . . "), while the Abbé Expilly gives a total of 21,852 for 1762, a figure almost certainly too low (Carrière, *La Population d'Aix,* pp. 34-35). For the cottage industry of Provence, see Michel Vovelle, "Le 18ème siècle provençal," in Edouard Baratier, ed., *Histoire de Provence* (Toulouse, 1969), p. 348.

6. Bib. Mej., Ms. 1191, Bouche, "Discours sur l'efat de Provence," pp. 57-58.

7. Ibid., p. 28.

8. For a description of the growth of Marseille in the eighteenth century, see Vovelle, in Baratier, ed., *Histoire de Provence,* pp. 344-45.

9. Bib. Mej., Ms. 1191, Bouche, "Discours sur l'état de Provence," p. 28.

10. Coste, *La Ville d'Aix,* 2:831-34.

11. These cities have inspired two excellent local studies: Hufton's *Bayeux* and John McManners, *French Ecclesiastical Society under the Ancien Régime; A Study of Angers in the Eighteenth Century* (Manchester, 1960).

12. Quoted in Coste, *La Ville d'Aix,* 2:771.

13. Ibid., 2:738.

14. Quoted in Carrière, *La Population d'Aix*, p. 63.

15. These figures on the clergy are from Coste, *La Ville d'Aix*, 2:735-38, 745.

16. This figure dates from 1695, and includes both the grande and petite robe, the avocats, the procureurs, and notaries, and various minor clerks of the law courts, the officials of the sénéchaussée court and the mint, the fiscal agents, the officers of the municipal administration and the administration of the pays d'état, as well as holders of purely honorific offices, the 23 secrétaires du Roi and the 19 trésoriers-généraux de France (Coste, *La Ville d'Aix*, 2:769-816).

17. Ibid., 2:801.

18. Charles de Brosses, *Lettres familières sur l'Italie*, ed. Yvonne Bezard (Paris, 1931), 1:25-26.

19. Coste, *La Ville d'Aix*, 2:751-766; Carrière, *La Population d'Aix*, pp. 70-74. Both of these studies were based on the same source: the capitation roll of 1695. Yet their findings differ. Carrière puts the number of nobles holding fiefs at 48.

20. In the last years of the Old Regime the figure for the nobility as a whole was 25-30 percent (Vovelle, in Baratier, ed., *Histoire de Provence*, p. 387).

21. Bib. Mej., Ms. 263, "Etat du diocèse d'Aix, par paroisses et par doyennes vers 1730."

22. Vovelle, in Baratier, ed., *Histoire de Provence*, p. 391.

23. Carrière, *La Population d'Aix*, p. 41.

24. Coste, *La Ville d'Aix*, 2:712, 960.

25. Ibid., 2:751-66.

26. A.D. (Aix), XXI H, II B 2, Hôpital de la Charité, Legs Bonnard.

27. A.D. (Aix), XXI H, II B 7, Charité, Legs LeGros; Coste, *La Ville d'Aix*, 2:761.

28. A.D. (Aix), XXVIII, E 19, Hôpital de la Pureté, Quêtes.

29. Maurice Agulhon, *La Sociabilété méridionale: Confréries et associations dans la vie collective en Provence orientale à la fin du 18ème siècle* (Aix, 1966).

30. The figures in this paragraph are from Coste, *La Ville d'Aix*, 2:819-38.

31. Ibid., 2:712.

32. For an example of such an estate see A.D. (Aix), XXI H, II E 274, Charité, "Second Registre des biens des pauvres . . .," estate of Marie Toulousan, widow of Jean Pierre Latil, domestic of the Baron de Très.

33. Coste, *La Ville d'Aix*, 2:712, 839-953.

34. Ibid., 2:846-49,881-910.

35. Ibid., 2:848-49,885.

36. Ibid., 1:206-9; 2:839-953.

37. Ibid., 2:712.

38. Vovelle, in Baratier, ed., *Histoire de Provence*, p. 387.

39. Maurice Agulhon, *La Vie sociale en Provence intérieure au lendemain de la Révolution* (Paris, 1970), p. 60; Vovelle, in Baratier, ed., *Histoire de Provence*, p. 389. A hectare equals approximately 2.4 acres.

40. René Baehrel, *Une Croissance: La Basse-Provence rurale, fin du XVIe siècle- 1789* (Paris, 1961), 1:60-61.

41. Coste, *La Ville d'Aix*, 2:981.

42. Achard, "Description," p. 178.

43. Coste, *La Ville d'Aix*, 1:61, 2:1034.

44. For an analysis of wage and cost-of-living levels for the travailleur and artisan, see Chapter IV.

45. Vovelle, in Baratier, ed., *Histoire de Provence*, p. 356.

46. Pierre-Joseph de Haitze, *Histoire de la Ville d'Aix, capitale de la Provence* (Aix, 1889), 6:397, 4:365.

47. Jean Pourrière, *Les hôpitaux d'Aix-en-Provence au moyen âge; 13, 14, 15e siècles* (Aix, 1969), pp. 15-16.

48. A.D. (Aix), XXI H, II E 29, Charité, Deliberations 1719-22.

49. Bib. Mej., 1884, M. Laforest, *De l'Influence du dépôt de Mendicité des Bouches-du-Rhône Sur les moeurs populaires, sur la diminution des crimes, et sur celle des*

criminals dans ce Département . . . (Aix, 1819), p. 7. This building is still standing, and at present houses the Ecole des arts et métiers.

50. Bib. Mej., F 884, *La Mendicité abolie Dans La Ville d'Aix Par L'Hôpital Général ou Maison de Charité, avec la Reponse aux principales objections que l'on peut faire contre cet établissement* (Aix, n.d.), p. 38.

51. Haitze, *Histoire d'Aix*, 5:399-400, 6:149-50.

52. Bib. Mej., Res. D 349, *Institutions et Règlements De L'Hôpital Notre Dame de Miséricorde établi dans la Ville D'Aix, pour le soulagement des Pauvres malades, des Honteux, et des Invalides* (Aix, 1688), p. 74.

53. A.D. (Aix), XXI H, II E 1, *Les Règlemens de l'Hôpital-Général La Charité d'Aix* (Aix, n.d.), p. 18.

54. Lib. Arb. 500, Prisons, "Délibérations de l'Oeuvre des Prisons d'Aix, portant de présenter requête à Mons. L'Archevêque, pour avoir rang avec les autres Hôpitaux . . . aux Processions solennelles, et de faire à cet effet une Bannière," April 1, 1698.

55. The Parlement deliberated on and registered the proper order for processions in 1710 (A.D. [Aix], XXI H, II A 2, Charité, "Cérémonial," and XXIII H, IV A 1, Insensés, "Règlement"). This did not, however, prevent serious disputes over rank between the Oeuvre des Prisons and the Penitents Noirs in 1727 (A.D. [Aix], XXIII H, IV A 1, Insensés, "Règlement"), and between the Charité and the sisters of the Third Order of St. Dominique in 1742 (A.D. [Aix], XXI H, II A 2, Charité, "Cérémonial.")

56. The charities as economic entities will be discussed in much greater detail in Chapter III.

57. From 1729 on the Charité held the right to grant the maîtrise after six years of work at the hospital (A.D. [Aix], XXI H, II E 31, Charité, Deliberations, 1726-32, December 11, 1729). This right was reconfirmed in 1779 (A.D., C 3220, Charité, De La Tour to Amelot, August 3, 1779).

58. Bib. Mej., F 884, *Mendicité abolie*, p. 3.

CHAPTER II

1. Bib. Mej., Ms. RA 10, Pierre-Joseph de Haitze, "Aix, ancienne et moderne, ou la topographie de la ville d'Aix-en-Provence," p. 63.

2. A.D., IG 235 bis, "Etat du Diocèse d'Aix," 1782; A.M., GG 519, Hôpital St. Eutrope, "Mémoire à Ms. Les consuls et assesseurs de la ville d'Aix."

3. See Nicole Sabatier, *L'Hôpital Saint-Jacques d'Aix-en-Provence, 1519-1789* (Aix, 1964) for a history of St. Jacques.

4. Bib. Mej., Res. D 349, *La Compagnie de la Miséricorde Etablie en La Ville D'Aix . . .* (Aix, 1636). Hereafter cited as Miséricorde, *Reglements*, 1636.

5. Haitze, *Histoire d'Aix*, 4:15, 142, 303, 316; Bib. Mej., Ms. RA 10, Haitze, "Aix, ancienne et moderne . . . ," p. 64.

6. A.M., GG 512, Enfants Trouvés, "Lettres Patentes du Roy . . . en faveur de tous ceux qu'ils établis à faire la Queste pour la Rédemption des Esclaves entre les mains des Turces."

7. Haitze, *Histoire d'Aix*, 4:357-59.

8. A.D. (Aix), XXI H, II E 1, *Les Règlemens de L'Hôpital-Général La Charité d'Aix* (Aix, n.d.). Hereafter cited as Charité, *Règlemens*.

9. Haitze, *Histoire d'Aix*, 5:399-401, 6:83, 149, 388; A.D., IG 235 bis, "État du Diocèse," 1782; Bib. Mej., F 739, *Institution et Règlements du Bureau Général de Charité . . .* (Aix, 1702). The other charity founded in this period was the Corpus Domini de St. Sauveur, which financed dowries and apprenticeships for poor girls and boys.

10. For Brancas' attempt to take the initiative in the field of charity, see Haitze, *Histoire d'Aix*, 6:308. The charities founded by Brancas were the Filles Orphelines, the Enfants Abandonnées (which provided food and shelter for homeless children), Ste. Marcelle (an institution for unemployed servant girls), and free charity schools.

11. A.D., C 3214, Diocèse d'Aix, "Enquête, Incurables," 1766; A.D., IG 235 bis, "Etat du Diocèse," 1782.

12. Pourrière, *Hôpitaux au moyen âge,* pp. 81-82, 172; Sabatier, *St-Jacques,* 1:20.

13. Pourrière, *Hôpitaux au moyen âge,* pp. 24-27, 88, 170-72.

14. The best analysis of Vives' writings on poverty is Natalie Z. Davis, "Poor Relief, Humanism, and Heresy: The Case of Lyon," *Studies in Medieval and Renaissance History* 5 (1966): 217-75. For the attitude of Lyon's merchants toward the problem of poverty, and their role in the founding of the Aumône Général, see Richard Gascon, *Grand commerce et vie urbaine au XVIe siècle: Lyon et ses marchands* (Paris, 1971), 2:733-811.

15. The will is quoted in Sabatier, *St-Jacques,* 1:161. See also 1:165-67. For the Miséricorde, see Bib. Mej., Res. D 349, Miséricorde, *Règlements,* 1636. See also ibid., *Catalogue des Recteurs Qui Ont exercé l'oeuvre de la Miséricorde en cette Ville d'Aix depuis l'année 1600* (Aix, 1684). This shows that no ecclesiastic served as rector from 1600 to 1684.

16. Isambert, Jourdan, and Decrusy, *Recueil Général Des Anciennes Lois Françaises Depuis l'an 420 jusqu' à la révolution de 1789* (Paris, 1822-33), 12:841-43, 897-900, 920-23; 13:41 (no text given); 14:105-7, 398-99.

17. Sabatier, *St-Jacques,* 1:249, 271-73.

18. Jean Imbert, "Les Prescriptions hospitalières du Concile de Trente et leur diffusion en France," *Revue d'histoire de l'Eglise de France* 42 (January-June, 1956): 7-8.

19. This demand was first voiced in the Estates-General of 1577. (Article I, "Cahier des remonstrances, plaintes, et doléances de L'Etat Ecclesiastique de France Presenté au Roi en l'Assemblée-générale de ses Etats à Blois le 8 février, 1577," *Recueil des Actes, Titres et Mémoires . . . du Clergé de France* [Paris, 1740], 1:1037-39.) It was also mentioned at the Assemblies of the Clergy of 1625, 1660, and 1675 (*Collection des procès-verbaux des Assemblées-Générales du Clergé de France, depuis l'année 1560, jusqu' à présent* [Paris, 1748-78], 2:491; 4:671-73; *Recueil du Clergé,* 1:1435-39). The latter is the most elaborate statement of the clerical position. I wish to thank my fellow student, Richard M. Golden, for drawing my attention to these sources.

20. Isambert et al., *Recueil des Lois,* 20:252, 309-13.

21. Ibid., 18:20.

22. Coste, *La Ville d'Aix,* 1:15-54, provides a survey of the history of Aix in the seventeenth century.

23. A.M., BB 99, "Délibérations Communales," pp. 398, 465.

24. For the Cascaveous see Roland Mousnier, *Fureurs paysans* (Paris, 1967), pp. 50-51.

25. The literature of the French Counter-Reformation is too vast to be more than indicated here. Especially influential on my views of the attitudes of figures of the Counter-Reformation toward charity and poverty were the following: for St. Vincent de Paul: R. P. Chalumeau, *St. Vincent de Paul* (Paris, 1959); for the Oratorians, Paul Milcent, "Spiritualité de la charité envers les pauvres selon St. Jean Eudes," *XVIIe siècle* 90-91 (1971): 17-44; for the Jansenists, R. Taveneaux, "Jansenisme et vie sociale en France au XVIIe siècle," *Revue d'histoire de l'Eglise de France,* 54:152 (January-June, 1968): 37-46. More general treatments include R. P. Chalumeau, "L'Assistance aux malades pauvres au dix-septième siècle," *XVIIe siècle* 90-91 (1971): 75-87; Orest A. Ranum, *Paris in the Age of Absolutism: An Essay* (New York, 1968), pp. 109-31, 229-51; and Gutton, *La Société et les pauvres,* pp. 215-46.

26. For the charitable activities of the Company of the Holy Sacrament as a whole see Ranum, *Paris in the Age of Absolutism,* and Emmanuel Chill, "Religion and Mendicity in Seventeenth Century France," *International Review of Social History* 7 (1962): 400-26. Little is known about the activities of the Company in Aix. The standard history of the Company, Raoul Allier, *La Cabale des Dévots, 1627-1666* (Paris, 1902) devotes a few pages to its work in Aix (pp. 233-38). There are also indications of the activities of the Company in Aix scattered through the documents published in Raoul Allier, ed., *La*

Compagnie du Très-Saint Sacrement de l'Autel à Marseille: Documents publiés (Paris, 1909). See also *Les Bouches-du-Rhône, Encyclopédie Départementale* (Marseille, 1931). Vol. 5.

27. I do not have the exact figures for the rate of literacy in Aix at any period during the seventeenth century. However, evidence from marriages recorded in parish registers in western Provence shows that in 1700 barely ten percent of the population in this area could sign their names. This is in contrast to a much higher national average of 21 percent (Michel Vovelle, "Provence Sage, 1750-88," in Baratier, ed., *Histoire de Provence,* p. 380). As Aix was a city, and a center for the diffusion of French into the Provençal-speaking countryside, the rate of literacy in Aix was probably slightly higher than that of western Provence.

28. M. Mollat, "La Notion de pauvreté au moyen âge: Position de problèmes," *Revue d'Histoire de l'Eglise de France* 52 (1966): 5-23, emphasizes the importance of the works of the Church Fathers in the formation of the doctrines of the Catholic Church on poverty and charity. See also Gutton, *La Société et les pauvres,* pp. 215-25. Brian Tierney, *Medieval Poor Law: A Sketch of Canonical Theory and Its Application in England* (Berkeley and Los Angeles, 1959) is an excellent further treatment of the doctrines of the medieval Church.

29. Bib. Mej., F 884, *Mendicité abolie,* p. 3.

30. Bib. Mej., Res. D 349, Miséricorde, *Règlements,* 1636, p. 3.

31. Bib. Mej., F 884, *Mendicité abolie,* p. 4.

32. Bib. Mej., 7694, Pierre-Joseph de Haitze, *Etat de L'oeuvre pour le secours des prisonniers . . .* (Aix, 1689), p. 2.

33. Bib. Mej., Res. D 349, Miséricorde, *Règlements,* 1636, pp. 12, 14.

34. Ibid., Miséricorde, *Règlements,* 1688, p. 7.

35. Bib. Mej., F 884, *Mendicité abolie,* pp. 33, 34.

36. Lib. Arb. 415, *Etat de la Maison de la Charité, de La Ville d'Aix, Depuis le 2 février 1687 jour du dernier enfermement des Pauvres, jusques au 20 mars 1702* (Aix, 1702).

37. Bib. Mej., Res. D 349, Miséricorde, *Règlements,* 1688, pp. 7-8.

38. Bib. Mej., 7694, *État/de L'oeuvre pour secours des prisonniers, Exercée Par la Compagnie des F. F. Pénitens Blancs . . .* (Aix, 1689), p. 5; Bib. Mej., F 884, *Mendicité abolie,* p. 23; For other examples of the use of the metaphor of investment and return, see ibid., p. 29, and *État . . . de la Charité.*

39. Bib. Mej., F 884, *Statuts et Règlements de la Confraire de Notre Dame D'Esperance En L'Eglise St. Sauveur de la Ville d'Aix* (Aix, 1637), p. 23.

40. A.D. (Aix), XXI H, II E 44, *Règlements de L'Hopital La Charité* (Aix, n.d.). I wish to thank my fellow student, Susan Kupper, for translating the Latin quotations in this work, hereafter cited as Charité, *Règlements.*

41. Ibid.

42. This description of the theories of the canonists relies on Tierney, *Medieval Poor Law,* pp. 23-39.

43. A.D. (Aix), XXI H, II E 44, Charité, *Règlements.* Italics mine.

44. Bib. Mej., F 884, *Mendicité abolie,* p. 3.

45. Bib. Mej. F 884, *Mendicité abolie.* This pamphlet was most probably written around 1680 by Père Guevarre, in connection with the publicity campaign for the hospital-general (see below, p. 36). At least he is credited with the authorship of a pamphlet of the same title. (Augustin and Aloys De Backer, *Bibliothèque de la Compagnie de Jèsus,* ed. Carlos Sommervogel, S.J. Brussels and Paris, 1892, 3:1924).

46. Bib. Mej., F 884, *Mendicité abolie,* pp. 40-43, 56.

47. Tierney, *Medieval Poor Law,* p. 57.

48. Mollat, "La Notion de pauvreté au moyen âge," pp. 5-7.

49. Tierney, *Medieval Poor Law,* p. 56.

50. Bib. Mej., F 884, *Mendicité abolie,* pp. 23, 87.

51. Bib. Mej., Res. D 349, Miséricorde, *Règlements,* 1688, pp. 5-6.

52. For the precautions taken against the disclosure of the identities of the pauvres honteux see Bib. Mej., Res. D 349, *La Compagnie de la Miséricorde Establie en la Ville d'Aix, pour le secours et assistance de tous les pauvres malades, et autres personnes affligées* . . . (Aix, 1671). p. 38.

53. Bib. Mej., Res. D 349, Miséricorde, *Règlements*, 1688, p. 9.

54. For an example of this rule, see ibid., Miséricorde, *Règlements*, 1671, p. 32.

55. Ibid., Miséricorde, *Règlements*, 1688, p. 43; Nicole Sabatier, *St-Jacques*, 1:155.

56. Tierney, *Medieval Poor Law*, p. 58.

57. This is quoted in Bib. Mej., F 884, *Mendicité abolie*, pp. 65-66.

58. Bib. Mej., Res. D 349, *Instructions et Règlemens Des Bureaux de Charité Etablis dans Toutes Les Villes et dans Tous Les Autres Lieux du Diocèse d'Aix Ou L'on n'a pas d'enfermer les Pauvres* (Aix, 1700) p. 23; Bib. Mej., F 884, *Mendicité abolie*, p. 74.

59. Bib. Mej., F 884, *Mendicité abolie*, p. 74.

60. Bib. Mej., Res. D 349, *Règlement des Bureaux de Charité*, p. 34.

61. Bib. Mej., F 884, *Mendicité abolie*, p. 75.

62. Bib. Mej., Res D 349, *Règlemens des Bureaux de Charité*, p. 27; Bib. Mej., F 884, *Mendicité abolie*, p. 63.

63. Bib. Mej., F 884, *Le Paradis Ouvert Aux Aumôniers de la Ville d'Aix, avec une instruction aux Personnes Charitables qui y assistent les pauvres et à ceux qui demandent quelque assistance* . . . (Aix, 1677), pp. 9-10, 20.

64. J.P. Gutton, "A l'aube du XVIIe siècle: Idées nouvelles sur les pauvres," *Cahiers d'histoire*, 10 (1965):93.

65. A.D. (Aix), XXVIII H, A 2, *Règlements pour Les filles de la pureté* (Aix, n.d.).

66. Bib. Mej., F 884, *Paradis Ouvert*, pp. 14-15.

67. Bib. Mej., F 884, *Mendicité abolie*, p. 11.

68. A.D. (Aix), XXI H, II E 44, Charité, *Règlements*.

69. Tierney, *Medieval Poor Law*, p. 12.

70. Bib. Mej., F 884, *Mendicité abolie*, p. 59.

71. Emmanuel Chill, "Religion and Mendicity," p. 415.

72. Such a conviction is expressed in A.D. (Aix), XXI H, II E 44, Charité, *Règlements*.

73. Michel Foucault, *Histoire de la folie à l'âge classique* (Paris, 1961), pp. 54-81.

74. Philippe Ariès, *L'Enfant et la vie familiale sous l'ancien régime*, (Paris, 1960), p. 466.

75. Bib. Mej. F 884, *Mendicité abolie*, p. 48.

76. Bib. Mej., Res. D 349, Miséricorde, *Règlements*, 1688, p. 11.

77. These instructions for such investigations undertaken by the Miséricorde, called "Informations extraordinaires," can be found in Bib. Mej., Res. D 349, Miséricorde, *Règlements*, 1688, p. 103. Similar investigations undertaken by the hospital-general are cited in Bib. Mej. F 884, *Mendicité abolie*, p. 40, while those of the bureaux de charité are outlined in Bib. Mej., Res. D 349, *Règlemens Des Bureaux de Charité*, p. 23.

78. Bib. Mej., Res. D 349, *Règlemens Des Bureaux de Charité*, p. 25.

79. Bib. Mej., F 884, *Mendicité abolie*, pp. 70, 71.

80. Ibid., pp. 47, 51-56, 68-69.

81. See Chill, "Religion and Mendicity," and Ranum, *Paris in the Age of Absolutism*.

82. Isambert et al. *Recueil*, 18:20.

83. Ibid., 20:20.

84. On Chaurand's career, see de Backer, *Bibliothèque de la Compagnie de Jésus*, 2:1101, and Charles Joret, "Le P. Guevarre et les bureaux de charité au XVIIe siècle," *Annales du Midi* 1 (1889):340-93. (I wish to thank Professor Mary Anglim of the University of Wisconsin for these references.)

85. Haitze, *Histoire d'Aix*, 6:277-78.

86. One of these, Père Guevarre, won fame in his own right as a preacher of enfermement. Formerly a teacher and chaplain at the Collège Royal du Bourbon in Aix, he was inspired by Chaurand's example to become a wandering evangelist. He accompanied Chaurand to Rome in 1693, when they organized a hospital-general in Saint-John-

Lateran. Later Guevarre preached throughout Languedoc, Gascony, and Dauphiné, as well as his native Provence, and he was even called to Turin in 1714 to advise the King of Piedmont on problems of public assistance. On Guevarre see Joret, "Le P. Guevarre et les bureaux de charité," and "Le P. Guevarre et la fondation de l'hôpital-général d' Auch," *Annales du Midi* 2(1890):27-35; also de Backer, *Bibliothèque de la Compagnie de Jésus,* 3:1924.

87. Haitze, *Histoire d'Aix*, 6:278.

88. Lib. Arb. 415, *Ordre de Mons. L'Archevêque Touchant les Aumônes Que les Fidèles font aux pauvres, qui mendiant contre la défense du Roy* . . . (Aix, 1702).

CHAPTER III

1. Bib. Mej., F 884, t. 4, *Etat de L'Hôpital La Miséricorde* . . . (Aix, 1709).

2. Bib. Mej., Res. D 349, Miséricorde, *Règlements*, 1688, pp. 22-23.

3. A.D. (Aix), XXI H, II E 1, *Les Règlemens de l'Hôpital-Général La Charité d'Aix* (Aix, 1779), p. 1.

4. A.D. (Aix), XXXII H, A 1, *Instructions pour les srs. Recteurs de l'Oeuvre Etablie pour le Secours des Pauvres Prisonniers* . . . (Aix, 1747), p. 7.

5. Lib. Arb. 415, *Règlemens pour l'hôpital des Incurables de cette Ville d'Aix* . . . (Aix, 1766).

6. Bib. Mej., 7694, *Etat de L'Oeuvre pour secours des prisonniers* . . . (Aix, 1689), pp. 40-41.

7. Bib. Mej., F 884, t. 4, *Etat de L'Hôpital la Miséricorde*, p. 4.

8. Of 66 rectors in the period 1600-22, 61 were described as "marchands," four as "bourgeois," and one was a notary (Bib. Mej., Res. D 349, *Catalogue des Recteurs Qui Ont exercé l'Oeuvre de la Miséricorde en cette Ville d'Aix depuis l'anneé 1600.)*

9. Haitze, *Histoire d'Aix*, 4:366.

10. A.D. (Aix), XXI H, II E 29-II E 36, Charité, Deliberations, 1720-85.

11. A.D. (Aix), XXI H, II E 29, Charité, Deliberations, 1719-22; II E 32, Deliberations, 1739-41; II E 33, Deliberations, 1741-62.

12. For the rectors of the Pureté, see Haitze, *Histoire d'Aix*, 6:183-85. For the Charité, see A.D. (Aix), XXI H, II E 29-II E 36, Charité, Deliberations, 1720-85.

13. A.D. (Aix), XXI H, II E 1, Charité, *Règlemens*, p. 17, includes a provision that "the Rectors cannot make the poor work for their own particular account, without giving the same price that the others give."

14. Lib. Arb. 415, *Consultation des Ms. Brès et Emerigon Pour les Créanciers de l'Hôpital de la Charité de la Ville d'Aix* . . . (Aix, 1763).

15. The Charité limited the service of its rectors to nine years. See A.D. (Aix), XXI H, II E 34, Charité, Deliberations, 1762-72, December 23, 1762.

16. A.D. (Aix), XXI H, II E 33, Charité, Deliberations, 1741-62, passim.

17. A.D. (Aix), XXI H, II E 34, Charité, Deliberations, August 7, 1763.

18. Lib. Arb. 415, *Consultation des Ms. Brès et Emerigon.*

19. Bib. Mej., Res. D 349, Miséricorde, *Règlements,* 1671, p. 29.

20. A.D. (Aix), XXI H, II E 34, Charité, Deliberations, July 10, 1763.

21. A.D. (Aix), XXI H, II E 31, Charité, Deliberations, February 8, 1731.

22. A.D., C 3214, Hôpitaux, "Enquête," 1766, reply of the Mont-de-Piété; and C 3217, Hôpitaux, mémoire to the Controller-General, September 7, 1760.

23. Bib. Mej., Res. D 349, Miséricorde, *Règlements,* 1688, p. 56.

24. A.D. (Aix), XXI H, II E 35, Charité, Deliberations, December 30, 1778.

25. A.D. (Aix), XXI H, II E 1, Charité, *Règlemens*, p. 3.

26. A.D. (Aix), XXI H, II E 33, Charité, Deliberations, November 20, 1749.

27. It was customary to will a sum for a large number of masses to be said after death.

(For an example, see A.D. [Aix], XXI H, II B 7, Charité, Legs Legros.) Alternatively, one could provide for one or two requiem masses to be repeated yearly, in perpetuity. (A.D. [Aix], XXI H, II B 5, Don Coriolis.)

28. A.D., IG 235 bis, "Etat du diocèse d'Aix," 1782.

29. A.D., C 3214, "Etat du Refuge," 1767; A.D. (Aix), XXI H, II E 71-II E 110, Charité, Accounts, 1720-62, passim.

30. Albert Soboul, *La France à la veille de la Révolution,* Vol. 1, *Economie et société* (Paris, 1969), p. 106.

31. A.D., IG 235 bis, "Etat du diocèse d'Aix," 1782.

32. Bib. Mej., Res. D 349, Miséricorde, *Règlements,* 1671, pp. 46, 47; Sabatier, *St-Jacques,* 1:386, 389.

33. Sabatier, *St-Jacques,* 1:391-92.

34. Bib. Mej., Res. D 349, Miséricorde, *Règlements,* 1671, pp. 47-48.

35. Bib. Mej., F 884, t. 4, *Etat de L'Hôpital La Miséricorde,* p. 91.

36. Bib. Mej., Res. D 349, Miséricorde, *Règlements,* 1688, p. 63.

37. A.D., C 3214, "Mémoire sur . . . l'hôpital des paralitiques Incurables . . . ," 1766; A.M., GG 517, "Situation de l'Hôpital-Général des Insensés . . . ," 1787.

38. G. Valran, *Misère et charité en Provence au XVIIIe siècle: essai d'histoire sociale* (Paris, 1889), pp. 97-98.

39. Bib. Mej., Res. D 349, Miséricorde, *Règlements,* 1671, pp. 49-50.

40. Ibid., p. 53.

41. Sabatier, *St-Jacques,* 1:393.

42. Valran, *Misère et charité,* pp. 99-100.

43. A.D. (Aix), XXI H, II E 33, Charité, Deliberations, June 19, 1749

44. Bib. Mej., F 739, *Départment des Employs des Officiers de l'Hôpital-Général de la Charité d'Aix, et autres choses concernant le bon ordre de la maison* (Aix, n.d.), pp. 3-7.

45. A.D. (Aix), XXI H, II E 71-II E 110, Charité, Accounts, 1720-62, passim.

46. A.D. (Aix), XXIII H, IV E 36, "Registre des officiers de l'hôpital-général de Insensés de cette ville d'Aix du premier janvier, 1782," p. 2. The register also covers later years.

47. A.D. (Aix), XXI H, II E 34, Charité, Deliberations, April 11, 1765, July 20, 1766; II E 35, July 7, 1774; II E 33, July 5, 1744.

48. For examples of orphan boys who earned their maîtrises in the Charité, see A.D. (Aix), XXI H, II E 34, Charité, Deliberations, April 11, 1765, and II E 36, May 24, 1781, September 20, 1781.

49. A.D. (Aix), XXI H, II E 34, Charité, Deliberations, July 17, 1746, February 16, 1769.

50. A.D. (Aix), XXIII H, IV E 36, "Registre des officiers de l'hôpital-Général des Insensés."

51. A.D. (Aix), XXI H, II E 34, Charité, Deliberations, August 30, September 3, 1767.

52. A.D. (Aix), XXIII H, IV E 36, "Registre des officiers de l'hôpital-Général des Insensés"; A.D. (Aix), XXI H, II F 9, Charité, "Registre des procès-verbaux d'admissions des pauvres," 1743-1812 passim.

53. For example, in the Charité the cooks received three loaves of bread, two bowls of soup, and a pot of wine diluted with water. This was much more abundant than the diet of the inmates (see below). (Bib. Mej., F 739, *Départment des Employs des Officiers de l'Hôpital-Général de la Charité . . .* [Aix, n.d.], pp. 19-20.)

54. The price rise at the end of the eighteenth century has been well documented by C. E. Labrousse, *Esquisse du mouvement des prix et des revenues en France au XVIIIe siècle* (Paris, 1933). Information on salaries is harder to find. The only two series presented by Baehrel which are reasonably complete for the period 1726-89—those of the agricultural laborer and a carter—show that salaries increased 25 percent and 28 percent from 1726-41 to 1771-89. (Baehrel, *Une Croissance,* 1:607-8.)

55. A.D. (Aix), XXI H, II E 34, Charité, Deliberations, January 29, 1764.

56. A.D. (Aix), XXI H, II E 1, Charité, *Règlemens,* pp. 45-55.
57. Bib. Mej., F 739, *Officiers de la Charité,* p. 14.
58. A.D. (Aix), XXI H, II E 1, Charité, *Règlemens,* p. 14.
59. See A.D. (Aix), XXI H, II E 33, Charité, Deliberations, May 4, 1741, July 24, 1749.
60. See ibid., November 6, 1749.
61. A.D. (Aix), XXI H, II E 1, Charité, *Règlemens,* p. 15.
62. Ibid. p. 15.
63. The will of de la Roque is reprinted in Sabatier, *St-Jacques,* 1:144-52.
64. A.D., C 3214, Hôpitaux, Enquête, "Mémoire sur l'etablissement, les revenues, les charges, depens et dettes de l'hôpital des paralitiques incurables de la ville d'Aix," 1766.
65. Lib. Arb. 415, *Etat de la Charité,* 1702.
66. For the Oeuvre des Prisons, see A.M., LL 349, "Déclarations et Inventaires des Hôpitaux," L'Oeuvre des Prisons, accounts; for the Insensés, ibid., "Inventaire du Insensés," July 12, 1791; for the Mont-de-Piété, A.D., C 3214, Hôpitaux, "Enquête," Mont-de-Piété, November 16, 1766.
67. See G. and M. Vovelle, "La Mort et L'Au-Delà en Provence," *Annales: E. S.C.,* 24:6 (Nov.-Dec., 1969): 1602-30, and Michel Vovelle, *Piété baroque et déchristianisation en Provence au XVIIIe siècle: les attitudes devant la mort d'après les clauses des testaments* (Paris, 1973).
68. Vovelle, *Piété baroque,* pp. 231, 232.
69. A.D. (Aix), XXI H, II B 2, Charité, Legs Bonnard.
70. Lib. Arb. 415, Incurables, "Règlements," 1766.
71. Vovelle, *Piété baroque et déchristianisation,* pp. 244, 245.
72. A.D. (Aix), XXVIII H, B 3, "Oeuvre de la Pureté, Dons et legs."
73. For example, in 1720 the Charité inherited from M. Allemandy his office of trésorier-général de France. (A.D. [Aix], XXI H, II E 29, Charité, Deliberations, 1719-22, July 28, 1720.)
74. A.D. (Aix), XXI H, II B 3, Charité, Legs Chambon.
75. Valran, *Misère et charité,* p. 341.
76. A.D. (Aix), XXI H, II B 7, Charité, Legs Le Gros.
77. Bib. Mej., Res. D 349, Miséricorde, *Règlemens,* 1688, p. 31.
78. Bib. Mej., Res. D 349, *Institutions et Règlemens Des Bureaux de Charité . . . d'Aix* (Aix, n.d.), p. 50.
79. Bib. Mej., Res. D 349, Miséricorde, *Règlemens,* 1671, pp. 24-25.
80. Bib. Mej., 7694, Haitze, *Le Secours des prisonniers,* pp. 36-37.
81. A.D. (Aix), XXIII H, IV A 1, Insensés, Rules
82. A.D. (Aix), XXVII H, E 19, Pureté, "Quêtes."
83. A.D. (Aix), XXI H, II E 33, Charité, Deliberations, 1741-62, May 1, 1746.
84. Bib. Mej., Res. D 349, Miséricorde, *Reglements,* 1671, pp. 26-27.
85. See Lib. Arb. 500, "Délibération de l'Oeuvre des Prisons d'Aix, portant présenter requête à Monseig L'Archevêque, pour avoir rang avec les autres Hôpitaux et Congrégations Charitables, aux Processions solemnelles . . . ," April 1, 1698. Also A.D. (Aix), XXI H, II A 2, Charité Processions.
86. George V. Taylor, "Non-Capitalist Wealth and the Origins of the French Revolution," *American Historical Review* 62: 2 (January, 1967): 470.
87. The standard work on the rente is Bernard Schnapper, *Les Rentes au XVIe siècle: histoire d'un instrument de crédit* (Paris, 1957). See also Taylor, "Non-Capitalist Wealth and the Origins of the French Revolution," p. 479; and Robert Forster, *The Nobility of Toulouse in the Eighteenth Century: A Social and Economic Study* (Baltimore, 1960), pp. 102-20.
88. A.M., LL 349, "Déclarations et Inventaires des Hôpitaux et oeuvres diverses," 1790-92, inventory of the Charité, 1790.
89. Ibid.
90. Ibid.

91. Ibid., inventory of the Oeuvre des Orphelines.
92. Ibid., inventory of Mont-de-Piété.
93. A.D. (Aix), XXI H, II E 33, Charité, Deliberations, 1741-62, October 1750; October 12, 1755.
94. A.D. (Aix), XXI H, II E 1, Charité, *Règlements,* 1779, pp. 5, 6.
95. A.D. C 3220, Correspondence between Charité and controlleur-général, 1760-70, passim.
96. For the background and purpose of the ordinance, see Chapter V. See also A.D. (Aix), XXI H, II E 187, "Etat des pauvres entrés le mois de septembre dans l'Hôpital-Général . . . ensuite de la déclaration du Roy, du 18 juillet, 1724."
97. A.D., C 3221, Refuge, passim.
98. A.D. (Aix), XXI H, II E 33, Charité, Deliberations, 1741-62, June 26, 1757.
99. This phrase occurs in Bib. Mej., F 739, *Département des Employs,* p. 1.
100. A.D. (Aix), XXI H, II E 1, Charité, *Règlemens,* 1779, pp. 12, 89-90; II E 239, "Second Registre des Distributions Semainiers commencé Le Premier janvier de L'Année 1773"; Valran, *Misère et charité,* p. 124.
101. Valran, *Misère et charité,* pp. 127-29, quotation, p. 129.
102. A.D. (Aix), XXI H, II E 33, Charité, Deliberations, 1741-62, July 6, 1747.
103. A.D. (Aix), XXI H, II E 35, Charité, Deliberations, September 23, 1779.
104. A.D. (Aix), XXI H, II E 33, Charité, Deliberations, 1741-62, February 18, 1742.
105. A.D. (Aix), XXI H, II E 29, Charité, Deliberations, 1719-22, June 15, 1721.
106. A.D. (Aix), XXI H, II E 33, Charité, Deliberations, 1741-62, November 23, 1749.
107. Ibid., December 14, 1749.
108. Ibid., January 24, 1754.
109. A.D., C 3220, Charité, 1760-80, "Etat," 1767.
110. Each prostitute cared for in the Refuge also cost the institution approximately seven sous per day to feed and clothe (A.D. C3221, Refuge, "Mémoire," 1770).
111. A.D. (Aix), XXI H, II E 114, Charité, Accounts, 1767.
112. A.D. (Aix), XXI H, II E 110, Charité, "Etat des Rentes et Revenues de l'Hôpital-Général de la Charité d'Aix Pendant l'Année, 1789."
113. A.D. (Aix), XXI H, II B 16, Charité, "Billets des Rentes, 28 mai, 1750-17 janvier, 1756."
114. A.D. (Aix), XXI H, II B 15, Charité, "Placements des rentes, du 10 janvier, 1745, au 18 mai, 1750."
115. Ibid; II B 16, "Rentes," 1750-56.
116. A.D. (Aix), XXI H, II B 15, "Rentes" 1745-50; II B 16, "Rentes," 1750-56; II B 17 "Rentes," 1756, ff.
117. A.D. (Aix), XXI H, II B 16, "Rentes," 1750-56.
118. A.D. (Aix), XXI H, II B 15, "Rentes," 1745-50.
119. The precise criterion for the use of these honorific addresses in the eighteenth century is unclear, although their use in the seventeenth century has been well described by Mousnier, *Fureurs paysans,* pp. 16-25. In eighteenth-century Aix the cut-off point between those who were called "sieur" and "demoiselle" and those who were not was at the level of large shopkeeper and substantial master craftsman. They often were honored with such forms of address while the journeyman and petty shopkeeper were not.
120. The men and women without honorific modes of address most probably belong to these social groups as well, thus making their numbers even larger than those which appear on the table.
121. A.D. (Aix), XXI H, II B 15, "Rentes," 1745-50; II B 16, "Rentes," 1750-56; II B 17, "Rentes," 1756, ff.
122. A.D. (Aix), XXI H, II B 17, "Rentes," 1756, ff.
123. A.D. (Aix), XXI H, II E 34, Charité, Deliberations, January 8, 1767; II B 17, "Rentes," 1756, ff.
124. A.D. (Aix), XXI H, II B 15, Charite, "Rentes," 1745-50; II B 16, "Rentes," 1750-56; II B 17, "Rentes," 1756, ff.

125. Ibid.
126. For an example of this argument, see Taylor, "Non-Capitalist Wealth," p. 472.

CHAPTER IV

1. Gutton, *La Société et les pauvres*, p. 53.
2. A.D. (Aix), XXI H, II E 274, "Second Registre des biens des Pauvres . . . d'l'hôpital-général de la Charité, commensé le 17e novembre, 1732."
3. These figures are rough estimates derived from Baehrel, *Une Croissance*, pp. 604-15, tables 38-42. The methodology was inspired by Hufton, *Bayeux*, p. 82.
4. Bib. Mej., Ms. 838, Miollis, "Mémoire sur les Enfans Trouvés," p. 34.
5. This percentage is based on a probable late-eighteenth-century population of 25,000. See above, pp. 4,132.
6. Gutton, *La Société et les pauvres*, p. 53.
7. Pierre Deyon, *Amiens, capitale provinciale: Étude sur la société urbaine au 17e siècle* (Paris and La Haye, 1967), p. 358. The figures are 1,149 of a total population of approximately 30,000.
8. Hufton, *Bayeux*, p. 86.
9. See Sabatier, *St-Jacques*.
10. Augustin Roux, *Les Fonds des Archives départementales des Bouches-du-Rhône*, Part II, Vol. 2 *Dépot annexe d'Aix-en-Provence* (Marseille, 1954), p. 124. The surviving register is A.D. (Aix), XXX H, E 1, "Registre ou sont inscrits tous les Enfans qui passent dans L'Oeuvre depuis 1770 jusqu' En [1792]."
11. Valran, *Misère et charité*, p. 189.
12. A.D., IG 235 bis, "Etat du diocèse d'Aix," 1782. The only other of Aix's charities with a fixed population was St. Joachim, which fed and housed six of the blind.
13. A.D. (Aix), XXX H, E 1, Enfants Abandonnées, "Registre."
14. It is impossible to tell what percentage of Aix's population professed the Reformed religion, either before or after the Revocation. It is estimated that there were from six to seven thousand Protestants in Provence, clustered mostly around the village of Lourmarin, in 1682. In 1685 the number was reduced to fourteen or fifteen hundred. (Bourde, in Baratier, ed., *Histoire de Provence*, p. 329). Aix probably had fewer than one hundred Protestants after 1685.
15. Coste, *La Ville d'Aix*, 2:982-83.
16. Haitze, *Histoire d'Aix*, 6:166.
17. Coste, *La Ville d'Aix*, 2:983.
18. There is no information available on the earnings of these craftsmen: the lifestyle of the urban artisanate is one of the great unresearched questions of Old Regime social history.
19. A.D. (Aix), XXI H, II E 274, "Second Registre des biens des Pauvres . . . de l'hôpital-général de la Charité, commençé le 17e novembre, 1732." See also Chapter I.
20. A.M., GG 524, "Extrait des Registres de Parlement . . . ," August 21, 1720.
21. Sabatier, *St-Jacques*, 2:876-888, 931.
22. Valran, *Misère et charité*, pp. 95-102.
23. With regard to the nursing staff, Valran states "since recruitment was difficult the personnel was not completely clerical." (*Misère et charité*, p. 102.) This would seem to imply that the majority of the nursing staff were in religious orders.
24. Ibid., pp. 104-5.
25. These figures date from the years 1780-83. Sabatier, *St-Jacques*, 2:931.
26. Valran, *Misère et charité*, p. 110; Lib. Arb. 415, "Reglemens pour l'hôpital des Incurables de cette Ville d'Aix," 1766.
27. A.D. (Aix), XXIII H, IV A 1, "Règlement de l'hôpital des Insensés de cette ville d'Aix," 1695. The classic history of the treatment of the insane is Foucault, *Histoire de la folie*.

28. All quotations in this paragraph come from A.D. (Aix), XXIII H, IV A 1, "Règlement de l'hôpital-général des Insensés," 1705.

29. Children under four received by the Charité are listed in its register as "sent to St. Jacques to be nourished in conformity with the règlement of 1688." (A.D. [Aix], XX H, II F 9, Charité, "Procès—verbaux d'admissions des pauvres," 1743-1812.)

30. Carrière, *La Population d'Aix,* pp. 54-55; Sabatier, *St-Jacques,* 3:1074.

31. Sabatier, *St-Jacques,* 3:1074.

32. Bib. Mej., Ms. 838, Miollis, "Enfans Trouvés," p. 3.

33. At Marseille and Lyon only one-half of the children in the hôtel-Dieu died before age seven; at Grenoble the figure was only one-fourth (ibid., p.6.)

34. Statistics in ibid, pp. 7, 8, 15, 64; for the letter to Grenoble, Bib. Mej., Ms. 841, "Mémoire dans lequel on répond aux demandes que Ms. les Recteurs de l'Hôpital d'Aix-en-Provence, ont faites à Ms. les Administrators de l'hôpital de Dijon"; See also Baron Guillibert, "Contribution à l'histoire des hôpitaux d'Aix et de Montpellier," *Annales de Provence* 3 (May-June, 1909):2-8.

35. Bib. Mej., Ms. 838, Miollis, "Enfans Trouvés," pp. 19, 21-22, 68. Real wages are my calculations.

36. Ibid., p. 85.

37. Ibid., pp. 66, 81, 106-7.

38. A.D. (Aix), XXI H, II E 1, Charité, *Règlemens,* p. 11.

39. A.D. (Aix), XXI, H, II E 1, Charité, *Règlemens,* 1779, pp. 81-83. These stipulations were considerably tightened in times of financial difficulty. For example, when the financial crisis of the 1760's necessitated a reduction in the number of the Charité's inmates, the rectors decreed that only true orphans would be admitted until the emergency passed. (A.D. [Aix], XXI H, II E 34, Deliberations, 1762-74.)

40. A.D. (Aix), XXI H, II F 9, Charité, "Registre," passim.

41. A.D. (Aix), XXI H, II E 34, Charité, Deliberations, June 14, 1764.

42. A.D. (Aix), XXI H, II E 33, Charité, Deliberations, May 17, 1753.

43. This figure is based on an analysis of the 256 cases which give information about the eventual disposition of the inmates in question.

44. A.D. (Aix), XXI H, II F 9, Charité, "Registre," June, 1770.

45. Both cases in A.D. (Aix), XXI H, II F 9, Charité, "Registre,"

46. Philippe Ariès, *Centuries of Childhood: A Social History of Family Life,* trans. Robert Baldick (New York, 1962), pp. 38-40.

47. A.D. (Aix), XXI H, II F 9, Charité, "Registre," passim.

48. I could not find mortality figures for children of comparable age groups in Aix. However, in Caen during the period 1774 to 1792, 21 percent of the children of *fermiers,* 27 percent of the children of artisans, and 30 percent of the children of *journaliers* died between the ages of one and nine.

49. A.D. (Aix), XXI H, II E 33, Charité, Deliberations, October 26, 1749, March 30, 1758.

50. For the text of the arrêt, see A.D. (Aix), XXI H, II E 45, "Arrest du Parlement de Provence, du 21 février 1742." For its ineffectiveness, A.D. (Aix), XXI H, II E 33, Deliberations, August 27, 1744, November 15, 1744.

51. A.D. (Aix) XXI H, II E 34, Deliberations, April 7, 1763, March 20, 1766.

52. Ibid., December 1, 1763, December 15, 1765, March 30, 1766; A.D. (Aix), XXI H, II E 36, Deliberations, June 15, 1780.

53. A.D. (Aix), XXI H, II E 45, arrêt of Parlement, February 21, 1742.

54. Ibid.

55. A.D. (Aix), XXI H, II E 1, Charité, *Règlemens,* 1779, pp. 16, 26-27.

56. A.D. (Aix) XXI H, II E 5, Charité, Deliberations, 1772 ff., February 25, 1779.

57. A.D. (Aix) XXI H, II E 34, Deliberations, 1741-62, January 8, 1741.

58. A.D. (Aix) XXI H, II E 1, *Règlemens,* pp. 20-23; *Règlemens,* 1779, pp. 89-90.

59. A.D. (Aix), XXI H, II E 1, *Règlements Généraux pour les Pauvres de l'hôpital-Général La Charité d'Aix* (Aix, 1687), p. 24.

60. A.D. (Aix) XXI H, II E1, Charité, *Règlemens,* 1779, p. 54. For an example, see A.D. (Aix), XXI H, II E 33, Charité, Deliberations, 1741-62, May 12, 1754.

61. A.D. (Aix), XXI H, II E 33, Charité, Deliberations, 1741-62, February 13, 1749.

62. For the permissive attitudes towards sexuality in children which prevailed in noble families, see Ariès, *Centuries of Childhood,* and David Hunt, *Parents and Children in History: The Psychology of Family Life in Early Modern France* (New York, 1970).

63. A.D. (Aix), XXI H, II E 1, Charité, *Règlemens,* p. 13.

64. A.D. (Aix), XXI H, II E 33, Charité, Deliberations, 1741-62, December 2, 1751.

65. A.D. (Aix), XXI H, II E 1, Charité, *Règlemens,* pp. 20-21.

66. A.D. (Aix), XXI H, II E 33, Charité, Deliberations, 1741-62, July 24, 1749; May 18, 1749.

67. See E. P. Thompson, "Time, Work-Discipline, and Industrial Capitalism," *Past and Present* 38 (December, 1967): 56-97, and *The Making of the English Working Classes* (New York, 1964); Neil Smelser, *Social Change in the Industrial Revolution* (Chicago, 1959), and Sidney Pollard, *The Genesis of Modern Management: A Study of the Industrial Revolution in Great Britain* (London, 1965).

68. I have no proof of this, but I think that the mid-seventeenth-century fabriques of the hospital-general were the first "factories" in Aix. Those few private textile workshops in the town came later, I believe. A similar case of charitable institutions pioneering in the development of industrial techniques occurred in Lyon a century earlier; it was Lyon's Aumône-Général which pioneered the manufacturing of silk in the city. (Gascon, *Grand commerce et vie urbaine au XVIe siècle* 2:795-801.)

69. A.D. (Aix), XXI H, II F 9, 1774, 1789.

70. A.D. (Aix), XXI H, II E 1, *Règlemens,* 1779, p. 85-87.

71. A.D. (Aix), XXI H, II E 1, *Règlemens,* 1779, p. 87.

72. A.D. (Aix), XXI H, II E 34, Deliberations, 1762-72, June 7, 1764.

73. A.D., IG 235 bis, "Etat du diocèse d'Aix," 1782.

74. A.D. (Aix), XXVII, F 1, "Livre des délibérations du Bureau de La maison hospitalière . . . de la Pureté commencé le 5 janvier 1711."

75. A.D. (Aix), XXXIII H, Corpus Domini, "3ème Registre des délibérations . . . ," March 19, 1786.

76. Bib. Mej., Ms. 1191, "Description Historique, Geographique et Topographique," pp. 118-19.

77. Bib. Mej., Ms. 1192, "Relation de la vie et de la mort de Catherine Tempier ditte argentine, fille orpheline de l'hôpital-général de la Charité de cette ville d'Aix, 1709."

78. Ibid., pp. 3, 95, 151, 152-53.

79. "These Instruments are bands of iron or of brass decorated with large points of different styles, with small blades of iron, ended in points decorated on each side with curved points, with knives, with scissors, with spikes, with pieces of pewter." Ibid., p. 53.

80. Ibid., p. 60.

81. A.D. (Aix), XXI H, II F 9, Charité, "Procès-verbaux."

82. A.D. (Aix), XXI H, II E 274, "Second Registre des biens des pauvres . . . ."

83. A.D. (Aix), XXI H, II E 229-36, Registers for the distribution of bread, 1692-99; II E 237, "Distribution du Pain . . ." 1703-5; II E 238, "Rolle des Pauvres de la Ville Auxquels on Distribué Le Pain Touts Les Dimanches," 1705-52.

84. Records show that such distributions took place in 1740-41, and scattered mentions, too numerous to list, occur in the minutes of the Charité throughout the century.

85. A.D. (Aix), XXI H, II E 1, *Règlemens,* pp. 7-8. The record surviving is A.D. (Aix), XXI H, II E 238, "Rolle des pauvres."

86. Bib. Mej., F 739, *Institution et Règlements du Bureau Général de Charité . . .* (Aix, 1702), p. 5, lists Guevarre as one of the founding directors.

87. A letter from De La Tour, the intendant of Provence, dating from January, 1778, states that these bureaux have ceased to operate. A.D., C 4181, De La Tour to Necker, January 16, 1778.

88. Bib. Mej., Res. D 349, *Règlemens Des Bureaux de Charité,* pp. 10-11.
89. Ibid., pp. 34-35.
90. Ibid.
91. For the years of crises, see Vovelle, in Baratier, *Histoire de Provence,* pp. 399-400. The quote is from A.D. (Aix), XXI H, II E 33, Charité, Deliberations, 1741-62, June 27, 1751. See also A.D. (Aix) XXI H, II E 34, Charité, Deliberations, 1762 ff., July 4, 1767.
92. Baehrel, *Une Croissance,* p. 103.
93. Carrière, *La Population d'Aix,* pp. 56-57.
94. Admissions to the Charité were suspended on the following occasions: July 4, 1767; November 1, 1767; Feburary 25, 1768; June 4, 1769; May 13, 1770; June 9, 1771 (A.D. [Aix], XXI H, II E 34, Deliberations, 1762-71.)
95. A.D. (Aix), XXXII H, H 1, "Extrait des Registres des Délibérations de L'Oeuvre des Prisons de la Conciergerie de cette ville d'Aix . . . ."
96. A.D. (Aix), XVI H, II F 17, "Livre . . . de la Fondation de Messire Antoine de Très, Conseiller du Roy en La Cour de Parlement . . . ."
97. *La Vie penible et laborieuse de Jean Joseph Esmieu: Marchand colporteur en Provence sous la Révolution française,* ed. Pierre Du Bois (Toulon, 1967), pp. 12-13.

CHAPTER V

1. A.M., BB 101, "Délibérations Communales," p. 161.
2. Haitze, *Histoire d'Aix,* 6:494.
3. A.M., FF 2, Règlements de Police, "Précis des Loix et arrêts de Règlements qui commettent Les Consuls-Lieutenants de Police, à L'expulsion des Mendians."
4. A.D. (Aix), XXI H, II E 1, Charité, *Règlemens,* p. 9.
5. A.M., BB 38, "Délibérations communales," June 19, 1541; A.M., BB 60, "Délibérations communales," July 15, 1564; A.D. (Aix), XXI H, II E 1, Charité, *Règlemens,* p. 9.
6. A.M., FF 2, Règlements de Police, "Arrest de La Cour de Parlement," 1743.
7. A.M., CC 512, Comptabilité de la Ville, "Distribution . . . aux pauvres qu'on expulsat de la Ville avec order de retourner dans leur lieu d'originé," April 12, 1588; A.M., AA 14, Documents de la Ville d'Aix, "Ordre aux Egyptiens et Bohemians de sortir de la Provence . . . ," August 14, 1614; "Injunction faite aux mendiants non domiciliés à Aix d'avoir à se retire chez cux," March 5, 1616; A.M., BB 99, Délibérations Communales, "Interdiction aux gardes des portes de laissir entrer les soldats ou pauvres étrangers . . . ," November 3, 1625; A.M., FF 2, Règlements de Police, "Précis des Loix . . . ," laws of August 17, 1644, January 15, 1683, January 13, 1710, February 5, 1714, October 5, 1716, and July 5, 1717.
8. A.M., FF 2, Règlements de Police, "Extrait des Registres du Bureau de Police de cette ville d'Aix," May 22, 1789.
9. A.M., FF 2, Règlements de Police, "Arrest de La Cour de Parlement," 1743.
10. A.D. (Aix), XXI H, II E 33, Charité, Deliberations, 1741-62, July 27, 1749.
11. Lib. Arb. 369, "Déclaration du Roy concernant le Mendiants et Vagabonds," July 18, 1724.
12. A.D. (Aix), XXI H, II F 11, "Livre d'entrée des mendiants enfermés en vertu de l'ordonance royale du juillet 1724." The entries range in date from January 16, 1725, to June 7, 1733. Doubtless numerous repeat offenders escaped the scrutiny of the Charité's officials; how many, we cannot tell.
13. It is impossible to know how the remaining 5 percent (61) had come to enter the hospital-general.
14. See the contemporary complaints about the inefficiency of the force in A.D., C 4178, "Police: Mendiants," 1763-64, *Mémoire Sur Les Vagabonds et Sur Les Mendiants* (Soissons and Paris, 1764), p. 45.
15. P. Crépillon, "Un 'Gibier des prévôts': mendiants et vagabonds au XVIIe siècle entre la Vire et la Dives," *Annales de Normandie* 17:3 (October, 1967): 226-27.
16. Carrière, *La Population d'Aix,* pp. 86-87.

17. Haitze, *Histoire d'Aix*, 6:494.

18. For a comparable caste of professional beggars in Paris, see Jeffry Kaplow, "Sur la population flottante de Paris à la fin de l'ancien régime," *Annales historiques de la Révolution française*, 39: 187 (January -March 1967): 2-14.

19. The Italian beggar persisted in Provence in later years. See A.D., C 4180, "Police: Mendiants," 1768-70, letter from Venetian Consul to De La Tour, October 5, 1768; and A.D., C 4184, "Police, Dépôt de Mendicité d'Aix," 1773-75, various documents concerning Italian beggars. The Genoese beggar was a familiar figure in Provence as late as 1798; see A.M., LL 247, "Mendicité et Vagabondage," Department to Municipality, 8 Vendémiaire, an 7.

20. For the depressed economy of these areas see Georges Lefebvre, *Etudes Orléanais* (Paris, 1962-63); Jeffry Kaplow, *Elbeuf During the Revolutionary Period: History and Social Structure* (Baltimore, 1964), and Hufton, *Bayeux*.

21. Abel Poitrineau, "Aspects de l'emigration temporaire et saisonnière en Auvergne à la fin du XVIIIe et au début du XIXe siècle," *Revue d'histoire moderne et contemporaire* 9 (1962):7-40.

22. A.D., C 4178, "Police: Mendiants", 1763-64, *Mémoire Sur Les Vagabonds*.

23. These calculations are based on the people noted in the register as captured in a group. Doubtless they do not show all the beggars who traveled together; in some cases the police may have been able to arrest only one or two people from a group. These people would not show up in these statistics as traveling in a group.

24. I was unable to find any interrogations of people arrested as beggars. But where such records exist, they usually show that, when questioned, the suspects maintained that they begged only to keep themselves alive while looking for work. See Thomas M. Adams, "The Phenomenon of Beggary in Eighteenth Century France: A Sample Taken from Rennes in 1777 and Some Notes on Relevant Writings," (unpublished seminar paper, Dept. of History, University of Wisconsin, 1971).

25. A.D., IG 235 bis, "Etat du diocèse d'Aix," 1782.

26. That these patterns of migration were standard for the area is confirmed by Michel Vovelle's study of immigration into Marseille, based on a survey of the geographical origins of the signers of marriage contracts. He found that most came from the valley of the Rhône, from Lyon, from Dauphiné, and from Italy, while few were from Languedoc. (Vovelle, *Piété baroque et déchristianisation*, p. 370, and in Baratier, ed., *Histoire de Provence*, p. 356).

27. Marseille was the home of 24 beggars, and Toulon of 10 (A.D., [Aix], XXI H, II F 11, "Livre d'entrée des mendiants").

28. Baehrel, *Une Croissance*, vol. 1, passim; A. Bourde, "La Provence baroque," and "La Provence au Grand Siècle," in Baratier, ed., *Histoire de Provence*, pp. 276-80, 316-18, respectively; M. Vovelle, "Le dixhuitième siècle provençal," in Baratier, ed., *Histoire de Provence*, pp. 349-54.

29. This cycle has been best described by Emmanuel LeRoy Ladurie, *Les Paysans de Languedoc* (Paris, 1966).

30. Baehrel, *Une Croissance*, 1:476; A.M., FF 97, Délibérations Communales, "Ordonnance du Bureau de la Police de la Ville d'Aix, Portant Règlement pour les Travailleurs, Instrumens de labeur, et forages des Bêtes," March 23, 1722.

31. Baehrel, *Une Croissance*, 1:495.

32. Bib. Mej., Ms. 263, "Etat du .diocèse d'Aix par paroisses et par doyennes vers 1730."

33. Ibid.

34. Ibid.

35. Vovelle, *Piété baroque et déchristianisation*, p. 253.

36. For example, in Lyon in the 1770's the majority of those arrested for beggary were agricultural laborers. And here too lack of organized aid in the rural areas was a factor in driving the country people into the city to beg (Gutton, *La Société et les pauvres*, pp. 162-70).

37. Bib. Mej., Ms. 263, "Etat du diocèse," 1730.

38. A.D., IG 235 bis, "Etat du diocèse d'Aix," 1782.

39. Crépillon, "Un 'Gibier des prévôts'," p. 225.

40. Adams, "Phenomenon of Beggary," p. 11.

41. Olwen Hufton has described how much easier it was for a man than a woman to "opt out" of the circumstances of poverty. See "Women in Revolution, 1789-96," *Past and Present* 53 (November, 1971): p. 93.

42. Adams, "Phenomenon of Beggary," Chart I. See also Crépillon, "Un 'Gibier des prévôts'," p. 225.

43. See, once again, Adams, "Phenomenon of Beggary," and Crépillon, "Un 'Gibier des prévôts.' " Gutton has found that among the urban beggars arrested in Lyon in 1770, the majority were aged fifty to eighty (Gutton, *La Société et les pauvres,* p. 116).

44. A.D. (Aix), XX H, I E 51, "Déclarations de grossesse," 1787-88.

45. Of the total of 254 thefts recorded for the years 1773-90, 57 can be definitely classified as this sort of "country thievery." In addition, numerous crimes among the 131 thefts identified in the record merely as "vol," with no details given, probably fall into this category.

46. A.D. (Aix), B, IV B 1253, Sénéchaussée d'Aix, "Procédures criminals," 1776; A.D. (Aix), B, IV B 1250, "Informations criminelles," 1774.

47. A.D. (Aix), B, IV B 1253, Sénéchaussée d'Aix, "Procédures criminals," 1776.

48. Ibid.

49. For the career of De Besse, see Vovelle, "Provence sage, 1750-1788," in Baratier, ed., *Histoire de Provence,* p. 374.

50. Richard Cobb, *The Police and the People: French Popular Protest, 1789-1820* (Oxford, 1970), pp. 131-50.

51. See A.D. (Aix), U, 120 bis, U 1, Brigandage, 1807-25; also Agulhon, *La Vie sociale en Provence intérieure,* pp. 369-405.

52. A.D. (Aix), B, IV B 1253, Sénéchaussée d'Aix, "Procédures criminals," 1776.

53. This figure is only the vaguest approximation. My figures for the crime rate per year come from the court of the sénéchaussée of Aix, whose jurisdiction covers not only Aix but much of the surrounding countryside. It is impossible to find exact population figures for this area. I have arbitrarily taken the figure of 70,000.

54. This low rate of murder was apparently typical of eighteenth-century France. See Robert Darnton, "French History: The Case of the Wandering Eye," *New York Review of Books* 20:5 (April 5, 1973): 28.

55. A.D. (Aix), B, IV B 989, "Sentences criminelles," 1780-90; IV B 988, "Sentences criminelles," 1773-79.

56. A.D., C 3221, Refuge.

57. Edward Shorter, "Illegitimacy, Sexual Revolution and Social Change in Modern Europe," *The Journal of Interdisciplinary History* 2:2 (Autumn, 1971): 236-72.

58. These examples and the statistics come from A.D. (Aix), XX H, I E 51, St. Jacques, "Déclarations de grossesse," 1787-88.

59. A.D. (Aix), B, IV B 1253, Sénéchaussée d'Aix, "Informations criminelles," 1789.

60. A.D. (Aix), B, IV B 1250, Sénéchaussée d'Aix, "Informations criminelles," 1774.

61. A.D. (Aix), XXI H, II E 274, "Second Registre des biens des Pauvres," 1732 ff. .

62. Ibid.

63. Ibid.

64. A.D. (Aix), B, IV B 1250, Sénéchaussée d'Aix, "Informations criminelles," 1774.

65. A.D. (Aix), B, IV B 1274, Sénéchaussée d'Aix, "Informations criminelles," 1789.

66. Bib. Mej., Ms. 263, "Etat du diocèse," 1730.

67. A.D. (Aix), B, IV B 989, "Sentences criminelles," 1780-90, August 1784, and March 1788.

68. A.D. (Aix), XXI H, II E 274, "Second Registre des biens des Pauvres," 1732.

69. In this I follow Jeffry Kaplow, "The Culture of Poverty in Paris on the Eve of the Revolution," *International Review of Social History* 12:2 (1967): 277-91.

70. Bib. Mej., Ms. 263, "Etat du diocèse," 1730.

71. One such charge was filed against an innkeeper of Aix and his servant girl in June of 1774. (A.D. [Aix], B, IV B 988, "Sentences criminelles," 1773-79.)

72. A.D. (Aix), B, IV B 1250, Sénéchaussée d'Aix, "Informations criminelles," 1774.

73. A.D. (Aix), B, IV B 1273, "Informations criminelles," 1789.

74. See the work by students of Pierre Chaunu in Normandy, for example, Bernadette Boutelet, "Etude par sondage de la criminalité dans la bailliage du Pont-de-L'Arche," *Annales de Normandie* 12:4 (December, 1962): 235-62; and Jean-Claude Gégot, "Etude par sondage de la criminalité dans le bailliage de Falaise: criminalité diffuse ou société criminelle?" *Annales de Normandie* 16:2 (June, 1966): 103-64.

75. Since the work of Enrico Ferri *(Criminal Sociology* [New York, 1898]), changes in patterns of crime have usually been tied to changes in the economy. Ferri suggests that crimes of violence are characteristic of preindustrial, peasant societies, while industrial and urbanized areas show a far greater proportion of crimes against property. Theft is seen as the weapon of the townsman, wise in the ways of the marketplace, while assault is traditionally the weapon of the slow-witted but "elemental" peasant. But this is not entirely convincing, for Aix at least. There most of the thefts were country thievery, while violence was connected with the urban marketplace and cabaret.

76. The deliberations of Aix's municipal council for the years from 1750 to 1789 do not disclose any major bread riots or other incidents of popular violence. Further confirmation of this rather doubtful evidence would, however, be desirable.

77. The attitude of the poor of the Old Regime toward the police is a subject of debate among historians. Timothy LeGoff and Donald Sutherland, studying a country district in Brittany, have found great distrust and suspicion of the police among the peasantry. (T. J. A. LeGoff and D. M. G. Sutherland, "Crime and Counter-Revolution in Brittany," unpublished paper, 1971). But Jeffry Kaplow finds among the Parisian poor the same willingness to run to the police with every complaint that I have postulated. Kaplow, however, nonetheless maintains that the poor hated the police ("Culture of Poverty," p. 284).

78. Both in A.D. (Aix), B, IV B 989, "Sentences criminelles," 1780-90.

79. Esmieu, *Vie pénible et laborieuse.*

CHAPTER VI

1. For population trends in France as a whole, see S. Dupaquier, "Sur la population française au XVIIe et au XVIIIe siècle," *Revue historique* 239:1 (January-March, 1968): 43-80, and L. Henry, "The Population of France in the Eighteenth Century," in *Population in History,* eds. D. V. Glass and D. E. C. Eversley (London, 1965).

2. Vovelle, in Baratier, ed., *Histoire de Provence* pp. 354-55.

3. Baehrel, *Une Croissance,* 1:236, 254

4. Ibid., 1:236.

5. A.D. (Aix), XXI H, II F 11, "Livre d'entrée des mendiants."

6. Christian Paultre, *De la repression de la mendicité et du vagabondage en France sous l'ancien régime* (Paris, 1906) p. 603. There were doubtless many factors other than a rise in the number of beggars which might have brought about the startling change reflected in these figures; for example, the effectiveness of enforcement might have changed. But such a large jump could hardly have come about without at least some increase in the number of beggars.

7. Labrousse, *Mouvement des prix,* and *La Crise de l'économie française à la fin de l'ancien régime et au début de la Révolution* (Paris, 1944).

8. Baehrel, *Une croissance,* 2:548, Table 4, "Le Prix du pain de boulangerie à Aix," and 2:608, Table 40, "Salaries de Charretiers."

9. Vovelle, in Baratier, ed., *Histoire de Provence,* p. 348.

10. Baehrel, *Une Croissance,* 1:75.

11. Sabatier, *St-Jacques*, Vol. 4, Annex I, This table groups gifts and legacies together with the product of the quête. See also Vovelle, *Piété baroque et déchristianisation*, p. 262, Planche 48.

12. Vovelle, *Piété baroque et déchristianisation*, p. 244, Planche 43.

13. A.D. (Aix), XXI H, II E 71-II E 110, Charité, Accounts, 1720-62.

14. A.D. (Aix), XXI H, II E 33, Charité, Deliberations, 1741-62, June 27, 1751; and Lib. Arb. 415, *Consultation de Ms. Brès et Emerigon.*

15. Grimaldi's will is printed in Edouard Mechin (ed.), *Annales du Collège Royal Bourbon d'Aix depuis les premières demarches faites pour sa foundation jusqu' qu 7 ventôse an III* (Marseille, 1891), 2:382-84.

16. A.D. (Aix), XXI H, II B 3, Charité, Legs Chambon.

17. A.D. (Aix), XXI H, II E 33, Charité, Deliberations, December 17, 1744;June 26, 1755; A.D. (Aix), XXIII H, IV A 1, *Lettres Patentes d'l'Hôpital des Insensés* (Aix, 1737).

18. Raymond Darricau, "L'action charitable d'une reine de France: Anne d'Autriche," *XVIIe Siècle* 90-91 (1971): 111-125, gives a rather superficial account of Anne's charitable activities. For her role in the founding of the Charité, see A.D. (Aix), XXI H, II E 1, Charité, *Règlements*, 1779, p. 4.

19. A.D. (Aix), XXI H, II A 1, *Lettres Patents, portant confirmation des privilèges de l'Hôpital-Général La Charité d'Aix*, 1741, p.2.

20. For a statement of the importance of letters patent to a charity, see A.D., C 3222, Mont-de-Piété, "Copie de Mémoire Envoyé le 9 avril, 1781, à M. Necker."

21. Valran, *Misère et charité*, p. 341.

22. Sabatier, *St-Jacques*, 1:152.

23. A.D. (Aix), XXI H, II E 29, Charité, Deliberations, August 14, 1721; August 17, 1721; September 7, 1721; October 12, 1721; XXI H, II E 33, February 6, 1749.

24. A.D. (Aix), XXIII H, *Lettres Patentes pour l'Hôpital des Insensés*, 1737.

25. A.D. C 3220, Charité, 1760-80, De La Tour to Trudaine, Feb. 29, 1760; Trudaine to De La Tour, March 31, 1760; De La Tour to Trudaine, April 28, 1760; Trudaine to De La Tour, May 30, 1760; Bertin to De La Tour, July 1, 1760.

26. A.M., BB 111, Aix, Délibérations communales, 1757-71, December 17, 1760.

27. For example see Lib. Arb. 415, *Consultation de Ms. Brès et Emerigon.*

28. Ibid.

29. Ibid.

30. Ibid.

31. Ibid.

32. Ibid.

33. Lib. Arb. 415, *Arrest du Conseil D'État du Roi, et Lettres Patents Sur Icelui, qui pourvoit à la reduction des dettes de l'Hôpital de la Charité d'Aix, et à leur payement* (Aix, May 30, 1762).

34. A.D., C 3213, Hôpitaux: *Commission générale des Hôpitaux, Lettres Patentes, Pourtant établissement d'une Commission pour procéder à la vérification des biens et charges, dettes actives et passives des Hôpitaux de Oeuvres de Charité du pays de Provence, ainsi qu'à leur administration* (Aix, 1762).

35. A.D., C 3213, Hôpitaux: Commission générale, Mayor and consuls of Aix to Vice Chancellor, April 22, 1765.

36. A.D., C 3213, Hôpitaux: Commission générale, De La Tour to De L'Averdy, July 24, 1765.

37. A.D., C 3213, Hôpitaux: Commission générale, Vice Chancellor to Mayor and Consuls of Aix, August 14, 1765.

38. A.D. (Aix), XXI H, II E 34, Charité, Deliberations, 1762 ff., February 6, 1766; June 8, 1766; April 12, 1767; March 10, 1768; July 28, 1768; January 29, 1769; April 9, 1769; January 21, 1770; January 24, 1771; April 3, 1771.

39. Ibid., July 15, 1764.

40. Ibid., July 4, 1767.

41. Ibid., November 1, 1767; May 15, 1768; June 4, 1769; May 13, 1770; June 9, 1771; May 6, 1779; October 31, 1779; November 14, 1779.

42. A.D. (Aix), XXI H, II F 9, "Procès-Verbaux," 1743-1812.

43. Bib. Mej. 415, "État de la Maison de la Charité de la Ville d'Aix, Depuis le 2 février 1687 jour du dernier enferment des Pauvres, jusques au 20 mars 1702;" A.D., 3217, Hôpitaux, Aix, Mémoire to Controller-General, September 7, 1760; A.D., 3220, Charité, 1760-80, "Etat de la Charité," April 24, 1780.

44. A.D. (Aix), XXI H, II E 34, Charité, Deliberations, 1762 ff., March 24, 1763; April 5, 1764; July 3, 1766. See also A.D., 3220, Charité, 1760-80, De La Tour to De L'Averdy, July 7, 1765.

45. Ibid., June 3, 1764.

46. A.D., 3220, Charité, 1760-80, "État des Remboursements faits de la Caisse des Créanciers de l'hôpital-général la Charité de la ville d'Aix depuis le 1 janvier 1763 jusques au 31 décembre 1766."

47. A.D. (Aix), XXI H, II E 112-II E 122, Charité, Accounts, 1765-77.

48. A.D. (Aix), XXI H, II E 34, Charité, Deliberations, 1762 ff., August 28, 1763; September 6, 1764; January 8, 1767.

49. A.D. (Aix), XXI H, II E 35, Charité, Deliberations 1772 ff., May 10, 1778.

50. Bib. Mej., 415, Lettres Patentes du Roi, Qui ordonnent l'execution d'un nouveau plan de libération pour l'Hôpital-Général de la Charité, de la ville d'Aix (Versailles, 1780). For Necker's reaction see A.C., 3220, Charité, 1760-80, Procureur du Pays to De la Tour, June 16, 1780; De la Tour to Necker, June 28, 1780; Necker to De La Tour, July 26, 1780; Necker to De La Tour, August 9, 1780.

51. For the hôtel-Dieu see Sabatier, St-Jacques, esp. Chapter IV, Annexe I. See also A.D., C 3217, Hôpitaux, Aix, Mémoire to Controller-General, September 7, 1760. This also details the situation of the Miséricorde. An account of the financial situation of all of Aix's charities is found in Valran, Misère et charité, pp. 191-241.

52. Valran, Misère et charité, pp. 245, 237-44; Gutton, La Société et les pauvres, p. 461; Camille Bloch, L'Assistance et l'état en France pendant la Révolution (Paris, 1908), pp. 260-315.

53. In earlier years deliberations of the bureaux contain long discussions about the health and morality, etc., of the charities' inmates, but after 1760 they refer only to financial matters.

54. A.D. (Aix), XXI H, II E 34, Charité, Deliberations, 1762 ff., November 18, 1762; December 23, 1762; December 8, 1762; May 8, 1768.

55. Valran, Misère et charité, pp. 219-20.

56. Bloch, L'Assistance et l'état, p. 308.

CHAPTER VII

1. Montesquieu, De l'Esprit des Lois, Bk. 23, Chapter 29, Voltaire, Philosophical Letters, Letter 20.

2. "Fondation," Encyclopédie, ou dictionnaire raisonné des sciences, des arts et des métiers, 2nd ed. (Geneva, 1778).

3. The standard works on Physiocracy are Georges Weulersse, Le Mouvement physiocratique en France (Paris, 1910) and Ronald L. Meek, The Economics of Physiocracy (Cambridge, Mass., 1963). A study which deals with not only the ideas of the Physiocrats but also their influence on government policy is John West Rogers, Jr., "The Opposition to the Physiocrats: A Study of Economic Thought and Policy in the Ancien Régime, 1750-1789" (unpublished Ph.D. dissertation, Dept. of History, The Johns Hopkins University, 1971).

4. This program is best treated in Bloch, L'Assistance et l'etat, pp. 157-77. Bloch puts far less emphasis on the Physiocratic contribution to the program than I have done.

5. The dépôts have been studied by Thomas M. Adams, "An Administrative Solution for the Problem of Beggary in Eighteenth Century France: The *dépôts de mendicité* (1764-1789)" (unpublished Ph. D. dissertation, Dept. of History, University of Wisconsin, 1972). Mr. Adams has kindly made available to me portions of this manuscript, which are the source of much of the following narrative.

6. A horrifying description of the ravages of these bands of beggars in the area of the Beauce can be found in A.C., C 4178, *Mémoire Sur Les Vagabonds,* a report printed and distributed by the royal government as propaganda for its new program.

7. For the text of the ordinance see A.D., C 4178: Police: Mendiants, 1763-64, "Déclaration du Roi concernant les Vagabonds et Gens sans aveu," August 3, 1764. The system of dépôts, although a logical extension of the policy behind the edict, was not a part of the original document. The dépôts were rather established by an arrêt de conseil of October 21, 1767.

8. A.D., C 4178, Police: Mendiants, 1763-64, Bertin to De La Tour, April 1, 1763; De La Tour to Bertin, April 13, 1763.

9. A.D., C 4178, Police: Mendiants, 1763-64, "Mémoire sur la déclaration du 3 août, 1764 . . . ."

10. A.D., C 4178, Police: Mendiants, 1763-64, "Lettre, Écrite par ordre de Sa Majeste, aux Archévêques et Evêques du Royaume, concernant les Mendiants," 1764.

11. A.D., C 4178, Police: Mendiants, 1763-64, archbishop of Aix, August 30, 1764; bishop of Fréjus, August 24 and August 29, 1764; diocese of Glandèves, undated; bishop of Riez, August 23, 1764.

12. A.D., C 4178, Police: Mendiants, Procureurs du Pays to De La Tour, August 31, 1764.

13. A.D., C 4178, Police: Mendiants, Rèsponse de M. le Controlleur-Général à M. de Regusse, président du Parlement de Provence.

14. A.D., C 4179, Police: Mendiants, De L'Averdy to De La Tour, October 19, 1766; De La Tour to Tarascon, Arles, Apt et al., November 24, 1766; de la Tour, "Etat des villes ou l'on pourvoit établie des entrepôts pour les Mandnias," January 26, 1767; De L'Averdy to De La Tour, February 21, 1767; De La Tour to l'Averdy, April 20, 1767; De L'Averdy to De La Tour, June 8, 1767, and September 23, 1767; De La Tour to De L'Averdy, October 12, 1767.

15. The controversy over the financing of the dépôts not only in Provence, but in the other pays d'états as well, is treated extensively in Adams, "Dépôts de mendicité," Chapter 9, "Political Problems: Resistance from Parlements and Estates," This section is based on Mr. Adams' treatment.

16. For the history of these complex claims, see Adams, "Dépôts de mendicité," also A.D., C 4181, Police, Mendiants, "Mémoire contenant des Observations Sur L'Ordinance du Roy Concernant Les Mendiants du 30 juillet, 1777;" letter from prévôt-général de Provence, October 14, 1777.

17. How this dispute was finally settled is unclear. Adams (p. 30) can find no evidence that Provence ever contributed its share of the costs for the dépôts, and argues that the royal government must have accepted its contention that it had already paid.

18. Paultre, *De la repression de la mendicité,* pp. 602-3.

19. A.D., C 4183, Police: Mendicité, "Dépôt de Mendicité d'Aix," 1770-72. For Mellon, see letter from l'abbé Marechal, prieur de Fromentière et archiviste du roy à Troyes en Champagne, November 22, 1774.

20. A.D., C 4182, Police, "Dépôt de Mendicité d'Aix," 1774-78; Intendant to Controller-General, undated.

21. A.D., C 4182, Police, "Dépôt de Mendicité d'Aix," 1774-78: report, undated and unsigned.

22. A.D., C 4182, Police, "Dépôt de Mendicité d'Aix," 1774-78, Intendant to Controller-General, undated.

23. For Turgot's views see *Oeuvres de Turgot,* ed. Gustave Schelle (Paris, 1913), 3:202-56.

24. The correspondence concerning the re-establishment of the dépôts can be found in A.C., C 4181 Police: Mendiants, Vagabonds, 1776-89.

25. Ibid., De La Tour to Clugny, June 1776.

26. Ibid., letter from prévôt-général de Provence, October 14, 1777; "Mémoire contenant des Observations Sur L'Ordinance du Roy Concernant Les Mendiants du 30 juillet, 1777."

27. In 1783 the intendant would write that "no dépôts have existed in Provence since May 1, 1776." (Ibid., De La Tour to Dormesson, June 13, 1783.)

28. There remains in the provincial archives no evidence that any ateliers de charité functioned in Provence. For a description of the program of ateliers elsewhere in France, see Jean-Louis Harouel, *Les Ateliers de charité dans la province de Haute-Guyenne* (Paris, 1969).

29. Victor Requetti, Marquis de Mirabeau, *L'Ami des hommes, ou traité de la population* (Paris, 1883), p. 43.

30. Ibid., p. 65.

31. Ibid., pp. 348-52.

32. Ibid., p. 220.

33. Ibid., p. 351.

34. Ibid., pp. 13-25.

35. At Aix, for example, in the 45 years from 1722 to 1767, the hôtel-Dieu cared for 4,844 abandoned infants, an average of 108 per year, while in the period from 1768 to 1775 the yearly average rose to 261. (Bib. Mej., Ms. 838, Miollis, "Mémoire sur les Enfans Trouvés," p. 3.)

36. Mirabeau, *L'Ami des Hommes*, pp. 353-55.

37. Bib. Mej., Ms. 1191, "Description Historique, Geographique et Topographique." See especially pp. 175-76; 183-85.

38. Bib. Mej., 7796, Miollis, *Réflexions Importantes Sur L'État Présent des Communautés de Campagne en Provence* (Avignon, 1772), and Bib., Mej., Ms. 838.

39. Bouches-du-Rhône, *Encyclopédie Départementale*, Part I, Vol. 2, *Dictionnaire Biographique des origins à 1800* (Paris and Marseille, 1931), pp. 265 (Haitze), 329 (Miollis).

40. Bib. Mej., 7694, Pierre Joseph de Haitze, *Le Secours des prisonniers;* Bib. Mej., F 884, t. 4, Haitze, *État de L'Hôpital La Miséricorde, des Pauvres Malades et Honteux de la Ville d'Aix* . . . (Aix, 1709); Haitze, *Histoire de la Ville d'Aix.*

41. Bib. Mej., 7694, Haitze, *Le Secours des prisonniers*, p. 3.

42. Ibid., p. 92.

43. Bib. Mej., F 884, t. 4, Haitze, *État de la Miséricorde*, p. 124.

44. Bib. Mej., Ms. 838, Miollis, "Mémoire sur les Enfans Trouvés," p. 135.

45. Bib. Mej., 7796, Miollis, *Réflexions Importantes*, 2:52-61.

46. Ibid., 1:69-70.

47. Valran, *Misère et charité*, pp. 398-99.

CONCLUSION

1. For the Revolutionary legislation on public assistance for the needy, see Jean Imbert, *Le Droit hospitalier de la Révolution et de l'Empire* (Paris, 1954).

2. Alfred Cobban, *The Social Interpretation of the French Revolution* (Cambridge, 1964), p. 170.

Bibliography

ARCHIVAL SOURCES

1. Archives of the Department of the Bouches-du-Rhône, Annex in Aix-en-Provence

This study is based for the most part on the records of Aix's hospitals and charities, found in Series H of the departmental archives, stored in the annex at Aix-en-Provence. These records are similar in type to those kept by hospitals and charities today. They include registers of the people entering the institutions, yearly account books, rules and regulations concerning the internal functioning of the charities, and notes of the deliberations of the institutions' governing boards. Citations for the specific documents consulted can be found in the notes.

The annex at Aix also houses the records of the town's various courts, classified under Series B of the departmental archives. Of these I found the criminal sentences handed down by the sénéchaussée court most useful in providing a profile of the criminal poor.

2. Archives of the Department of the Bouches-du-Rhône, main depository, Marseille

Series C, containing the records of the provincial administration of Provence, is housed in the main depository of the departmental archives at Marseille. Consisting mostly of correspondence between the intendant and his subdélégués, or between the intendant and his various agencies of the central administration, this series provides a record of the royal government's initiatives in the field of public assistance from the 1760's on. The series also contains the reports of government investigations into agencies of public assistance, which present much useful information about the history, financing, and functioning of Aix's municipal charities.

Another useful survey which provides information on the amount and type of charity available throughout Provence is a report on the state of the diocese of Provence undertaken by the Church in 1782. This is classified with other ecclesiastical records in Series G of the departmental archives.

3. Municipal Archives, Aix-en-Provence

Because the records of the city's hospitals have been removed to the departmental archives, the municipal archives of the city have relatively little to offer the historian of poverty and charity. Series EE, the deliberations of the communal council, has scattered references to the problems of poverty, while Series GG contains a few documents pertaining to Aix's charities. Series FF, the records of the municipal police, provide revealing sidelights on the life of the poor.

4. The Bibliothèque Méjanes

Aix's municipal library, the basis of which is the private collection of an eighteenth-century parlementaire, has a fine selection of the printed fund-raising pamphlets issued by the charities. It also has a few manuscripts of interest to the historian of charities, including Miollis's analysis of the care of the enfant trouvé, and the anonymous life of Catherine Tempier, an inmate of La Charité. The Méjanes also contains Pierre Joseph de Haitze's indispensable *Histoire de la ville d'Aix.*

5. The Libraire Arbaud

This little known collection, tucked away in the unheated back room of a usually deserted museum devoted to eighteenth-century porcelain, has a number of useful printed sources, both pamphlets issued by the charities and printed copies of royal and municipal ordinances on beggary.

OTHER ORIGINAL SOURCES

Bloch, Camille, and Tuetey, Alexandre (eds.). *Procès-verbaux et rapports du Comité de mendicité de la Constituante, 1790-1791.* Paris, 1911

Brosses, Charles de. *Lettres familières sur l'Italie*, ed. Yvonne Bezard. Paris, 1931

Collection des procès-verbaux des Assemblées-Générales du Clergé de France, depuis l'année 1560, jusqu'à présent. Paris, 1748-78

Encyclopédie, ou dictionnaire raisonné des sciences, des arts, et des métiers. Geneva, 1778

Esmieu, Jean Joseph. *La vie pénible et laborieuse de Jean Joseph Esmieu: Marchand colporteur en Provence sous la Révolution française*, ed. Pierre du Bois. Toulon, 1962

Haitze, Pierre-Joseph de. *Histoire de la Ville d'Aix, capitale de la Provence.* Aix, 1889.

Isambert, Jourdan, and Decrusy (eds.). *Recueil Général Des Anciennes Lois Françaises Depuis l'an 420 jusqu'à la révolution de 1789.* Paris, 1822-33

Mirabeau, Victor Requetti, Marquis de. *L'Ami des Hommes, ou traité de la population.* Paris. 1883

Montesquieu, Charles Louis Secondat, Baron de. *De l'Esprit des Lois.* Many editions

Necker, Jacques. *Oeuvres complètes de M. Necker,* Vol. 5, *De l'administration des finances.* Paris, 1820

Recueil des Actes, Titres et Mémoires . . . du Clergé de France. Paris, 1740

Turgot, Anne Robert Jacques, Baron de l'Aulne. *Oeuvres de Turgot,* ed. Gustave Schelle. 6 Vols. Paris, 1913

Voltaire (François-Marie Arouet). *Philosophical Letters.* Many editions

Young, Arthur. *Travels in the Kingdom of France.* Dublin, 1793

SECONDARY WORKS

Adams, Thomas M. "An Administrative Solution for the Problem of Beggary in Eighteenth Century France: The *dépôts de mendicité* (1764-1789)." Unpublished Ph.D. dissertation, Dept. of History, University of Wisconsin, 1972

Agulhon, Maurice. *La Sociabilité méridionale: Confréries et associations dans la vie collective en Provence orientale à la fin du 18ème siècle.* Aix, 1966

――――. *La Vie sociale en Provence intérieure au lendemain de la Révolution.* Paris, 1970

Allier, Raoul. *La cabale des dévôts, 1627-1666.* Paris, 1902

――――. (ed.) *La Compagnie du Très-Saint-Sacrament de l'Autel à Marseille: Documents publiés,* Paris, 1909

Ariès, Philippe. *Centuries of Childhood: A Social History of Family Life.* Trans. Robert Baldick, New York, 1962

Baehrel, René. *Une Croissance: La Basse-Provence rurale, fin du XVIe siècle-1789.* 2 Vols. Paris, 1961

Baratier, Edouard (ed.). *Histoire de Provence.* Toulouse, 1969

――――. *La Demographie provençale du XVIIe au XVIe siècle, avec chiffres de comparison pour le XVIIIe siècle.* Paris, 1961

Barber, Elinor G. *The Bourgeoisie in Eighteenth Century France.* Princeton, 1955

Blaug, M. "The Myth of the Old Poor Law and the Making of the New," *Journal of Economic History* 23:2 (June, 1963): 151-85

Bloch, Camille. *L'Assistance et l'état en France pendant la Révolution.* Paris, 1908

Bouches-du-Rhône. *Encyclopédie Départementale.* Part I, Vol. 4: *Dictionnaire biographique des origines à 1800.* Marseille, 1913-37

Bouchet, Michel. *L'assistance publique en France pendant la Révolution.* Paris, 1908

Boutelet, Bernadette. "Étude par sondage de la criminalité dans la bailliage du Pont-de-L'Arche," *Annales de Normandie* 4 (December, 1962):235-62

Brucker, Père Joseph. *La Compagnie de Jésus: Esquisse de son institut et de son histoire, 1521-1773.* Paris, 1919

Busquet, R., Bourrilly, L. L., and Agulhon, Maurice. *Histoire de la Provence.* Paris, 1966

Cahen, L. "Les idées charitables à Paris au XVIIe et au XVIIIe siècles, d'après les règlements des compagnies paroissiales," *Revue d'histoire moderne et contemporaire* 2(1900-1901):5-22

Carrière, Jacqueline. *La Population d'Aix-en-Provence à la fin du XVIIe siècle: Etude de démographie historique d'après le registre de capitation de 1695.* Aix, 1958

Chalumeau, R. P. "L'Assistance aux malades pauvres au dix-septième siècle," *XVIIe Siècle* 90-91 (1971):75-87

———. *St. Vincent de Paul.* Paris, 1959

Chill, Emmanuel. "Religion and Mendicity in Seventeenth Century France," *International Review of Social History* 7(1962):400-26

Coats, A. W. "Changing Attitudes to Labour in the Mid-18th Century," *Economic History Review* 11:1 (August, 1958):35-52

———. "Economic Thought and Poor Law Policy in the 18th Century," *Economic History Review* 9:1 (August, 1960):39-52

Cobb, Richard. *The Police and the People: French Popular Protest, 1789-1820.* Oxford, 1970

Cobban, Alfred. *The Social Interpretation of the French Revolution.* Cambridge, 1964

Cole, Charles W. *French Mercantilist Doctrines Before Colbert.* New York, 1931

Coste, Jean Paul. *La Ville d'Aix in 1695: Structure urbaine et société.* 2 Vols. Aix, 1970

Crépillon, P. "Un 'Gibier des prévôts': Mendiants et vagabonds au XVIIIe siècle entre la Vire et la Dives," *Annales de Normandie* 17:3 (October, 1967):223-53

D'Anders, P. Julien-Eymard. "Richesse et pauvreté dans l'oeuvre d'Yves de Paris," *XVIIe Siècle* 90-91 (1971): 17-47

Darricau, Raymond. "L'action charitable d'une reine de France: Anne d'Autriche," *XVIIe Siècle* 90-91 (1971):111-27

Darnton, Robert. "French History: The Case of the Wandering Eye," *New York Review of Books* 20:5 (April 5, 1973): 25-30

Davis, Natalie Z. "Poor Relief, Humanism and Heresy: The Case of Lyon," *Studies in Medieval and Renaissance History* 5(1966):217-75

De Backer, Augustin and Aloys. *Bibliothèque de la Compagnie de Jesus,* ed. Carlos Sommervogel, S. J. Vols. 2 & 3. Brussels and Paris, 1891-92

Deyon, Pierre. *Amiens, capitale provinciale: étude sur la société urbaine au 17e siècle.* Paris and La Haye, 1967

Dupaquier, S. "Sur la population française au XVIIe et au XVIIIe siècle," *Revue histoirque* 239:1 (January-March, 1968):43-80

Ferri, Enrico. *Criminal Sociology.* New York, 1898

Forget, Mireille. "Des prisons au bagne de Marseille: la charité a l'égard des condamnés au dix-septième siècle," *XVIIe Siècle* 90-91(1971):147-75

Forster, Robert. *The Nobility of Toulouse in the Eighteenth Century: A Social and Economic Study.* Baltimore, 1960

Foucault, Michel. *Histoire de la folie à l'âge classique.* Paris, 1961

Gascon, Richard. *Grand commerce et vie urbaine au XVIe siècle: Lyon et ses marchands.* 2 Vols. Paris, 1971

Gégot, Jean-Claude. "Etude par sondage de la criminalité dans le bailliage de Falaise: criminalité diffuse ou société criminelle? " *Annales de Normandie* 16:2 (June, 1966): 103-64

Groethuysen, Bernhard. *The Bourgeois: Catholicism vs. Capitalism in Eighteenth Century France.* New York, 1968

Guillibert, Baron. "Contribution à l'histoire des hôpitaux d'Aix et de Montpellier," *Annales de Provence* No. 3 (May-June, 1909):2-8

Gutton, J.-P. "A l'aube du XVIIe siècle: Idées nouvelles sur les pauvres," *Cahiers d'histoire* 10 (1965): 87-97

———. "Compte rendu d'un doctorat d'État: La Société et les Pauvres: l'exemple de l'aumône-générale de Lyon 1534-1789,"*L'Information historique* No. 2 (March-April, 1971):86-88

———. "La Mendicité au dix-huitième siècle," *L'Information historique* No. 2 (March-April, 1969):36-38

———. *La Société et les pauvres: L'Exemple de la generalité de Lyon, 1534-1789.* Paris, 1970

Harouel, Jean-Louis. *Les Ateliers de charité dans la province de Haute-Guyenne.* Paris, 1969

Henry, Louis. "The Population of France in the Eighteenth Century." In *Population in History: Essays in Historical Demography*, eds. D. V. Glass and D. E. C. Eversley. London, 1965

Hufton, Olwen. *Bayeux in the Late Eighteenth Century: A Social Study.* Oxford, 1967

———. "Begging, Vagrancy, Vagabondage and the Law: An Aspect of the Problem of Poverty in Eighteenth Century France," *European Studies Review* 2:2 (April, 1972):97-123

———. "Life and Death among the Very Poor." In *The Eighteenth Century*, ed. Alfred Cobban. New York, 1969

———. "Women in Revolution, 1789-96," *Past and Present* 53 (November, 1971): 90-108

Hunt, David. *Parents and Children in History: The Psychology of Family Life in Early Modern France.* New York, 1970

Imbert, Jean. *Le Droit hospitalier de la Révolution et de l'Empire.* Paris, 1954

———. *Les hôpitaux en droit canonique.* Vol. 7 of *L'Eglise et l'état au moyen âge.* Paris, 1947

———. "Les Prescriptions hospitalières du Concile de Trente et leur diffusion en France," *Revue d'histoire de l'Eglise de France* 42 (January-June, 1956):6-28

Joret, Charles. "Le P. Guevarre et la fondation de l'hôpital-général d'Auch," *Annales du Midi* 2(1890):27-35

———. "Le P. Guevarre et les bureaux de charité au XVIIe siècle," *Annales du Midi* 1(1889):340-93

Jordan, W. K. *The Charities of Rural England, 1480-1660: The Aspirations and Achievements of the Rural Society.* New York, 1962

———. *Philanthropy in England, 1480-1660: A Study in the Changing Pattern of English Social Aspiration.* London, 1956

Kaplow, Jeffry, "The Culture of Poverty in Paris on the Eve of the Revolution," *International Review of Social History* 12:2 (1967):277-91

———. *Elbeuf During the Revolutionary Period:History and Social Structure.* Baltimore, 1964

———. (ed.). *New Perspectives on the French Revolution: Readings in Historical Sociology.* New York, 1965

———. "Sur la population flottante de Paris à la fin de l'ancien régime," *Annales historiques de la Révolution française* 39:187 (January-March, 1967):2-14

Kingdon, Robert M. "Social Welfare in Calvin's Geneva," *American Historical Review* 76:1 (February, 1971):50-70

Labrousse, C. E. *Esquisse du mouvement des prix et des revenues en France au XVIIIe siècle.* 2 Vols. Paris, 1933

———. *La Crise de l'économie française à la fin de l'ancien régime et au début de la Révolution.* Paris, 1944

Lallemand, L. *La Révolution et les pauvres.* Paris, 1898

Lefebvre, Goorges. *Etudes Orléanais.* 2 Vols. Paris, 1962-63

LeGoff, T. J. A. and Sutherland, D. M. G. "Crime and Counter-Revolution in Brittany." Unpublished paper, Brock and York Universities, St. Catherines and Toronto, 1971

LeRoy Ladurie, Emmanuel. *Les Paysans de Languedoc.* Paris, 1966

Marshall, Dorothy. *The English Poor in the Eighteenth Century: A Study in Social and Administrative History.* London, 1969

McCloy, Shelby T. *Government Assistance in Eighteenth Century France.* Durham, N. C. 1946

McManners, John. *French Ecclesiastical Society under the Ancien Régime: A Study of Angers in the Eighteenth Century.* Manchester, 1960

Meek, Ronald. *The Economics of Physiocracy.* Cambridge, Mass., 1963

Milcent, Paul. "Spiritualité de la charité envers les pauvres selon St. Jean Eudes," *XVIIe Siècle* 90-91 (1971):47-57

Mollat, M. "La Notion de pauvreté au moyen âge: Position de problèmes," *Revue d'histoire de l'Eglise de France* 52(1966):5-23

Mousnier, Ronald. *Fureurs paysans.* Paris, 1967

Murtin, M.-Cl. "Les Abandons d'enfants à Bourg et dans le département de l'Ain à la fin du 18e siècle et dans le première moitié du 19e," *Cahiers d'Histoire* 102(1965):135-66

Owen, David. *English Philanthropy, 1660-1960.* Cambridge, Mass., 1964

Paultre, Christian. *De la Repression de la mendicité et du vagabondage en France sous l'ancien régime.* Paris, 1906

Poitrineau, Abel. "Aspects de l'émigration temporaire et saisonnière en Auvergne à la fin du XVIIIe et au début du XIXe siècle," *Revue d'histoire moderne et contemporaire* 9(1962):7-40

Pourrière, Jean. *Les Hôpitaux d'Aix-en-Provence au moyen âge: 13, 14, 15e siècles.* Aix, 1969

Poutet, Yves. "L'Enseignement des pauvres dans la France du dix-septième siècle," *XVIIe Siècle* 90-91 (1971):87-111

Poynter, J. R. *Society and Pauperism: English Ideas on Poor Relief, 1795-1834.* London and Toronto, 1969

Raimbault, Maurice. "Les oeuvres d'assistance en Provence de 1453 à 1789," *Encyclopédie Départementale des Bouches-du-Rhône.* Vol. 3. Marseille, 1931

Ranum, Orest A. *Paris in the Age of Absolutism: An Essay.* New York, 1968

Rogers, John West, Jr. "The Opposition to the Physiocrats: A Study of Economic Thought and Policy in the Ancien Régime, 1750-1789." Unpublished Ph.D. dissertation, Dept. of History, The Johns Hopkins University, 1971

Rothman, David J. *The Discovery of the Asylum: Social Order and Disorder in the New Republic.* Boston and Toronto, 1971

Roux, Augustin. *Les Fonds des Archives départementales des Bouches-du-Rhône.* Part II, Vol. 2, *Dépôt annexe d'Aix-en-Provence.* Marseille, 1954

Russell-Wood, A. J. R. *Fidalgoes and Philanthropists: The Santa Casa da Miséricordia of Bahia, 1550-1755.* Berkeley, 1968

Sabatier, Nicole, *L'Hôpital Saint-Jacques d'Aix-en-Provence, 1519-1789.* 4 Vols. Aix, 1964

Schnapper, Bernard. *Les Rentes au XVIe siècle: histoire d'un instrument de crédit.* Paris, 1957

Sheppard, Thomas Frederick. "A Provincial Village in Eighteenth Century France: Lourmarin, 1680-1800." Unpublished Ph.D. dissertation, Dept. of History, The Johns Hopkins University, 1969

Shorter, Edward. "Illegitimacy, Sexual Revolution, and Social Change in Modern Europe," *The Journal of Interdisciplinary History* 2:2 (Autumn, 1971):236-72

Soboul, Albert. *La France à la veille de la Révolution.* Vol. 1, *Economie et Société.* Paris, 1966

Traveneaux, R. "Jansenisme et vie sociale en France au XVIIe siècle," *Revue d'histoire de l'Eglise de France* 54:152 (January-June, 1968): 27-46

Taylor, George V. "Non-Capitalist Wealth and the Origins of the French Revolution." *American Historical Review* 62:2 (January, 1967):469-97

Tierney, Brian. *Medieval Poor Law: A Sketch of Canonical Theory and Its Application in England.* Berkeley and Los Angeles, 1959

Valran, G. *Misère et charité en Provence au XVIIIe siècle: essai d'histoire sociale.* Paris, 1889

Venard, Marc. "Les Oeuvres de charité en Avignon à l'aube du XVIIe siècle," *XVIIe Siècle* 90-91 (1971):128-46

Viguier, Jules. *Les Débuts de la Révolution en Provence.* Paris, 1894

Vovelle, G. and M. "La Mort et L'Au-Delà en Provence," *Annales: E. S. C.* 24:6 (November-December, 1969):1602-30

Vovelle, Michel. *Piété baroque et déchristianisation en Provence au XVIIIe siècle: Les Attitudes devant la mort d'après les clauses des testaments.* Paris, 1973

Weulersse, Georges. *Le Mouvement physiocratique en France.* Paris, 1910

Index

Library of Congress Cataloging in Publication Data

Fairchilds, Cissie C
    Poverty and charity in Aix-en-Provence, 1640-1789.

    (Johns Hopkins University studies in historical
and political science; 94th ser., no. 1)
    1. Aix, France—Charities. 2. Aix, France—
Poor. I. Title. II. Series: Johns Hopkins University. Studies in historical and political science; 94th ser., no. 1.
HV270.A5F34   362.5'0944'91   75-36938
ISBN 0-8018-1677-7